A MASTER CLASS

FRESH, PASSIONATE NEW ENGLAND COOKIN

Sensational Recipes from the Chefs of the

A MASTER CLASS

NEW ENGLAND CULINARY INSTITUTE

and Ellen Michaud

For Amanda

♥ Ellen

NEW ENGLAND CULINARY INSTITUTE®

By the Chefs of the NEW ENGLAND CULINARY INSTITUTE and ELLEN MICHAUD

University Press of New England Hanover and London

Published by University Press of New England,
One Court Street, Lebanon, NH 03766
www.upne.com
© 2008 by New England Culinary Institute
Printed in the United States of America
5   4   3   2   1

Photographs on pages xii, 1, 38, 211, and 231 © 2007 John Churchman

Library of Congress Cataloging-in-Publication Data

Michaud, Ellen.
A master class : sensational recipes from the Chefs of the New
England Culinary Institute and Ellen Michaud / by the Chefs
of the New England Culinary Institute and Ellen Michaud.
    p.   cm.
Includes index.
ISBN 978-1-58465-680-7 (cloth : alk. paper)
1. Cookery, American — New England style. 2. Natural foods — New England.
I. New England Culinary Institute. II. Title. III. Title: Sensational recipes
from the chefs of the New England Culinary Institute and Ellen Michaud.
TX715.2.N48M53   2008
641.5974—dc22   2008021310

CONTENTS

FOREWORD

At 28, Gavin Kaysen is one of the youngest chefs to have been named "Best New Chef" by *Food & Wine* Magazine. In just the few short years since he graduated from the New England Culinary Institute, he has won the right to represent the United States in the prestigious Bocuse d'Or competition at Lyon, won a bronze medal at the International Trophy of Cuisine and Pastry in Paris, been profiled in *Forbes* and *Time*, and appeared on the *Today Show* and *The Next Iron Chef*.

As a student at the New England Culinary Institute, I would go to the farmers' markets every morning. There I would see the hands of farmers covered in calluses, dirt, and wrinkles from the hours of unrelenting work under the sun that they put into the food they sold. It made me think about the amazing effort and the unstinting care that went into the produce, meat, poultry, wines, and cheeses they created. And I began to realize that these men and women were giving me a gift.

This is something that I've carried with me throughout my career. Whether I was in London or Switzerland, California or New York, I realized that if I wanted to honor these farmers and show my respect for their gift, I needed to take the perfection they offered and turn it into art on a plate.

You might want to keep that in mind as you work your way through *A Master Class*, offered within these pages by the chefs of the New England Culinary Institute. The recipes here honor the farmer and respect the food he or she produces—and are intended to free the amazing flavors inherent in foods produced by people who care about taste rather than shelf life.

As chefs we learn how to grow with our cuisine, both personally and professionally, from the farmers with whom we work. I hope you get to know the farmers in your community, and support them with your business. They not only allow us to create fabulous food, they connect us to the earth.

Gavin Kaysen

INTRODUCTION

Master Chef Michel LeBorgne was inducted into the exclusive Maître Cuisinier de France (M.C.F.) in 1988. Eight years later, the organization named him "Chef of the Year," its highest honor. Chef Michel is also a member of the Académie Culinaire de France, Master Chefs of America, Golden Toque, Les Amis d'Escoffier Society, and the Société des Cuisiniers de Paris.

When I was a young boy on the coast of Brittany, my family and I would eat fresh-caught fish from the sea, mushrooms gathered from a nearby forest, and vegetables pulled from the earth only minutes before they went on the table. The flavors were superb. I learned there and then that, when food is that fresh, it needs little from the chef who prepares it except a little skill, a sharp knife, some fresh herbs, a good sea salt, and my grandmother's cast iron sauté pan.

Working in some of the world's finest restaurants and becoming a Master Chef of France have not changed my mind, and, in many ways, I have tried to recreate that environment here at the New England Culinary Institute.

I came to the school some twenty-five years ago. During that time somewhere around ninety chefs have left the crazed kitchens found in many of the world's top restaurants to join me in a life that grounds us in the authenticity of country life, surrounds us with the sustainable farms, greenhouses, and artisanal food producers necessary to develop contemporary flavors, energizes us with several hundred enthusiastic young people wanting

to know why and how and what about this—then stimulates us with a collaborative of chefs with whom to argue, debate, cook, and compete.

The result has been the steady development of an authentic American cuisine that has ignited a passion for fresh, regionally sourced foods and artisanal products—an authenticity and passion that led *Saveur Magazine* to call the Culinary Institute "one of the nation's finest culinary schools" and to name Vermont—home to a travel guide's-worth of inns and restaurants created by the Institute's graduates—the "coolest food state in the union."*

That's an amazing accolade. But with most of its 500 students a year moving into the nation's top kitchens, the school has also sent a sizzle of creative energy flowing from Vermont to New York, Chicago, New Orleans, Honolulu, Tokyo, San Francisco, the British Virgin Islands, Antarctica, and everywhere in between.

That sizzle led 150 leading food editors, culinary journalists, and restaurateurs to name the Institute one of the top ten cooking schools in the United States and Canada. It also led many of the Institute's graduates—Alton Brown, Gavin Kaysen, and Steve

---

Saveur Magazine 48 (January/February 2001): p. 61.

Corry are a few—to be named chef of the year, best chef, or best new chef by *Food & Wine*, *Bon Appétit*, and others. What's more, it recently led the International Association of Culinary Professionals to name the New England Culinary Institute as the number one cooking school in America.

At the number one cooking school in America, however, recipes are not a blueprint but a starting point. And that includes every recipe in this book. Each and every recipe in *A Master Class* is drawn from the school's database and has been tested by an experienced chef instructor. But each and every chef here at the Institute urges you to look at the recipes, look at the ingredients, go to a farmers' market, farm, or fish monger's, see what's fresh, see what's local, see what's in season, then use the book as a catalyst to explore your *own* creativity.

With a handful of exceptions, the recipes we've included have a contemporary New England accent that relies on the authentic flavors of sustainably grown vegetables and produce from all four seasons. They also rely on wild-caught fish and shellfish from sustainable species; pastured beef, veal and pork; free-range chicken and eggs; handmade pastas from rich, artisanal flours; cheeses from small farms; potatoes, grains, and beans from heirloom varieties; and desserts that include chocolate produced in areas where workers are paid a fair wage.

That makes *A Master Class* a real-world cookbook that focuses on the intersection of flavor and a sustainability that will preserve the land and water for future generations and encourage biological diversity, fair wages, the growth of communities, and respect for animals.

You can find a farmers' market near you by logging on to www.ams.usda .gov/farmers/map.htm or www.localharvest.org. You can find a local source of pastured meat at www.eatwild.com. And you can find a listing of sustainable fish and shellfish at www.montereybayaquarium.org/cr/SeafoodWatch/ web/sfw_factsheet.aspx.

Where there are sustainably sourced ingredients available, we urge you to use them. Where there are not sustainably sourced ingredients available, we suggest you make the best decision based on what's at hand — then work within your community to make better choices available to all of us.

Michel LeBorgne, M.C.F.

SPRING

Smoke rises from the old sugarhouse on the ridge, cords of wood that were neatly stacked by the Congregational church in the valley are just about gone, and Saturday morning shoppers at the local natural foods co-op in Middlebury, Vermont, are so hungry for a ripe, red tomato that they'll willingly pay $6.99 a pound for the succulent globes raised in David Miskell's Shelburne greenhouse.

The hills surrounding this area of Vermont are freshly covered with a heavy spring snow that will keep skiers, snowshoers, and ice-sculpting New England Culinary Institute students happy for weeks. But down here in the valley along Lake Champlain, patches of icy mud are beginning to appear amid the stubble of last year's corn stalks, and the brooks that tumble over rocks and wander through our pastures toward the lake are beginning to swell with snowmelt.

In another couple of weeks, definitely by the end of March, peepers and croakers will be announcing the birth of spring, mud will be sucking whole vehicles underground, and the first burnished amber of this year's maple syrup will be drizzled on paper cups filled with snow at every village's spring fair. Lambs will make their appearance, and fiddleheads—baby ferns with their stems still tightly furled—will be harvested from leaf-mulched beds beside tumbling brooks in the forest. Once in the kitchen, they'll be rinsed, sautéed with a splash of this and a sprinkle of that, and served steaming hot over angel hair pasta as a celebration of spring.

By April, farmers throughout the state will be checking out their tractors, getting ready to move a winter's worth of cow compost out into the fields, and debating this year's planting dates with their neighbors.

In seemingly no time at all, NECI Chef Joe Buley will have a gaggle of students pulling on Wellies and tramping around his farm to study sustainable farming practices. Arugula, spinach, asparagus, and baby beets will appear on our tables, pots of pea soup will simmer on the stove, and steelhead trout from the Choiniere-Willoughby River will be smoking over outdoor firepits.

Neighbors will be coming out of hibernation along with the bears, and while the bears are checking our backyard birdfeeders for their favorite sunflower seeds, the neighbors will be checking and debating heirloom seeds at the local Agway.

Finally, in May, lilacs will begin to bloom beside every farmhouse door. Their fragrance will begin in the valley along the lakeshore, then rise ever higher into the mountains until it fills valleys and mountains alike in a haze of fragrance.

The Eastern Cherokee who roamed these hills in an earlier time believed that God inhabits this place.

So do those of us who live here today.

I

FIRST FLAVORS

Watching student waiters circulate at a New England Culinary Institute party high in the hills of Vermont, it's hard to focus on the conversation as the subtle aromas emanating from the students' trays blend together in a fragrant haze that fills the room and captivates the senses.

Is that a hint of thyme? A whisper of fennel?

The questions and the effect are endless — which means that the foods circulating among the Institute's guests are doing exactly what they're intended to do.

Whether you call them "appetizers," "tapas," or "little plates," the array of small dishes, soups, salads, or breads served before a main meal, or on their own at a nibble fest for a group of friends, are usually intended as the evening's first flavor. And as such they have a huge responsibility: to demonstrate to one and all that the food coming out of *this* kitchen will offer flavors that delight body, mind, and soul — and set guests to puzzling over what's been married with which and who knew that this, that, or the other ingredient had the potential to taste like *this*?

In some cases, those flavors will be classic New England, like the simple tower built by New England Culinary Institute chefs from alternating layers of farm-fresh goat cheese, just-picked heirloom tomatoes, and a basil spinach vinaigrette. In other cases, those flavors will offer the unexpected — the pea soup made from a rich farm-fresh cream, freshly picked and shelled peas, and a sprinkling of finely chopped mint.

The key to offering first flavors that will have your guests closing their eyes in ecstasy? Fresh ingredients sustainably produced and purchased in season from local sources. The less time from field to mouth, farm to mouth, or sea to mouth, the better. The flavors will be intense, subtle, unexpected, classic, and every gradation in between. And because they're grown with an eye toward making sure the source from which they came will be enriched rather than depleted by their cultivation, those same incredible flavors will be available during the next growing season and the next.

To help you make sure the flavors you offer your guests are at peak, the "first flavors" on the following pages reflect ingredients taken from all four seasons. Serve Asparagus and Scallop Brochettes in the spring, Tomato Basil Bruschetta late summer into the fall, White Bean, Tomato, and Rosemary Soup in the winter, and our sweet Vidalia Onion Tarts in the summer.

Flavor just doesn't get any better than this.

HEIRLOOM TOMATO AND GOAT CHEESE SALAD WITH BASIL VINAIGRETTE

Serves 4

CHEF'S NOTE: These "towers" of fresh goat cheese and heirloom tomatoes straight from the garden are incredibly simple to make, but they'll evoke a murmur of delight from your guests every time.

Dressing

1 bunch fresh basil, stems removed

3 spinach leaves

1 cup olive oil

¼ cup lemon juice

Salad

4 small heirloom tomatoes

2 logs (4 ounces each) goat cheese

Salt and freshly ground black pepper to taste

¼ cup fresh thyme, stems removed, chopped

¼ cup fresh rosemary, stems removed, finely chopped

½ cup fresh parsley, chopped

1 bag (8 ounces) mesclun greens

To make the dressing: In a blender, combine the basil, spinach, oil, and lemon juice. Process on high until thoroughly blended, about 4 minutes. Set aside.

To make the salad: On a cutting board, use a sharp knife to cut the tomatoes into 12 slices, each ¼ inch thick. Cut each cheese log into 4 slices. One at a time, place the cheese slices between 2 sheets of plastic wrap and press lightly until they are the same diameter as the tomato slices.

Spread the tomatoes and cheese on a work surface and sprinkle with the salt, pepper, thyme, rosemary, and parsley. Form a stack by alternately layering 3 slices tomato with 2 slices cheese, then transfer to a serving plate. Repeat with the remaining tomatoes and cheese.

In a medium bowl, dress the greens with some of the vinaigrette and season with the salt and pepper. Drizzle the tomato and cheese stacks with dressing. Arrange the greens around the stacks and serve.

TOMATO FENNEL SALAD

Serves 6

CHEF'S NOTE: A fresh summer addition to every table.

Dressing

1 large ripe heirloom tomato

¼ cup extra-virgin olive oil

¼ cup white balsamic vinegar

Salt and freshly ground black
pepper to taste

1 bunch fresh tarragon, stems
removed, chopped

Salad

2 tablespoons extra-virgin olive
oil

2 tablespoons white truffle oil

Juice of 1 lemon

Salt and freshly ground black
pepper to taste

2 bulbs fennel

2 pounds heirloom tomatoes,
assorted colors, diced

To make the dressing: Process the tomato in a blender until smooth. Drizzle in the oil and vinegar and season with the salt and pepper. Transfer to a bowl and fold in the tarragon.

To make the salad: Slice the fennel paper-thin in a food processor or with a mandolin. In a small bowl, whisk together the olive oil, truffle oil, and lemon juice. Season with the salt and pepper. Add the fennel and toss to coat evenly. Toss with the dressing and season again with salt and pepper if desired.

Arrange the diced tomatoes on a serving plate, top with the fennel, and serve immediately.

SHRIMP CAESAR SALAD IN PARMESAN BOWLS

Serves 4

CHEF'S NOTE: This is an amazingly easy and flavorful salad.

Bowls

¾ cup grated Parmesan cheese

Dressing

2 free-range egg yolks or 2 teaspoons mayonnaise

6 anchovy fillets

2 cloves garlic, chopped

½ cup grated Parmesan cheese

2 tablespoons lemon juice

1 cup olive oil

¼ cup cold water

Salt and freshly ground black pepper to taste

Salad

¼ cup (½ stick) butter, cubed

2 cloves garlic, chopped

4 jumbo shrimp, peeled, deveined, and halved vertically

½ cup fresh parsley, chopped

2 heads romaine lettuce, diced

½ cup croutons

To make the bowls: Preheat the oven to 350°F. Coat a baking sheet with nonstick cooking spray.

Divide the cheese into 4 portions on the baking sheet and form into flat circles. Bake just until they begin to melt and bubble, 3 to 5 minutes. Remove the circles from the baking sheet and mold each over the bottom of an upside-down glass.

To make the dressing: In a blender, process the egg yolks, anchovies, garlic, and cheese for 30 seconds. Drizzle in the lemon juice, then the oil, and finally the water, then process until well incorporated. Season with the salt and pepper.

To make the salad: Melt the butter in a nonstick skillet over high heat. Add the garlic and shrimp and cook until the shrimp is pink throughout, about 2 minutes.

Carefully remove the Parmesan bowls from the glasses and place 1 on each plate. In a small bowl, lightly toss the shrimp, parsley, and 2 tablespoons dressing. Toss the lettuce with the remaining dressing and place in the bowls.

Top the salads with croutons and a shaving of Parmesan. Spoon the shrimp and dressing onto the plates around the bowls and serve immediately.

GRILLED CHICKEN AND SNOW PEA SALAD WITH SESAME VINAIGRETTE

Serves 6 to 8

CHEF'S NOTE: This salad is a great way to use snow peas when they're fresh from the garden, and substituting broccoli stems for the more traditional water chestnuts utilizes a good ingredient that often goes to waste. When we first started making this salad, we used Boston and red leaf lettuce. Now, with a variety of salad mixes grown locally, we like to use a mix of baby greens and Asian greens like tatsoi and mizuna. If you don't have time to prepare chicken, the snow pea salad by itself is a nice alternative to the usual mixed green salad.

Marinade

½ cup soy sauce

¼ cup sesame oil

¼ cup thinly sliced scallions (green and white parts)

1½ tablespoons red wine vinegar

1½ tablespoons minced fresh ginger

1 tablespoon sugar

¾ teaspoon minced garlic

Dash of chili garlic sauce or other moderately hot pepper sauce

Salad

4 boneless skinless chicken breasts (3 ounces each)

20 snow peas, stems removed

4–6 ounces Soy and Sesame Vinaigrette (recipe on page 9)

8 cups salad greens (see Chef's Note), washed and dried well

½ cup grated carrot

3 or 4 broccoli stems, peeled and cut into rounds

To make the marinade: In a medium metal bowl, whisk together the soy sauce, sesame oil, scallions, vinegar, ginger, sugar, garlic, and chili sauce.

To make the salad: Place the chicken between two sheets of plastic wrap and use a mallet to flatten to an even thickness. Arrange in 1 layer in a rectangular ceramic or glass dish and pour the marinade over it. Cover with plastic wrap and refrigerate for 1 to 2 hours.

In a large saucepan, bring 4 quarts salted water to a boil and prepare a medium bowl of water and ice. Cook the snow peas in the boiling water until their color brightens, 10 to 20 seconds. Use a slotted spoon to transfer to the ice water. When chilled, remove from the water and pat dry with a towel. Set aside.

Thirty minutes to an hour before serving, preheat a gas or charcoal grill. Grill the chicken until cooked through, about 3 minutes per side (discard the marinade). Let stand for 5 minutes, then slice into thin strips.

In a large bowl, toss the greens with the dressing, reserving 1 tablespoon, and mound in the center of individual plates or a large bowl. Moisten the grated carrot with the reserved dressing and place on top of the greens. (Alternatively, serve the dressing on the side.) Arrange the snow peas in a pyramid over the greens and place chicken strips and sliced broccoli stems in between.

❧ *The Final Touch:* Arrange half-slices of cucumber around the base of the salad and sprinkle with chopped roasted cashews.

SOY AND SESAME VINAIGRETTE

Makes 1¾ cups

CHEF'S NOTE: This Asian-style dressing is also a nice alternative dressing for a tossed green salad. The amount of tamari or soy sauce will vary depending on its strength; if you use good-quality tamari, you won't need as much.

1½–2 tablespoons tamari or soy sauce

1 teaspoon minced fresh ginger

½ teaspoon minced garlic

⅓ cup rice wine vinegar

1⅓ cups vegetable oil

2 teaspoons sesame oil

In a medium bowl, combine the tamari, ginger, garlic, and vinegar. Pouring slowly, gradually whisk in the vegetable oil, then the sesame oil. Taste the dressing by dipping a lettuce leaf, then add more tamari or sesame oil if desired.

SPRING SPINACH SALAD
WITH WARM BACON VINAIGRETTE

CHEF'S NOTE: This is a great recipe for a summer evening, especially when made with fresh-picked spinach. Make and add the dressing just before serving.

Salad

½ pound Vermont Smoke and Cure Bacon

1 pound tender spinach, rinsed, drained, and stems removed

5 button mushrooms, thinly sliced

5 hard-cooked free-range eggs, sliced (or separated and put through a strainer)

1 medium red onion, cut into small dice

¼ cup sunflower seeds

3 ounces Jasper Hill Bayley Hazen blue cheese, crumbled

Dressing

1 tablespoon bacon fat

½ small onion, diced

1 teaspoon Dijon mustard

1 teaspoon sugar

¼ cup cider vinegar

Salt and freshly ground black pepper to taste

¾ cup extra-virgin olive oil

To make the salad: Cook the bacon in a medium skillet until crisp, 5 to 7 minutes, turning halfway through. Drain, reserving 1 tablespoon fat. Transfer the bacon to paper towels to cool.

In a serving bowl, combine the spinach, mushrooms, eggs, onion, and sunflower seeds. Crumble the cooled bacon, add to the salad, and toss to combine.

To make the dressing: In a small skillet, cook the onion in the bacon fat until translucent, about 3 minutes. Remove from the heat and whisk in the mustard, sugar, vinegar, salt, and pepper, then slowly whisk in the oil.

Add ½ cup warm dressing to the salad, toss to combine, and serve immediately, garnished with the cheese.

PURPLE FINGERLING SALAD

Serves 4

CHEF'S NOTE: This is a delicious spin on traditional potato salad, utilizing fresh, local fingerlings. If you can't find purple fingerlings, use all yellow or all red. The amount of olive oil may be adjusted to suit, depending on the size of the potatoes. Cutting the potatoes after cooking helps keep them moist.

Potatoes

1 sprig thyme, stems removed, finely chopped

1 sprig rosemary, stems removed, finely chopped

1 sprig sage, stems removed, finely chopped

Salt and freshly ground black pepper to taste

1 tablespoon extra-virgin olive oil

6 purple fingerling potatoes

6 yellow or red fingerling potatoes

Dressing

1 teaspoon + 1 tablespoon extra-virgin olive oil

1 small onion, finely chopped

2 tablespoons cider vinegar

Salt and freshly ground black pepper to taste

1 tablespoon Dijon mustard

2 bunches chives, chopped

To make the potatoes: Preheat the oven to 400°F. In a medium bowl, combine the thyme, rosemary, sage, salt, pepper, and oil. Add the potatoes and turn to coat. Spread on a baking sheet and roast until tender, about 20 minutes. Be careful not to overcook, or they will be mushy.

To make the dressing: Meanwhile, heat 1 teaspoon oil in a medium skillet. Add the onion and cook, stirring occasionally, until golden brown and caramelized, about 5 minutes. Transfer to a plate.

Place the vinegar in a large bowl and stir in the salt and pepper, then add the mustard, chives, and 1 tablespoon oil. Stir in the onion.

When the potatoes are done, let stand until completely cool or refrigerate to speed up the process. When cool, cut in half lengthwise with a moistened knife, add to the dressing, and stir to coat. Serve immediately or refrigerate until ready to serve.

GREEN MOUNTAIN BLUE CHEESE DRESSING

Makes about 1 cup

CHEF'S NOTE: This delicious dressing is best when made with a Vermont blue cheese. Try Bayley Hazen blue, made from the milk of a select group of 27 local Ayrshire cows. The taste varies more in summer when the cows are pastured and is more consistent in winter when they're fed local hay. Either way, the cheese is superb. Look for cheese that's been aged for three months. Use on fresh greens.

½ cup mayonnaise

4 ounces Vermont blue cheese, crumbled

3 tablespoons buttermilk

¼ cup sour cream

2 tablespoons fat-free milk

1 tablespoon fresh lemon juice

1 tablespoon minced garlic

1 tablespoon finely chopped onion

Salt and freshly ground black pepper to taste

In a large bowl, combine the mayonnaise, cheese, buttermilk, sour cream, milk, lemon juice, garlic, onion, salt, and pepper. Refrigerate until well chilled.

MAPLE BALSAMIC DRESSING

Makes about 1 cup

CHEF'S NOTE: The sweetness of the maple in this dressing is balanced by the acidity of the vinegar and by the mustard. The mustard also acts as an emulsifier as well as a flavoring agent, lightly binding the oil and vinegar together. The dressing nicely complements tossed salads and grilled vegetables.

---

1 tablespoon Maple Mustard
(recipe below)

¼ cup balsamic vinegar

1¼ cups vegetable oil

Salt and freshly ground black
pepper to taste

Place the mustard in a medium bowl and gradually whisk in the vinegar. Continue whisking while adding the oil in a slow stream. Once the oil has been incorporated, dip a lettuce leaf into the dressing to taste it. If it's too acidic, whisk in additional oil and/or mustard; if it's too sweet, add more vinegar. Season with the salt and pepper. Drizzle on fresh greens and toss, or across grilled vegetables.

MAPLE MUSTARD

Makes 1 cup

CHEF'S NOTE: While fancy grade syrup is prized by many for pancakes, the lower grades have more flavor for cooking. This mustard can also be used as a glaze for grilled chicken or pork or baked ham.

½ cup Grade B maple syrup

¼ cup Dijon mustard

¼ cup whole-grain mustard

In a medium bowl, whisk together the syrup and mustards. Transfer to a container and refrigerate until needed; if it hasn't been in contact with meat, it will keep for weeks.

VERMONT ONION SOUP

Makes 4 cups

CHEF'S NOTE: This is a flavorful après-ski warmup.

¼ stalk celery leaves

1 bay leaf

1 teaspoon black peppercorns

1 sprig fresh thyme

1 sprig fresh rosemary

6 tablespoons canola oil

1 Vidalia onion, sliced

2 tablespoons flour

1 cup port wine

4 quarts vegetable broth or stock

Salt to taste

4 slices French bread

6 ounces Gruyère cheese, cut into 4 slices

Make a bouquet garni by tying the celery leaves, bay leaf, peppercorns, thyme, and rosemary in a piece of cheesecloth.

Heat the oil in a soup pot over medium heat, then add the onion and cook until golden brown. Add the flour and stir until combined.

Deglaze the pot with the wine, cooking until the liquid is reduced by ¾. Add the stock slowly and bring to a boil. Season with the salt and attach the bouquet garni to the pot handle with a piece of string so it hangs into the soup. Simmer for 20 minutes, occasionally skimming off any foam that forms on the surface.

Remove the bouquet garni and add more seasoning if desired. Ladle the soup into 4 ovenproof bowls, then add a crouton and lay a slice of cheese across the top. Bake at 350°F or place under the broiler until the cheese is golden brown.

❧ *The Final Touch:* Serve each bowl in a napkin folded like an artichoke.

SWEET CORN SOUP

Makes 6 to 8 cups

---

6 ears corn

½ cup small-dice onion

¼ cup small-dice peeled carrot

¼ cup small-dice peeled celery

2 tablespoons (¼ stick) butter or
canola or sunflower oil

1 quart chicken broth or stock

½ cup flour

¼ cup (½ stick) butter, melted

½ cup heavy cream

1½ teaspoons salt

¼ teaspoon cayenne pepper

1½ tablespoons sherry vinegar

Remove the kernels from the corn and set aside in a bowl. Scrape the cobs with the back of a knife.

In a small, heavy-bottomed, stainless steel soup pot, cook the onion, carrot, and celery in the butter for 10 minutes. Add the broth and corn cobs and cook until the liquid is reduced by ⅓.

Meanwhile, make a roux by combining the flour and melted butter in a small saucepan. Cook, stirring often, over low heat for 5 minutes; do not brown. Remove from the heat and let cool slightly.

Remove the corn cobs from the stock and discard. Add the roux and whisk vigorously until incorporated. Add the corn kernels, reserving ½ cup, and simmer for 20 minutes, occasionally skimming off any foam that forms on the surface.

Purée the soup in a food processor or with an immersion blender. Add the cream and season with the salt, pepper, and vinegar. Strain through a stiff cone-shaped strainer, forcing the liquid and some solids through with a rubber spatula. If the soup is too thick, thin with additional broth. If it's too thin, return to the heat and cook until reduced to the desired consistency.

Season the reserved corn kernels with salt and pepper. Ladle the soup into bowls and top each serving with a spoonful of corn.

ROASTED GARLIC SOUP

Makes 6 to 7 cups

CHEF'S NOTE: This is a creamy, rich soup that honors garlic's place in country cooking. Be careful not to overcaramelize the garlic, or it will add a bitter note to the soup. Since store-bought broths are often high in sodium, you may want to cut back on the amount of salt in the recipe or add it to taste.

---

4 heads garlic

3 shallots

1 medium carrot

1 stalk celery

1 medium onion

1 small potato

2 tablespoons (¼ stick) butter

1½ teaspoons salt

1 bay leaf

1 tablespoon fresh thyme leaves, stems removed

1 quart chicken broth or stock

1 cup heavy cream

2 teaspoons sherry vinegar

½ teaspoon ground white pepper

Preheat the oven to 325°F. Lightly oil a small roasting pan.

Remove the tops of the garlic heads to expose about ¼ inch of the cloves. Remove ⅛ inch from each end of the shallots, but do not peel. Place the garlic and shallots in the roasting pan and bake until the shallots are soft and lightly browned, about 40 minutes. Remove the shallots and continue to roast the garlic until soft and lightly browned, about 20 minutes. Let cool.

Squeeze the garlic heads to extrude the garlic. Peel the shallots.

Peel and cut the carrot, celery, onion, and potato into medium dice. Melt the butter in a small soup pot and add the diced vegetables, bay leaf, thyme, and a pinch of salt. Cook over low heat until the vegetables are soft but not browned, 30 minutes.

Add the broth, garlic, and shallots and simmer over low heat until the vegetables are tender and the mixture is reduced by about ¼, 30 minutes.

Add the cream and return to a simmer. Remove and discard the bay leaf. Purée the soup with an immersion or stick blender until smooth. If the soup is too thick, thin with additional broth. If it's too thin, return to the heat and cook until reduced to the desired consistency. Add the vinegar, pepper, and remaining salt.

WHITE BEAN, TOMATO, AND ROSEMARY SOUP
Makes 8 cups

CHEF'S NOTE: Perfect for family gatherings after winter outdoor activities, this soup is hearty and satisfying.

1¾ cups cannellini beans

1 bay leaf

1 sprig (4") rosemary

1 small head garlic

9 plum tomatoes

1 small onion

½ small stalk celery

½ small carrot

4 tablespoons extra-virgin olive oil

2 teaspoons minced rosemary

2 quarts chicken or vegetable broth or stock

4 teaspoons balsamic vinegar

1 tablespoon salt

½ teaspoon freshly ground black pepper

Place the beans, bay leaf, and rosemary sprig in a small soup pot and add enough water to cover. Simmer until the beans are tender, 1 hour, adding more water if necessary. Remove from the heat and let the beans cool in the liquid. Strain off the liquid and set the beans aside.

Preheat the oven to 350°F. Lightly oil a baking pan.

Remove the top of the garlic head to expose ¼ inch of the cloves and place in the baking pan. Halve the tomatoes lengthwise and add to the pan. Roast until the garlic is soft and lightly browned, about 40 minutes. Let cool. Squeeze the garlic head to extrude the garlic or individually peel the cloves. Set aside.

Peel and cut the onion, celery, and carrot into small dice. Heat 1 tablespoon oil in a small soup pot. Add the diced vegetables, cover, and cook over low heat until soft but not browned, 20 minutes.

Add the beans, garlic, tomatoes (reserving 8 halves for garnish), minced rosemary, and broth and simmer for 15 minutes. Purée the soup with an immersion blender until smooth. If the soup is too thick, thin with additonal broth. If it's too thin, return to the heat and cook until reduced to the desired consistency. Add the vinegar, the remaining 3 tablespoons oil, and the salt and pepper.

Ladle ½ cup soup into each bowl, then top with a roasted tomato half, add some freshly ground pepper, and drizzle with a bit of oil.

❧ *The Final Touch:* Stir 1 teaspoon pesto into each bowl just before serving.

SPRING PEA SOUP WITH MINT AND LEMON
Makes 8 cups

CHEF'S NOTE: A far cry from the heavy split-pea soup we all know, this fresher-tasting vegetarian version is a wonderful quick soup when you're short on time. Hints of lemon and fresh mint add a new twist.

1 tablespoon unsalted butter

1 cup thinly sliced white onion

1 tablespoon thinly sliced peeled shallot

1 cup small-dice peeled white potato, kept in cold water until ready to cook

2 cups shelled fresh peas

2 teaspoons grated lemon zest

4 teaspoons finely chopped mint leaves

½ cup heavy cream

½ teaspoon finely ground white pepper

4–5 teaspoons sea salt

Melt the butter in a 3-quart saucepan over medium heat. When it begins to foam, add the onion and shallot, reduce the heat, and cook gently until translucent. Add the potatoes and 1 quart water and bring to a boil. Reduce the heat and simmer gently until the potatoes are very tender, about 10 minutes. Add the peas and return to a simmer, then add the lemon zest and mint and remove from the heat.

Working in small batches, transfer the soup to a blender and process until completely smooth, then strain through a fine-mesh strainer back into the pan. Stir in the cream, pepper, and salt to taste. Reheat, then add more seasoning if desired and serve immediately.

CAULIFLOWER AND BRIE SOUP WITH SAGE

Makes 10 to 12 cups

CHEF'S NOTE: Brie adds richness to this cauliflower purée and is balanced by the lemon and sage.

1½ tablespoons olive oil

1 medium onion, cut into small dice

½ stalk celery, cut into small dice

1 clove garlic, finely chopped

1 teaspoon thyme leaves

6½ cups chicken broth or stock

1 medium head cauliflower (1 pound), trimmed and cut into large dice

1 medium potato, peeled and cut into large dice

5 ounces Brie cheese, including rind

3–4 tablespoons fresh lemon juice

5 ounces heavy cream

2 tablespoons chopped fresh sage

1 tablespoon salt

1 teaspoon ground white pepper

½ cup Crispy Vermont Croutons (recipe on page 35)

Heat the oil in a small soup pot over low heat. Add the onion, celery, and garlic and cook until soft but not browned, 20 minutes. Add the thyme and cook for 1 minute. Add the broth, cauliflower, and potato and simmer until soft, 20 to 30 minutes. Add the cheese.

Purée with an immersion blender until completely smooth. Add the lemon juice, cream, sage, salt, and pepper. If the soup is too thick, thin with additional broth. If it's too thin, return to the heat and cook until reduced to the desired consistency.

Place a tablespoon of croutons in the center of each bowl before serving.

TOMATO-BASIL BRUSCHETTA

Serves 4

CHEF'S NOTE: This simple but delicious appetizer makes a nice starter before the main course or can be prepared quickly for a spontaneous get-together. Vary the toppings according to seasonal availability. You may also top with cheese if desired.

---

2 medium heirloom tomatoes, cut into small dice

1 medium onion, cut into small dice

2 cloves garlic, minced

¼ cup shredded fresh basil

1 tablespoon balsamic vinegar

Salt and freshly ground black pepper to taste

1 baguette, cut into ½" slices and lightly toasted

In a large bowl, combine the tomatoes, onion, garlic, basil, vinegar, salt, and pepper. Spoon onto the baguette slices and serve immediately.

BELGIAN ENDIVES WITH GOAT CHEESE

Serves 6

CHEF'S NOTE: A perfect meal starter, this dish is very simple and very Vermont.

---

6 Belgian endives
1 quart hot vegetable stock
2 teaspoons butter
2 teaspoons sugar
Salt and freshly ground black
   pepper to taste

12 ounces Vermont Butter and
   Cheese goat cheese (chèvre)
2 teaspoons chopped chives
1 sheet puff pastry dough

Preheat the oven to 350°F. Butter a baking pan and an ovenproof nonstick skillet.

Place the endives in the baking pan and cover with the stock. Add the butter and sugar and season with salt and pepper. Cover the pan with a sheet of parchment paper and bake until soft, 30 minutes. Transfer to a rack to drain and cool.

Place the cheese in a large bowl and gently stir in the chives. Season with salt and pepper.

Split the endives in half lengthwise and arrange in the skillet, outside leaves down. Cook over low heat until golden brown, about 20 minutes. Remove from the heat and crumble the cheese on the endives. Cover with the pastry dough and cut a hole in the center to let the steam escape. Bake until the pastry is golden brown, about 30 minutes.

Place a plate on top of the skillet and carefully flip it over. Cut the "pie" into 6 wedges, place a wedge on each plate, and serve immediately.

❧ *The Final Touch:* Top each serving with mesclun greens tossed with balsamic vinaigrette and spoon a few drops of vinaigrette around each wedge.

NEW ENGLAND SEAFOOD QUESADILLAS

Serves 4

CHEF'S NOTE: Although quesadillas originated south of the border, this New England coast version is great. The seafood filling can be made up to one day in advance. Be sure to drain off any liquid before adding it, or the quesadillas may be soggy. Poblano peppers are available in most supermarkets and are moderately hot. If you prefer nonspicy quesadillas, substitute an Anaheim long green pepper for the poblano and use cheddar instead of pepper Jack cheese.

---

2 tablespoons (¼ stick) butter

¼ cup medium-dice roasted, peeled, and seeded poblano pepper

¼ cup medium-dice cored and seeded red bell pepper

1 tablespoon minced garlic

¾ cup medium-dice sea scallops

¾ cup medium-dice cooked and peeled Maine shrimp

¾ cup cleaned fresh Maine crabmeat

1 tablespoon chopped fresh parsley

1 tablespoon chopped fresh cilantro

Salt and freshly ground black pepper to taste

4 (10") flour tortillas

1 cup (4 ounces) shredded pepper Jack cheese

1 cup salsa

½ cup sour cream

Preheat the oven to 300°F.

Melt the butter in a 12-inch sauté pan over medium-high heat. Add the poblano pepper, bell pepper, and garlic and cook until the peppers are tender, 1 to 2 minutes. Add the scallops and cook for 1 minute. Add the shrimp, crab, parsley, and cilantro and cook for 2 minutes. Remove from the heat, season with the salt and pepper, and transfer to a bowl.

Place the tortillas on a work surface and sprinkle the top halves with equal amounts of cheese. Spoon equal amounts of filling over the cheese. Fold the top halves of the tortillas over the bottom halves and press down.

Heat a large sauté pan over medium-high heat. Add 2 quesadillas and cook until golden brown, 3 to 4 minutes per side. Using a spatula, transfer to a baking sheet and place in the oven while you cook the remaining quesadillas.

Transfer the quesadillas to a cutting board and cut each into 4 wedges. Place on individual plates, add sour cream and salsa to each, and serve immediately.

❧ *The Final Touch:* To round out this appetizer, add a small portion of tossed green salad with citrus dressing. It's light and goes well with the quesadillas.

ASPARAGUS AND SCALLOP BROCHETTES WITH RISOTTO

Serves 4

CHEF'S NOTE: To prepare an ice bath to blanch vegetables, put ice in a bowl of cold water and set aside. After cooking the vegetables, place them in the bath for just a few minutes. This will keep their color bright.

Risotto

4 stalks asparagus

1 shallot, peeled and finely chopped

¼ cup olive oil

2 cups Arborio rice

3 cups vegetable broth or stock

2 cups heavy cream

½ cup Parmesan cheese

6 tablespoons (¾ stick) butter

Brochettes

8 large scallops

2 teaspoons olive oil

Salt and freshly ground black pepper to taste

Sauce

2 cups carrot juice

6 tablespoons (¾ stick) butter

1 teaspoon ground nutmeg

Salt and freshly ground black pepper to taste

To make the risotto: Cut the bottom 2 inches off each asparagus stalk and chop into 1-inch pieces. Set the asparagus and chopped stalks aside.

In a medium saucepan, cook the shallot in the oil until translucent. Add the rice and mix well to coat with oil. Add the broth ½ cup at a time, stirring until the rice absorbs each addition. When all the broth has been added, stir in the cream, cheese, butter, and chopped asparagus.

To make the brochettes: Bring 6 quarts water to a boil in a large pot. Add the asparagus stalks and cook until bright green, about 2 minutes. Prepare an ice bath (see Chef's Note). When the asparagus is done, transfer to the bath for about 2 minutes. Transfer to a plate.

Using a wooden skewer, pierce the side of a scallop. Replace the skewer with an asparagus stalk, then add a second scallop. Repeat with the remaining asparagus and scallops and refrigerate until ready to cook.

Heat the oil in a nonstick sauté pan until smoking. Season the brochettes with the salt and pepper and carefully add to the pan. Cook until golden, 2 to 3 minutes per side, then transfer to paper towels.

To make the sauce: In a small saucepan over high heat, bring the carrot juice to a boil and cook for 3 to 5 minutes. Remove from the heat and add the butter. Add the nutmeg and season with the salt and pepper.

Divide the risotto evenly among 4 shallow bowls. Place a brochette on top of each and pour sauce around the risotto.

ROASTED BEETS WITH MÂCHE

Serves 4

CHEF'S NOTE: Dig beets fresh from your garden for a fresh, earthy taste. They can be cooked a day in advance and refrigerated.

---

6 medium beets

2 tablespoons vegetable oil

Salt to taste

3 shallots, finely chopped

1½ tablespoons red wine vinegar

5 tablespoons peanut oil

1 bunch mâche (lamb's lettuce)

Preheat the oven to 375°F.

Lightly rub the beets with the vegetable oil and sprinkle with salt. Bake for 1½ hours, then wrap in foil and let cool.

Peel and slice 4 beets and pulse into small dice in a food processor. Transfer to a bowl. Peel and dice 2 beets by hand.

In the food processor, pulse the hand-diced beets, shallots, vinegar, and peanut oil until coarsely pureed. Fold into the diced beets. Reserve ¼ of the mixture.

Place a 3⅓-inch round mold in the center of each plate and pack with the beet mixture, then remove the mold. Form 3 small ovals around the molded beets by filling a teaspoon with some of the reserved beet mixture and shaping it into a round with another teaspoon. Top with mâche.

VERMONT CHEDDAR, APPLE, AND
BACON PHYLLO POCKETS

Serves 4

CHEF'S NOTE: This recipe takes some preparation, but the end result is delicious and worth the effort. The pockets are best served warm from the oven, so timing is key in making them. You can find phyllo dough in the freezer section of the supermarket. It's easier to handle when still slightly frozen.

---

4 slices Vermont Smoke and
    Cure Bacon, cooked, drained,
    and crumbled (¼ cup)

1 medium onion, julienned

1 Vermont apple, peeled, cored,
    and chopped

Salt and freshly ground black
    pepper to taste

½ cup (2 ounces) shredded
    Cabot Seriously Sharp cheddar
    cheese

6 sheets phyllo dough

¼ cup (½ stick) butter, melted

In a medium skillet, warm the bacon, then add the onion and cook until browned, about 4 minutes. Add the apple and cook until soft, about 3 minutes. Remove from the heat, season with the salt and pepper, and let cool. Add the cheese, stir, and set aside.

Preheat the oven to 375°F. Lay a sheet of phyllo on a work surface and brush with butter. Add 2 more layers, brushing each with butter. Cut the dough into 4 equal squares. Place 2 tablespoons filling on each square, fold over diagonally, and seal each pocket by brushing with butter as necessary. Repeat with the remaining phyllo.

Place the pockets on a baking sheet and bake until golden brown, 3 to 4 minutes. Serve immediately.

FRIED CHICKEN, HEIRLOOM TOMATO, AND BUFFALO MOZZARELLA SKEWERS

Serves 4

CHEF'S NOTE: You can find organic arugula and heirloom tomatoes at your local farmers' market. Buffalo mozzarella is made by the Woodstock Water Buffalo Company in South Woodstock, Vermont (see the store locator at www.woodstockwaterbuffalo.com). If you don't wish to make the arugula oil, you can use good-quality extra-virgin olive oil.

Arugula Oil

4 ounces arugula

2 tablespoons salt

½ cup canola oil

Tapas

4 medium heirloom tomatoes, seeded and cut into wedges

2 tablespoons extra-virgin olive oil

3½ cups canola oil

1 cup bread crumbs

1 cup flour

3 free-range eggs

1 tablespoon freshly ground black pepper

2 boneless skinless Misty Knoll chicken breasts, cut into 1" cubes

8 (1") cubes fresh Woodstock Water Buffalo mozzarella

8 small fresh basil leaves

To make the arugula oil: Fill a medium saucepan with water and add salt to taste (it should be very salty, almost like seawater). Fill a bowl with water and some ice, then place a strainer in it and set aside. When the water in the pot is boiling vigorously, add the arugula and cook for 30 seconds. Transfer to the strainer until very cool; the arugula should be very bright green. Strain and squeeze as dry as possible with a kitchen towel. Place in a blender, add the oil, and process until liquefied. Transfer to a bowl and set aside.

To make the tapas: In a medium bowl, toss the tomatoes with the olive oil and sprinkle with a heavy pinch of salt. Grill or broil until slightly charred, then transfer to a plate.

Heat the canola oil to 350°F in a small pot, testing with a candy or deep fat thermometer.

Place the bread crumbs, flour, and eggs in individual shallow dishes. Gently stir the eggs. Season the chicken cubes with salt, then dredge them in the flour and shake off any excess. Dip in the eggs and shake off any excess, then toss in the bread crumbs to coat all sides. Fry until the internal temperature reaches 160°F, 2 to 3 minutes. Transfer to paper towels to drain.

Thread the mozzarella cubes, basil leaves, chicken cubes, and tomato wedges alternately onto 8 long toothpicks. (Be sure to make the skewers small enough so they can be eaten in one bite for more balanced flavor.) Put a splash of arugula oil on a serving plate and place the skewers on top. Season with salt and pepper to taste (the tomatoes and cheese require a good amount of salt).

❧ *The Final Touch:* To make this dish into an appetizer or light lunch, increase the ingredient amounts and place the chicken, mozzarella, tomatoes, and basil on a scattering of arugula tossed with citrus vinaigrette.

LE SOMMELIER: Since this tapas-style dish will probably be served at the start of a meal, it should be accompanied by a dry light white—that is, an aperitif-style wine. One local possibility is Cowtipper White from Boyden Valley Winery in Cambridge, Vermont, which has delightful fruit supported by crisp acidity. A Sauvignon Blanc from France's Loire Valley or California would also be good.

SCALLOPS WITH BEET CARPACCIO
AND WASABI CREAM

Serves 4

CHEF'S NOTE: A Vermont chef's spin on the right use of wasabi. When cooking scallops, it's best to use a cast-iron skillet or nonreactive nonstick pan. Aluminum pans conduct heat well, so they heat up fast but can cool too quickly, causing their temperature to fluctuate. Steel pans, which take the longest to heat but hold heat the best, can cause the scallops to stick and pull apart when you turn them.

---

12 large diver scallops	Zest of ½ lemon
4 medium beets	½ cup extra-virgin olive oil
2 cups sea salt or kosher salt	½ cup heavy cream
1 head garlic	¼ teaspoon wasabi powder
6 anchovy fillets	Fleur de sel sea salt

Place 4 square or rectangular appetizer or salad plates in the refrigerator. Remove the muscles from the scallops. Rinse the scallops, then dry with paper towels and refrigerate.

Preheat the oven to 400°F. Wash the beets. Spread the 2 cups sea salt on a baking sheet and place the beets and garlic on top. Bake for 10 minutes, then remove the garlic. Continue to bake the beets until tender when pierced with a fork, 30 to 45 minutes.

Extrude the garlic by squeezing each clove with your fingers. In a blender, process the garlic, anchovies, and lemon zest while slowly adding the oil.

Let the beets cool, then peel them. Using a mandolin or sharp knife, cut into very thin slices. Arrange the slices on a sheet of waxed paper, overlapping them in straight lines like roof shingles, then refrigerate.

In a medium bowl, whip the cream to a peak. Stir in the wasabi to taste and refrigerate.

Lightly oil a cast-iron skillet or nonstick pan. Cook the scallops over low heat for 1 minute on each side, then remove from the heat.

Cut the beet-covered waxed paper into four 5 x 7–inch rectangles. Place each piece beet side down on one of the cold plates and peel off the paper. If the dressing has separated, return it to the blender and pulse once or twice. Brush the beets with the dressing. Cut the scallops in half horizontally and arrange 6 halves on top of the beets on the left side of each plate. Sprinkle with the fleur de sel salt.

Using a pastry bag, pipe 5 or 6 stars of wasabi cream onto the beets on the right side of the plate. (If you don't have a pastry bag, you can use a resealable plastic bag. Cut off a corner of the bag to make a small hole, add the cream, and gently squeeze the bag to push it out.)

VERMONT GOAT CHEESE SOUFFLÉS

Serves 6

CHEF'S NOTE: These are a lovely accompaniment to any main course, starter, or salad. One secret of making soufflés is to carefully prepare the ramekins prior to spooning in the batter. Without this step, the soufflés get stuck inside the ramekins instead of puffing up beyond the rims, as the name implies. In this recipe, Japanese (panko) bread crumbs, which are coarse, pale in color, and very delicate, are perfect for this use. Pulse them into fine crumbs in a spice grinder. Chèvre is a mild, versatile goat cheese that can be used as part of a cheeseboard or in cooking.

---

2 tablespoons (¼ stick) butter, softened

¼ cup panko (Japanese) bread crumbs, ground into fine crumbs

6 tablespoons (¾ stick) butter

⅔ cup all-purpose flour

2 cups whole or 2% milk

1 cup Vermont Butter and Cheese goat cheese (chèvre)

4 free-range egg yolks

2 teaspoons chopped fresh thyme

2 teaspoons salt

1 pinch freshly ground nutmeg

6 free-range egg whites

Coat six 6-ounce ramekins with the softened butter and then the bread crumbs. Tap the bottoms to remove any excess from the bottoms and around the rims.

Melt the butter in a large saucepan over medium heat. Add the flour and cook, stirring with a wooden spoon or heat-resistant spatula, for 2 minutes. Do not let the mixture brown.

Reduce the heat to low and slowly add the milk, whisking constantly. Cook until thick and without lumps, 3 to 5 minutes.

Add the cheese and stir until completely incorporated. Remove from the heat and let stand until slightly cooled. Add the egg yolks one at a time, whisking after each addition. Add the thyme, salt, and nutmeg and stir to incorporate.

Preheat the oven to 375°F. In a medium bowl, whip the egg whites into soft peaks. Working in 3 batches, gently fold into the cheese mixture. Be careful not to overmix and deflate the egg whites.

Spoon the mixture into the ramekins, leaving ¼ inch of the top. Bake until the tops are golden brown, 25 to 30 minutes. Serve immediately.

VIDALIA ONION AND TOMATO TARTS WITH PESTO

CHEF'S NOTE: Each mouthful of this dish offers a taste of fresh herbs and vegetables from a summer garden, carried by the rich flavor of goat cheese.

---

1 sheet puff pastry dough
¼ cup olive oil
1 Vidalia onion, thinly sliced
1 cup fresh parsley, basil, and oregano (or others of your choice), chopped

4 small heirloom tomatoes
Salt and freshly ground black pepper to taste
3 ounces Vermont Butter and Cheese goat cheese (chèvre)
4 teaspoons basil pesto

Preheat the oven to 400°F. Dust a baking sheet with flour.

Roll out the pastry dough and cut into 4 thin rounds. Place on the baking sheet and brush with olive oil. Set aside in the refrigerator.

Heat a sauté pan, add the oil and onion, and cook until the onion is translucent. Sprinkle with the herbs. Divide into 4 equal portions and place in the centers of the dough rounds.

Cut the tomatoes into very thin slices and place on the rounds, covering as much of the onion as possible. Drizzle a bit of olive oil on the tomatoes and season with salt and pepper. Divide the cheese into 4 equal portions and place on top of the tomatoes. Bake for 25 minutes. Drizzle the pesto around the tomatoes and serve hot.

❧ *The Final Touch:* Sprinkle with a few drops of balsamic vinegar and arrange a few mesclun greens on top of each tart.

SLOW-ROASTED PLUM TOMATOES
Serves 4

CHEF'S NOTE: This dish is a nice accompaniment to just about any meal. When making it, it's important to cut the garlic into very thin slices so it cooks along with the tomatoes.

---

6 plum tomatoes
2 cloves garlic
½ teaspoon salt

3 tablespoons extra-virgin olive oil

Preheat the oven to 350°F. Lightly oil a baking sheet.

Halve the tomatoes lengthwise and place cut side up on the baking sheet. Using a sharp paring knife, peel the garlic and shave into ⅛-inch-thick slices. Insert into the tomato halves, then season with salt and drizzle with oil. Roast until the garlic is browned and the tomatoes are wrinkled and beginning to brown, 40 minutes. Serve warm.

SHALLOT MARMALADE

Makes about 1½ cups

CHEF'S NOTE: This "preserve" stores well and is a nice accent with pâtés, grilled meats, and poultry. Sweating the shallots (cooking slowly without browning) develops their sweetness, which is balanced by the acidity of the vinegar.

---

1 tablespoon extra-virgin olive oil

1 pound shallots, peeled and cut into ⅛" slices

¼ cup sugar

½ cup red wine

¼ cup red wine vinegar

Pinch of ground allspice

½ teaspoon salt

Heat the oil in a medium saucepan over low heat. Add the shallots and cook until soft and translucent but not browned, 10 minutes. Add the sugar and cook for 10 minutes. Add the wine and vinegar and simmer until thickened to a paste-like consistency, about 10 minutes. Season with the allspice and salt. Serve at room temperature.

GOUGÈRES

Serves 4

CHEF'S NOTE: Gougères (pronounced *goo-zhairs*) are savory little cheese pastries that go well with soups and appetizers. Both the gougères and the raw batter freeze well.

¼ cup (½ stick) butter

¼ teaspoon salt

1 cup flour

3 free-range eggs

1 tablespoon finely chopped fresh parsley

2 ounces cheese, such as Highgate Springs Boucher Blue or Thistle Hill Tarantaise

¼ teaspoon freshly ground black pepper

Preheat the oven to 375°F.

In a small saucepan over medium-high heat, bring the butter, salt, and 1 cup water to a boil. Remove from the heat, add the flour, and stir vigorously with a wooden spoon. Return to low heat and cook, stirring, for 3 minutes (do not let the mixture brown). Remove from the heat and let cool slightly.

Add the eggs one at a time, stirring well with the wooden spoon after each addition. Add the parsley, cheese, and pepper and stir until the cheese melts.

Using a pastry bag, pipe nickel-size portions of batter about 2 inches apart on a baking sheet. (Alternatively, use 2 spoons to place teaspoon portions, dipping the spoons in warm water if necessary to keep the mixture from sticking.) Bake until puffed and golden brown, 20 to 25 minutes.

⁂ *The Final Touch:* Grate additional cheese over the gougères as they come from the oven.

CRISPY VERMONT CROUTONS

Makes about 1½ cups

CHEF'S NOTE: These croutons made from brioche, an egg- and butter-enriched bread, add texture to puréed soups. If you can't find brioche, you can use another white bread, and you can vary the herbs as well.

---

3 (½"-thick) slices brioche

6 tablespoons (¾ stick) butter, melted

¼ teaspoon salt

Pinch of ground white pepper

1 tablespoon finely chopped fresh parsley (optional)

1 tablespoon grated Asiago or Pecorino Romano cheese (optional)

Preheat the oven to 350°F.

Using a serrated knife, cut the brioche into ½-inch squares. In a medium bowl, combine the butter, salt, and pepper. Add the bread and toss to coat. Spread on a baking sheet and bake until golden brown, 15 to 20 minutes. If desired, return the croutons to the bowl and toss with parsley and cheese.

SWEET TOMATO SUMMER JAM

CHEF'S NOTE: This jam will add color and sweetness to a variety of dishes. Use on appetizers such as pâtés or rillettes or on entrées such as duck and grilled meats.

1 pound heirloom tomatoes, cut into small dice

1 cup sugar

1 clove garlic, minced

3 bay leaves

⅔ cup white vinegar

Heat ⅔ cup water and the sugar in a medium saucepan over low heat until the sugar is dissolved. Add the garlic, bay leaves, and vinegar, then increase the heat to medium and simmer until the mixture reaches the consistency of thick syrup, 30 to 40 minutes. Transfer to jars with lids or cover and refrigerate (it will keep for 1 month). Serve at room temperature.

NEW ENGLAND CAPONATA

Serves 4

CHEF'S NOTE: This New England translation of a Sicilian dish is delicious with pasta and meats. It probably originated in Spain: The name comes from the Catalan word *caponada,* which refers to a similar relish and first appeared in 1709. Caponata is best served lukewarm as an appetizer or a side dish. It can be kept in a sealed container in the refrigerator for several days.

½ cup olive oil

2 Spanish onions, cut into small dice

1 stalk celery, washed, peeled, and finely chopped

2 large eggplants, peeled and cut into small dice

3 heirloom tomatoes, peeled, seeded, and cut into small dice

12 Picholine or green olives, pitted and finely chopped

2 tablespoons capers, coarsely chopped

4 anchovies, rinsed, dried, and minced

2 tablespoons tomato paste

5 tablespoons red wine vinegar

¼ cup sugar

Salt and freshly ground black pepper to taste

½ cup pine nuts, lightly toasted

In a sauté pan over medium-low heat, cook the onions and celery in ¼ cup oil until the onions are translucent and fragrant. Add the remaining ¼ cup oil and the eggplants and cook until slightly soft and cooked through.

Add the tomatoes, olives, capers, anchovies, and tomato paste. Increase the heat to medium and cook for about 5 minutes. Add the vinegar and sugar and season with the salt and pepper. Remove from the heat and stir in the pine nuts.

SUMMER

Summer has little to do with the calendar in Vermont. With snows still in the higher elevations until Memorial Day around the New England Culinary Institute's Montpelier campus, and nighttime temperatures low even in the valleys around the Inn at Essex where their fine dining program is based, every gardener — that is to say, every Vermonter — assembles his or her tools, starts, and seedlings on May 1, puts the Wellies beside the back door, and forks the first wheelbarrow's worth of cow manure into the garden on Mother's Day weekend.

Over the next two weeks, indoor seedlings grown under plant lights since March are removed from their warm corners, shifted to the porch during the day and back into the mudroom at night. Cold frames are planted, the garden cleared of winter debris, peony supports set up. Then most of us sit back, visit Gardeners' Supply or the local AgWay, and impatiently wait until the Memorial Day weekend.

After that, no one in the state goes back indoors except to sleep. Once the garden is in, green plants bolt from the ground as though aware of how little time there is to grow before the next cycle of darkness and cold. Farmers' markets open from one end of the state to the other, festivals are thrown on every village green, and the Vermont Fresh

Network, an organization of local farmers and restaurateurs committed to sustaining Vermont's farms, holds the first of its "meet the farmer" (and cheesemaker or vintner) dinners at restaurants throughout the state.

The Strolling of the Heifers, an annual celebration of young cows who step sweetly through the town of Brattleboro adorned in wildflower wreaths, is held the first weekend in June, and the Green Mountain Chew Chew Festival takes over Burlington's waterfront with huge white tents of our favorite restaurateurs and a celebration of Vermont food.

A week or so later, Vermont's heavy, intensely flavored strawberries are ready for picking and the Vermont Mozart Festival Orchestra launches its season with a concert on the grounds of the Shelburne Inn—an old, rambling estate that covers hundreds of acres of open meadows, barns, and carefully tended woods along Lake Champlain. As the white-coated musicians tune their instruments on the South Porch, a thousand Vermonters from all over the area spread out plaid blankets, open wicker hampers, uncork bottles of local wines, wave to friends they haven't seen since last summer, and watch across the lake as a molten sun sinks behind the Adirondacks' high peaks.

By July 4, most Vermonters have finally been able to stick a toe, a line, or a boat in one of our pristine freshwater lakes, and the midpoint of our summer season is celebrated in Middlebury with a passionate outdoor performance of Tchaikovsky's *1812 Overture* by the Vermont Symphony Orchestra—complete with authentic cannon fire, wildly applauding children, and fireworks over the Middlebury College campus.

Raspberries, blackberries, and blueberries arrive in quick succession, writers from all over the world gather at the Bread Loaf Writers Conference, performances of Shakespeare in the Barn begin again at the Inn at Baldwin Creek, farmers take their first cutting of hay, the corn is up, and—finally!—the first heirloom tomatoes of the season ripen in our gardens.

Once that happens, many of us are happy just to stay home. We take a colander out to the garden just before dark, listen to the cricket choir, watch the sun set, ask the lady garter snake to move away from the beans, and decide what to have for dinner.

Cherry tomatoes and sugar peas usually are popped directly into our mouths since few can resist the heavenly burst of flavor a just-picked veggie can offer. Earthy carrots, cukes, arugula, beans, and fennel go right into the colander, while a precious few ears of corn — their tassels damp and silky and smelling of the earth — are lovingly cradled in our arms.

Sitting on the back porch as the moon rises over the garden, we know that shucking them will not only feed our bellies. It will feed our souls.

2

FISH AND SHELLFISH

People who visit the New England Culinary Institute's restaurants—particularly the Main Street Grill or Butler's at the Inn at Essex—often ask why our seafood tastes better than theirs. Generally they think we've got some secret spice mix back in our kitchens that makes the difference. Or maybe we've got some technical skill that just brings out the best in everything that swims.

If you could hang out in our kitchens for an afternoon, you'd find that, to some extent, both notions are correct. But the real secret to the cooking successes that have won us the nation's top culinary honors is simply that we do our homework. Most of the New England states border the Atlantic Ocean, and NECI is a straight shot down the highway to the coast. So we know who catches our fish and shellfish, what they do to it, and when they do it; we also know where our fish and shellfish have lived, what the waters are like where it swims or scuttles, and whether or not it had a healthy life. We buy shrimp from Maine, scallops from Cape Cod, mussels and oysters from Fisher Island—the list is endless.

Each of these factors has a bearing on the seafood's flavor. Our recipes and technical skills can bring out the best in any fish or shellfish, and we're happy to share them with you. But to make sure you put the purest seafood flavor possible on your table, here's what else you need to do:

- Get to know your local fishmonger and find out where and how his fish and shellfish were raised.

- Buy American-sourced fish and shellfish. Much of the imported fish and shellfish is raised abroad in fish farms under unhealthy conditions. The fish has little flavor, as well — in part because it travels halfway around the world. Instead, use products like Maine shrimp. They're smaller than some of the jumbo jets from abroad, but they have superb flavor and are perfect in dishes like seafood pies.

· Find out what days seafood arrives at your fish store, shop only on those days, and cook the seafood the day you buy it.

· Look for the seal of the Marine Stewardship Council, which certifies that the seafood was harvested from sustainable sources using harvesting methods that will sustain our oceans.

· Look for shellfish with tightly closed shells.

· Look for wild-caught Pacific or Alaskan salmon. Atlantic salmon has been overfished and needs time to regenerate.

· Buy only whole fish — simply because it's easier to tell whether the fish is fresh. Look for clear, not cloudy, eyes. Look for firm, moist flesh that doesn't hold an indentation when you press it with a finger.

· Sniff. If there's a "fishy" odor anywhere in the shop, go elsewhere. Fresh fish has a sweet, fresh odor, not like the Jersey mudflats.

· Once you've chosen your fish, ask your fishmonger to wrap your purchase and bury it in a plastic bag of ice.

· If you can't buy and cook fresh fish or shellfish on the same day, buy frozen fish instead that's labeled "FAS" — frozen at sea. Just beware of the supermarket practice in which FAS fish are defrosted in the store, then placed on a bed of ice and offered as though they've just been caught. If you look carefully, nearby will be a tiny sign that says "previously frozen." If you see one of those, simply ask the fishmonger to go out back in his freezer and get you a fish that's still frozen. Then defrost it in your own refrigerator right before cooking.

Follow these tips and the fish and shellfish you place on your table will be superb. And why not? With what fish costs today, why you should be eating something a seal would turn down is a mystery!

CLASSIC NEW ENGLAND SALT COD CAKES

Serves 4

CHEF'S NOTE: Many historians feel that the salt cod industry was a major factor in the development of our nation. This recipe uses salt cod just as cooks did centuries ago. The key is to soak it in water for 24 hours in the refrigerator, changing the water several times. It's also important to make the cod mixture at least 6 hours before cooking, or it will be difficult to keep the cakes together. If you follow these basic rules, you'll be rewarded with the same tasty cod cakes New Englanders have enjoyed for hundreds of years.

---

1 pound dried salt cod, rinsed and soaked at least 24 hours

1 cup large-dice onion

3 cups milk

¼ cup (½ stick) butter

¼ cup small-dice onion

2 tablespoons minced garlic

2 scallions, minced

¼ cup chopped fresh parsley

1 tablespoon minced fresh tarragon leaves

⅓ cup heavy cream

3 cups bread crumbs

2 free-range eggs

2 teaspoons freshly ground black pepper

1 cup vegetable oil

1 lemon, cut into 8 wedges

Drain the cod. In a 2-quart saucepan over medium heat, bring the cod, milk, and large-dice onion to a simmer, stirring occasionally. Cook until the cod begins to flake apart, about 10 minutes. Transfer to a plate to cool and discard the milk and onion.

When the cod is cool enough to handle, flake it with your fingers into a medium bowl, discarding any skin or bones.

Melt the butter in a small sauté pan over medium-high heat. Add the small-dice onion and garlic and cook for 2 minutes. Remove from the heat and let cool, then add to the cod. Add the scallions, parsley, tarragon, cream, 1 cup bread crumbs, eggs, and pepper and combine thoroughly with your hands. Cover and refrigerate for at least 6 hours.

Place the remaining 2 cups bread crumbs in a shallow dish. Divide the cod mixture into eight ⅓-cup portions and form each into a tight cake. Carefully dredge the cakes in the bread crumbs, coating thoroughly.

Heat the oil in a 12-inch sauté pan over medium heat. Carefully add the cod cakes (if they don't start to sizzle immediately, the oil is not hot enough). Cook until golden brown, about 2 minutes. Carefully turn and cook the other side until golden brown and heated through. Transfer to paper towels to drain. To serve, place 2 cod cakes and 2 lemon wedges on each plate.

❧ *The Final Touch:* Coleslaw and roasted steak fries are great with cod cakes, especially this recipe. Any mayonnaise-based sauce, such as tartar sauce, works well and is in keeping with New England tradition.

LE SOMMELIER: The salty elements of this dish provide a nice counterpoint to the slight sweetness of Snow Farm Winery's American Riesling. Snow Farm was one of the original Vermont wineries, and their beautiful property in South Hero sits on the shores of Lake Champlain, where the climate is moderated by the lake's influence. Their Riesling has just a touch of sweetness and all the elegance of traditional Riesling.

WINTER STEW

Serves 4

CHEF'S NOTE: This stew featuring cod, kale, and sausage is the perfect cold-weather entrée in New England. When using kale, cut out the stem entirely and chop the leaves. When choosing the sausage, look for locally made cooked pork sausage with the consistency of kielbasa, which works well. If you can't find a local brand, a Portuguese linguica works well and is the most authentic; if you prefer to go spicier, andouilli is a good alternative. You can make your own vegetable stock or buy it readymade.

3–5 tablespoons olive oil

8 cod fillets (3 ounces each)

2 cups sliced fully cooked pork sausage

1 bunch kale, washed, stem removed, and leaves cut into ½" squares

8 medium red potatoes

2 cups medium-dice peeled seeded heirloom tomatoes

3 cups vegetable stock

2 tablespoons chopped fresh parsley

Salt and freshly ground black pepper to taste

Cut the potatoes into 6 pieces each. Place in a medium saucepan with water to cover and cook until tender, 20 to 30 minutes. Drain and set aside.

Heat a heavy 3-quart pot over medium-high heat. Add 3 tablespoons oil and the cod and cook until lightly browned, 4 to 5 minutes per side. Using a spatula, transfer to a plate or tray. Add the sausage to the pot and cook, stirring occasionally, until lightly browned, 8 to 10 minutes. If there isn't enough fat, add another 1 or 2 tablespoons oil.

Add the kale and stir for about 1 minute. Add the potatoes, tomato, stock, and parsley and bring to a simmer. Return the cod to the pot, cover, and return to a simmer. Reduce the heat to medium low and cook until the cod is cooked through, about 6 minutes.

Using a slotted spoon, place 2 fillets in each serving bowl. Season with salt and pepper, then ladle the stew into the bowls and serve immediately.

❧ *The Final Touch:* Top the stew with a sprig of fresh parsley and serve with dinner rolls.

LE SOMMELIER: We think this robust, warming winter stew will be even more enjoyable served with a cool Vermont ale. Try Rock Art Brewery's Whitetail Ale, a golden American-style ale whose dry, hoppy flavor nicely contrasts with the rich, spicy sausage and earthy kale. If you prefer wine, we recommend a medium-bodied, not-too-tannic red with good acidity. Some possibilities are a Chianti from Tuscany or the 2005 Leon Millot, an estate-bottled hybrid from Snow Farm Winery in South Hero, Vermont.

OVEN-POACHED COD WITH
SMOKED SALMON–HORSERADISH CRUST

Serves 4

CHEF'S NOTE: This dish may sound complex, but it's fairly easy to prepare. The key is to add the topping when the cod fillets are cooked about halfway through. Don't be surprised if you find yourself sampling the topping with some crackers as you're preparing the rest of the dish!

Topping

6 ounces smoked salmon, skin removed, cut into chunks

¼ cup heavy cream

¼ cup cream cheese

1 tablespoon fresh lemon juice

2 tablespoons prepared horse-radish, drained

2 tablespoons minced fresh dill

2 tablespoons diced red onion

Salt and freshly ground black pepper to taste

Cod

4 cod fillets (5 ounces each)

2 tablespoons fresh lemon juice

Salt and freshly ground black pepper to taste

½ cup bread crumbs

1 lemon, cut into 8 wedges

Preheat the oven to 400°F. Lightly butter or oil a 10 x 10–inch baking dish.

To make the topping: In a food processor, purée the salmon and cream until smooth, about 1 minute. Add the cream cheese and purée for 1 minute. Add the lemon juice, horse-radish, dill, onion, and a pinch of salt and pepper and pulse until combined. (You can make this 2 days ahead and refrigerate it until needed.)

To make the cod: Place the cod in the baking dish and pour in the lemon juice and ½ cup water. Season with salt and pepper. Bake until cooked about halfway through, about 6 minutes. Spread the salmon mixture evenly onto the cod, being careful not to break the fillets. Sprinkle the top with the bread crumbs and bake until the cod is cooked through, about 5 minutes. Carefully transfer to plates, garnish with the lemon wedges, and serve immediately.

The Final Touch: Many starches and vegetables complement this dish. Mashed potatoes and steamed asparagus make an especially nice combination that works well with the smoked salmon and cod flavors. Another option is to serve the fish over fettuccini with crisp, fresh green beans tossed in dill butter.

LE SOMMELIER: The texture and slight spiciness of this dish call for a slightly sweet ("off-dry") wine to balance them. Since it's a cod dish with a salmon element, a white wine seems like the best bet. Try Ballet of Angels from Sharpe Hill Vineyards in Connecticut. It's a blend of several grapes with a crisp texture and a bit of sweetness on the palate that make it a perfect complement.

COD WITH STEAMED MUSSELS

Serves 4

CHEF'S NOTE: This dish is a great combination of fresh seafood flavors that offers balanced nutrition in an appealing presentation. The key to success with this recipe is to have everything prepared before the final cooking stages.

Croutons

¼ cup canola oil

2 tablespoons olive oil

1 tablespoon minced garlic

1 tablespoon salt

1 tablespoon freshly ground black pepper

2 tablespoons chopped parsley

½ baguette, cut into ¼"-thick slices (at least 20 slices)

Cod and Mussels

4 cod fillets (5 ounces each)

Salt and freshly ground black pepper to taste

2 tablespoons olive oil

1 tablespoon minced garlic

1 cup ¼"-thick leek rings, soaked and drained

28 mussels, washed well and beards removed

½ cup white wine

1 cup drained canned Great Northern beans

2 tablespoons fresh lemon juice

3 tablespoons chopped fresh parsley

Preheat the oven to 400°F. Lightly butter or oil a 10 x 10–inch baking dish.

To make the croutons: In a small bowl, combine the canola oil, olive oil, garlic, salt, pepper, and parsley. Using a pastry brush, coat one side of the bread slices with the mixture and place oiled side up on a 12 x 18–inch baking sheet. Bake until lightly browned, about 5 minutes. Set aside. (The croutons can be made up to 1 day ahead and stored at room temperature but are best when made within an hour of serving.)

To make the cod and mussels: Place the cod in the baking dish and season with salt and pepper. Bake for about 10 minutes. If the cod is ready before the mussels, remove from the oven and cover with foil to keep warm.

Asparagus and Scallop Brochettes with Risotto

Heirloom Tomato and Goat Cheese Salad with Basil Vinagrette

Roasted Beets with Mâche

Scallops with Beet Carpaccio and Wasabi Cream

Tomato Fennel Salad

Shrimp Caesar Salad in Parmesan Bowls

Belgian Endives with Goat Cheese

Salmon-Wrapped Scallops

Heat a 3-quart saucepan over medium-high heat. Add the oil, garlic, and leeks and cook, stirring, until the leeks are tender, 2 to 3 minutes. Add the mussels, wine, beans, and ½ cup water. Cover and steam the mussels until they open, about 3 minutes. Remove from the heat, discard any unopened mussels, and add the lemon juice and parsley.

Using a spatula, carefully place the cod fillets in the center of 4 warmed plates. Arrange the mussels around the cod with the open ends facing up and out. Spoon or ladle the broth, beans, and leek mixture over the cod and mussels. Place the croutons around the rims of the plates and serve immediately.

❧ *The Final Touch:* Instead of using croutons, you can serve this dish with grilled bruschetta, which are great for soaking up the broth. Cut the baguette slices slightly on the diagonal, about ⅓ inch thick. Brush with the oil mixture and quickly broil the bread just before serving. You can also serve the dish in bowls with wide rims instead of on plates.

HERB-BAKED COD WITH CUCUMBER DILL SAUCE

Serves 4

CHEF'S NOTE: In this dish, the fresh fish, wilted greens, and cold summer sauce bring out the best in each other. All the components are rather easy to prepare, but when combined on the same plate, they create a nice medley of textures, flavors, and colors. Spinach, kale, or almost any other wilting green can be substituted for the escarole, although each will have a slightly different cooking time. Be sure to use fresh dill in the sauce. You may substitute rice wine vinegar or cider vinegar for the champagne vinegar and any fresh thyme for the lemon thyme.

Sauce

1 cup medium-dice peeled seeded cucumber

¼ cup small-dice red onion

2 tablespoons minced fresh dill

½ cup sour cream

3 tablespoons champagne vinegar

Cod

2 tablespoons chopped fresh lemon thyme leaves

3 tablespoons chopped fresh parsley

4 cod fillets (6 ounces each)

¼ cup (½ stick) butter, melted

Salt and freshly ground black pepper to taste

½ cup bread crumbs

½ cup water

½ cup white wine

2 tablespoons olive oil

1 head escarole, stem removed, washed well, and chopped

1 lemon, cut into 8 wedges

Preheat the oven to 400°F. Lightly butter or oil a 10 x 10–inch baking pan.

To make the sauce: In a medium bowl, stir together the cucumber, onion, dill, cream, and vinegar. Season with salt and pepper and set aside.

To make the cod: In a small bowl, combine the thyme and parsley. Place the cod in the baking pan and brush with some of the butter. Sprinkle generously with the herb mix and season with salt and pepper.

In a small bowl, combine the remaining butter with the bread crumbs and evenly distribute the crumbs on top of the cod. Add the water and wine to the pan, being careful not to pour them onto the fish. Bake for about 12 minutes.

Heat the oil in a 10-inch sauté pan over medium-high heat. Add the escarole and cook until wilted, about 5 minutes. Season with salt and pepper.

Pile equal portions of escarole in the center of 4 plates. Using a spatula, carefully place the cod on the greens. Top with a spoonful of sauce and serve the rest on the side. Garnish the plate with lemon wedges and serve immediately.

✺ *The Final Touch:* To nicely round out this meal, serve with a crusty bread.

BUTTER-POACHED COD WITH CREAMED LEEKS
Serves 4

CHEF'S NOTE: This is an excellent dish to make when cod from local fishermen is available (day-boat cod). When buying the cod, look for thicker fillets, which will be easier to keep intact when removing them from the poaching liquid. You can make your own vegetable stock or buy it readymade.

---

2 leeks, washed well and julienned (white parts only)

1 cup white wine

1 cup heavy cream

2 teaspoons salt

¼ teaspoon ground white pepper

1 tablespoon fresh lemon juice

2 cups vegetable stock

1 pound (4 sticks) salted butter, cut into 1" pieces

4 cod fillets (6 ounces each)

In a heavy 1-quart saucepan over medium-high heat, cook the leeks in the wine until the wine is reduced by ¾. Add the cream and cook until the cream is reduced by ½. Add the salt, pepper, and lemon juice and remove from the heat.

Bring the stock to a simmer in a 3-quart pot. Reduce the heat and whisk in the butter piece by piece until melted. Return to a low simmer and add the cod. Cook for about 7 minutes, being careful not to let the liquid boil. Remove from the heat.

Using a solid spoon, place equal portions of the leek mixture on 4 plates. Using a slotted spatula or spoon, carefully remove the cod from the liquid, pat with paper towels, and place on top of the leeks.

❧ *The Final Touch:* Asparagus and boiled red parsley potatoes are a perfect vegetable and starch to serve with this dish. If asparagus isn't available, green beans or sugar snap peas work well.

MICROBREWERY FISH AND CHIPS

Serves 4

CHEF'S NOTE: This old English classic has benefited from the development of the great microbreweries in New England; pick a flavorful local favorite. You can use homemade chips and tartar sauce or buy readymade products; the fish will steal the show either way.

---

12 ounces microbrewery beer or ale

6 tablespoons + 1½ quarts vegetable oil

2 free-range eggs

3 cups all-purpose flour

½ cup cornstarch

1 tablespoon salt

¼ tablespoon cayenne pepper

8 cod fillets (3 ounces each)

1 pound cooked french fries

1 cup tartar sauce

1 lemon, cut into 8 wedges

In a medium bowl, combine the beer, 6 tablespoons oil, and eggs. In a large bowl, combine the flour, cornstarch, salt, black pepper, and cayenne. Add the liquid ingredients and whisk until smooth. The consistency should be similar to slightly thick pancake batter. If it's too thick, thin with a little cold water.

Heat the 1½ quarts oil to 375°F in a deep fryer.

Place the cod in the batter and turn to coat all sides. One at a time, remove 3 or 4 fillets, drain off any excess, and place in the hot oil, being careful not to splash. Cook, carefully turning after a few minutes, until golden brown, about 6 minutes. Using tongs or a slotted spoon, transfer to a pan lined with paper towels and keep warm. Repeat with the remaining fillets.

To serve, place 2 fillets on each plate with a handful of french fries, 2 lemon wedges, and some tartar sauce.

❧ *The Final Touch:* Freshly made coleslaw rounds this dinner off nicely.

LE SOMMELIER: Using a wine or beer when preparing a recipe and then serving the beverage with the dish is a great way to pair a food and beverage. Magic Hat's #9 is a unique and flavorful beer to try for this dish. It has distinct but subtle apricot notes that add character and flavor.

BAKED HADDOCK WITH SEAFOOD STUFFING

Serves 4

CHEF'S NOTE: After serving this dish once, you may find that you're bombarded with pleas from your family and friends to make it again. The sauce is the trickiest part of the recipe, but the key to success is using real butter. The stuffing is very moist and doesn't use as much bread as most stuffings; it can be made several days ahead and refrigerated.

---

3 tablespoons butter

2 tablespoons minced red bell pepper

2 tablespoons minced green bell pepper

2 tablespoons minced onion

2 tablespoons minced mushrooms

¼ pound cooked small Maine shrimp

¼ pound pasteurized crabmeat, picked through for shells

⅓ cup sour cream

1 teaspoon dried thyme

2 tablespoons chopped parsley

2 tablespoons fresh lemon juice

⅔ cup bread crumbs

Salt and freshly ground black pepper to taste

4 haddock fillets (5 ounces each)

2 tablespoons (¼ stick) butter, melted

1 cup Lemon Butter Sauce (recipe on page 57)

Preheat the oven to 400°F. Lightly butter or oil a 10 x 10–inch baking pan.

Melt the butter in a 10-inch sauté pan over medium-high heat. Add the bell peppers and onion and cook, stirring occasionally, for 2 minutes. Add the mushrooms and cook until they give up their moisture and reabsorb it. Add the shrimp and crabmeat and cook gently for 1 minute. Remove from the heat and transfer the mixture to a medium bowl. Add the sour cream, thyme, parsley, lemon juice, and bread crumbs. Mix well and season with salt and pepper. If the stuffing seems too loose, add more bread crumbs.

Divide into four ½-cup portions and space them equidistant from each other in the pan. Form into tight ovals approximately 1 inch thick. Place a fillet on each portion and press down gently, shaping the fish around the stuffing. Brush the top of the haddock with melted butter and season with salt and pepper. Bake until cooked throughout, about 17 minutes.

Place a stuffed haddock fillet in the center of each plate and top with the sauce.

❧ *The Final Touch:* Fresh green beans, boiled red potatoes, and lemon wedges are the perfect accompaniment to this classic New England dish.

> LE SOMMELIER: A dry Riesling from upstate New York is wonderful with this dish. The cool climate of the Finger Lakes helps preserve the acidity of the grapes, making this wine a good match with the lemon butter sauce, and the weight of a dry or off-dry Riesling is balanced by the weight of the haddock. Try Dr. Konstantin Frank's 2006 Dry Riesling.

LEMON BUTTER SAUCE
Makes 1 cup

¼ cup white wine

2 tablespoons lemon juice

1 tablespoon minced shallot

3 black peppercorns

2 parsley stems

¼ cup heavy cream

½ cup (1 stick) butter, cut into 1-tablespoon pieces and kept refrigerated

Salt and freshly ground black pepper to taste

In a 1-quart stainless steel saucepan over medium-high heat, simmer the wine, lemon juice, shallots, peppercorns, and parsley stems until only a few tablespoons of liquid are left. Add the cream and simmer until reduced by ½. Reduce the heat to medium low and whisk in the cold butter 2 pieces at a time until melted. Strain the sauce through a fine-mesh strainer into a small saucepan and season with salt and pepper. Cover the pan to keep warm until ready to use.

ALMOND-CRUSTED HADDOCK
WITH BRAISED LEEKS

Serves 4

CHEF'S NOTE: This well-rounded entrée offers a nice combination of textures and flavors. As usual, be sure to wash the leeks very well, as they tend to be sandy. Panko bread crumbs work great in the almond crust and can be found in most supermarkets, but plain bread crumbs are also fine.

---

2 tablespoons (¼ stick) butter

½ cup panko (Japanese) bread crumbs

½ cup sliced almonds, lightly toasted

Salt and freshly ground black pepper to taste

2 leeks, washed well, halved lengthwise, and cut into 1"-wide half moons

2 tablespoons olive oil

1 cup white wine

2 teaspoons salt

2 teaspoons chopped fresh thyme leaves

4 haddock fillets (6 ounces each)

2 tablespoons (¼ stick) butter, melted

2 tablespoons fresh lemon juice

½ cup white wine

Preheat the oven to 400°F. Lightly butter a 10 x 10–inch baking dish.

Melt the butter in an 8-inch sauté pan over medium heat. Add the bread crumbs and cook, stirring, until the crumbs begin to toast, then add the almonds and season with salt and pepper. Remove from the heat.

Place a 2-quart saucepan over medium-high heat and add the oil. Add the leeks and cook until quite soft, about 5 minutes. Add the wine and cook until almost all the liquid has evaporated, then add 1 cup water and the salt and thyme. Cover and simmer, stirring occasionally, for 15 minutes. Reduce the heat and cook for 5 minutes, then remove from the heat and keep warm.

Place the haddock in the baking dish, brush with the melted butter, and season with salt and pepper. Evenly distribute the almond topping among the fillets. Pour the lemon juice, wine, and ¼ cup water into the pan and bake for 8 to 10 minutes.

Spoon the leeks onto warmed plates and top with the haddock.

❧ *The Final Touch:* Roasted garlic mashed potatoes and brussels sprouts complement this dish nicely, especially in the fall and winter.

> LE SOMMELIER: Snow Farm vineyards in South Hero, Vermont, produces an estate wine from Seyval Blanc grapes, a hybrid variety that's tolerant of Vermont's cold climate but capable of producing a crisp, fruity white wine that pairs nicely with the light, delicate haddock in this dish.

NEW ENGLAND HADDOCK
WITH STEAMED LITTLENECKS

Serves 4

CHEF'S NOTE: This dish will make any seafood lover happy. The salt pork used with the cabbage adds incredible flavor, but don't use more than the recipe calls for, or the dish will be too salty. You can find salt pork, often frozen, in many supermarkets, but you can substitute drained cooked bacon if necessary. Leaving the skin on the haddock helps keep the fish intact when it's seared, but if you can't find it with skin or prefer not to use it, be sure to buy thicker cuts.

¼ cup olive oil

Freshly ground black pepper to taste

4 tablespoons chopped fresh parsley

4 haddock fillets (5 ounces each), with skin

1 head green cabbage, cored and quartered

4 tablespoons (½ stick) butter

¼ cup small-dice salt pork

1 cup small-dice onion

2 tablespoons minced garlic

2 teaspoons celery seed

2 teaspoons chopped fresh thyme

1 teaspoon chopped fresh tarragon

16 littleneck clams, washed well

1 cup white wine

Freshly ground black pepper to taste

In a medium bowl, combine the oil, pepper, and 1 tablespoon parsley. Place the haddock skin-side up on a cutting board. Using a sharp knife, cut the skin in several places to help prevent curling. Coat with the oil mixture and refrigerate for several hours.

Preheat the oven to 375°F. Bring 2½ quarts water to a boil in a 4-quart saucepan. Break the cabbage apart with your hands, add to the pan, and cook until tender, about 8 minutes. Drain in a large strainer in the sink and rinse with cold water. Cut into ¼-inch-thick strips and set aside.

Melt 2 tablespoons butter in a 4-quart saucepan over medium-high heat. Add the pork, onion, and 1 tablespoon garlic and cook, stirring, until the onion is translucent, about 3 minutes. Add the cabbage, celery seed, thyme, tarragon, 1 tablespoon parsley, and pepper and stir well. Reduce the heat to medium and cook for about 12 minutes.

Heat a 12-inch ovenproof sauté pan over medium-high heat until very hot. Add the haddock skin-side down and cook until the skin is very crisp. Turn the fillets, transfer to the oven, and bake for about 7 minutes.

Meanwhile, in a 2-quart saucepan over medium-high heat, combine the clams, wine, the remaining 2 tablespoons garlic, and ⅔ cup water. Cover and simmer until the clams open, about 5 minutes. Discard any unopened clams and reserve the broth.

Pile equal portions of cabbage in the center of 4 warmed plates or bowls. Using a spatula, place the haddock skin-side up on top of the cabbage. Using tongs, place 3 clams around the haddock with the open ends facing up and out. Stir the remaining 2 tablespoons parsley and 2 tablespoons butter into the clam broth and season with pepper. Ladle a generous amount of broth over the haddock and clams and serve immediately.

❧ *The Final Touch:* This meal is really perfect as is, but if you serve a crusty bread or garlic bread with it, you and your guests will be able soak up and enjoy the delicious broth.

CEDAR-PLANKED HALIBUT
WITH ROASTED ROOT VEGETABLES

Serves 4

CHEF'S NOTE: This dish works well in the late fall and winter months. The combination of flavors, textures, and colors is fantastic. You can buy cedar planks at specialty food shops and online, but it's less expensive to have one cut to size at a local home improvement store; just be sure the cedar is untreated. Soak the plank in water for 12 hours, weighed down so it doesn't float. If it's more than ½ inch thick, soaked properly, and placed on the grill for only a short time, you can reuse it once after washing it well.

---

2 cups cubed (¾") peeled Yukon Gold potatoes

2 cups cubed (¾") peeled carrots

1 cup cubed (¾") peeled beets

1 cup cubed (¾") peeled turnip

1 cup cubed (¾") peeled parsnip

1 cup cubed (¾") red onion

8 tablespoons olive oil

Salt and freshly ground black pepper to taste

4 halibut fillets (6 ounces each)

1 bunch kale, stems removed, washed well, and cut into ½"-wide strips

2 tablespoons cider vinegar

Preheat the oven to 425°F. Preheat the grill to high.

In a large bowl, combine the potatoes, carrots, beets, turnip, parsnip, onion, and 3 tablespoons oil. Season with salt and pepper and toss. Transfer to a 12 x 18–inch baking sheet and roast until lightly browned and tender, 20 to 30 minutes, stirring after about 12 minutes.

Lightly brush the halibut with 2 tablespoons oil and season with salt and pepper. Place on a cedar plank, transfer to the grill, and cook until the plank begins to smoke, 3 to 5 minutes. Close the grill, reduce the heat to medium, and cook for 4 minutes. Using tongs and a hot pad, transfer to the oven and bake for 5 to 10 minutes, depending on the thickness of the fish. (A good rule of thumb is that firm fish such as halibut takes 10 minutes cooking time per inch of thickness.)

Heat the remaining 3 tablespoons oil in a 12-inch sauté pan over medium-high heat. Add the kale and cook, stirring, until wilted, about 2 minutes. Season with salt and pepper. Stir in the vinegar, then remove from the heat.

Place equal portions of kale in the center of 4 plates and spread it out so it forms a circle larger than the size of the halibut. Using a spatula, carefully place the halibut on the kale. Scatter the vegetables around the outer edges of the plate so they surround the halibut.

❧ *The Final Touch:* Place a lemon twist and a sprig of fresh thyme or parsley on the halibut and a bowl of lemon wedges on the table.

LE SOMMELIER: The smoky cedar flavor of the halibut and the slight sweetness of the root vegetables in this dish cry out for a nice ale. Pair it with the great Copper Ale from Otter Creek. The sweet roasted malt of the ale works well with the cedar, and the slight bitterness of the kale is perfectly balanced by the ale's hops.

BAKED MUSTARD-CRUSTED SALMON

Serves 4

CHEF'S NOTE: This is an outstanding way to serve salmon during the hotter months of the year. Preparation is quick, and the dish is light and flavorful. Local cucumbers work in this recipe, but European-style cucumbers are fine as well. It's important to use fresh dill. If you don't have champagne vinegar, you may substitute rice wine vinegar or cider vinegar.

---

1 cup medium-dice peeled seeded cucumber

¼ cup small-dice red onion

2 tablespoons minced fresh dill

½ cup sour cream

3 tablespoons champagne vinegar

Salt and freshly ground black pepper to taste

½ cup Dijon mustard

1 cup bread crumbs

¼ cup (½ stick) butter, melted

4 wild-caught salmon fillets (6 ounces each)

1 lemon, cut into 8 wedges

Preheat the oven to 400°F. Lightly butter or oil a 10 x 10–inch baking pan.

In a medium bowl, combine the cucumber, onion, dill, sour cream, and vinegar. Season with salt and pepper.

In a small bowl, combine the mustard, bread crumbs, butter, and a pinch of salt and pepper. Season the salmon with salt and pepper and pack the crumb mixture evenly on top of each fillet. Place in the pan with the crumb side facing up. Bake until the fish is cooked to desired doneness, 10 to 12 minutes. Transfer to plates, drizzle with sauce, garnish with the lemon wedges, and serve immediately.

LE SOMMELIER: This dish pairs very nicely with the delicate but fruity elements of a Pinot Noir, such as the one produced by Wolffer Estate in Sagaponack, New York. Their estate Pinot Noir offers enough fruit to match the mustard and is nuanced enough to complement the salmon.

🐿 *The Final Touch:* A tossed mesclun or spinach salad goes well with this dish. Simply place a handful of dressed greens on each plate.

GRILLED SALMON WITH SQUASH SAUCE AND A CRANBERRY PILAF

Serves 4

CHEF'S NOTE: This hearty yet low-fat entrée is a good fall and winter dish. While grilling the salmon adds great flavor that goes well with the other components of the dish, pan searing or broiling it also works well. You may find that you need to make adjustments to the consistency of the sauce because of the variables involved.

Sauce

1 tablespoon vegetable oil

½ cup cubed (½") peeled carrot

¼ cup cubed (½") onion

2 cups cubed (½") peeled seeded butternut squash

½ cup white wine

2 cups chicken broth or stock

1 teaspoon chopped fresh thyme leaves

1 tablespoon chopped fresh sage leaves

2 tablespoons fresh lemon juice

2 tablespoons (¼ stick) butter

Salt and ground white pepper to taste

Pilaf

⅓ cup wild rice

2⅓ cups chicken broth or stock

⅔ cup converted white rice

¼ cup walnuts, lightly toasted and chopped

¼ cup dried cranberries

1 tablespoon chopped fresh thyme leaves

Salt and freshly ground black pepper to taste

Salmon

4 wild-caught salmon fillets (6 ounces each)

2 tablespoons olive oil

To make the sauce: Heat the oil in a 2-quart saucepan over medium heat. Add the carrot and onion and cook until soft, about 2 minutes. Add the squash, wine, broth, and 1 cup water and simmer until soft, 15 to 20 minutes. Add the thyme and sage. Remove from the heat and let cool for 5 minutes.

Working in 2 batches, transfer to a blender, put the lid on, and place a kitchen towel over the top (in case any of the contents splash out). Pulse a few times, increase the speed to low and blend until smooth, then increase the speed again and purée until very smooth. If the mixture is too thick to purée, add some water or broth.

Transfer to a small saucepan over low heat. Stir in the lemon juice and butter and season with salt and white pepper. Cook until the mixture reaches the consistency of thick cream.

Preheat the grill. Preheat the oven to 375°F. Lightly butter or oil a 10 x 10–inch baking pan.

To make the pilaf: In a small saucepan, cook the wild rice in 1 cup broth until tender, about 45 minutes. In a 1-quart saucepan, bring the remaining 1⅓ cups broth to a boil over high heat. Add the converted rice, cover, and reduce the heat to medium low. Cook until tender, about 17 minutes. Remove from the heat and add the wild rice, cranberries, walnuts, and thyme. Season with salt and pepper and stir carefully with a fork.

To make the salmon: Place the fillets on a large plate, coat with olive oil, and season with salt and black pepper. Transfer skin-side up to the grill. After 2 minutes, use a spatula to give the fillets a quarter sideways turn. Cook for 2 minutes, then turn and cook for 1 minute on the other side. Transfer to the baking pan and bake for about 5 minutes.

Spoon equal portions of the pilaf into the centers of 4 plates. Ladle the sauce around the rice and place the salmon on top with the grill marks facing up.

LE SOMMELIER: While Pinot Noir seems like the natural wine to match with this dish, it's fun to mix it up a little bit. Westport Rivers Winery in Westport, Massachusetts, makes a rosé sparkling wine from Pinot Noir grapes. It's dry but has many of the characteristics of Pinot Noir, which make it a great match for this dish: crisp acid, light berry and cherry fruit, and a delicate texture.

The Final Touch: Garnish one side of the plate with fresh sage leaves and add a few re-hydrated cranberries around the plate.

SUGAR SNAPPED SALMON CAKES
WITH ROASTED POTATO WEDGES

Serves 4

CHEF'S NOTE: It's best to make salmon cakes when you have extra salmon after making another dish or there's a sale on certain pieces, such as from the tail. To test the doneness of the boiled potato that will be shredded and put into the cake mixture, pierce it with a paring knife. If the knife slides out slowly, the potato should be ready.

Salmon Cakes

1 pound wild-caught salmon

1½ cups grated peeled boiled potato

2 scallions, chopped

2 tablespoons chopped fresh parsley

3 tablespoons small-dice onion

¼ cup sour cream

¼ cup bread crumbs

2 tablespoons fresh lemon juice

2 tablespoons minced capers

Salt and freshly ground black pepper to taste

8 tablespoons vegetable oil

1 cup Lemon Butter Sauce (recipe on page 57)

Potatoes

2 baking potatoes, cut into wedges

2 tablespoons olive oil

Salt and freshly ground black pepper to taste

2 tablespoons (¼ stick) butter

Peas

2 cups sugar snap peas, stems removed

Salt and freshly ground black pepper

Preheat the oven to 400°F.

To make the salmon cakes: Mince the salmon with a knife until it has the consistency of ground beef. In a medium bowl, combine the salmon, potatoes, scallions, parsley, onion, sour cream, bread crumbs, lemon juice, capers, salt, and pepper and mix well. Taste the mixture and add more seasoning if desired. Form into eight ¼-cup cakes. Heat 2 tablespoons oil in a 12-inch sauté pan over medium heat, then add 2 cakes and cook until golden brown, about 2 minutes per side. Transfer to a 12 x 12–inch baking sheet and repeat with the remaining cakes, adding oil to the pan as needed.

To make the potatoes: In a medium bowl, toss the potatoes with the olive oil, salt, and pepper. Transfer to a 12 x 16–inch baking sheet and roast for 12 minutes. Using a spatula, turn the potatoes, then roast until golden brown, 2 minutes.

To make the peas: Melt the butter in a 10-inch sauté pan over medium-high heat. Add the peas and sauté for 2 minutes. Add 2 tablespoons water and season with salt and pepper.

Reduce the oven temperature to 300°F and place the salmon cakes in the oven to heat while you make the sauce.

Place a salmon cake in the center of each serving plate, then add another, leaning against the first. Place a pile of potatoes on one side of the plate and peas on the other. Spoon the sauce around the salmon cakes.

The Final Touch: A lemon twist and a fresh herb sprig are attractive on this plate. Other sauce options are remoulade sauce, mustard cream sauce, or fruit salsa.

> LE SOMMELIER: The texture of the salmon and the lemon butter provide a nice backdrop for the flavors of New World Pinot Gris. Wolffer Estate in Sagaponack, New York, produces an excellent example of Pinot Gris from their vineyards on Long Island. Find one at your local wine shop (or online) and see how well it works with this dish.

POACHED SALMON WITH PAELLA RISOTTO

Serves 4

CHEF'S NOTE: This hearty dish is especially good in fall and winter. Although wild Pacific salmon is the most flavorful choice, farm-raised Atlantic salmon also works well. If you can't find chorizo sausage, any spicy sausage will work.

---

1 quart apple cider

1 cup large-dice Spanish onion

1 cup large-dice celery

1 cinnamon stick

5 whole cloves

6 black peppercorns

1 teaspoon salt

1 quart chicken broth

½ teaspoon saffron threads (about 12 strands)

3 tablespoons unsalted butter

1 cup small-dice Spanish onion

1½ cups Arborio rice

¼ cup grated Parmesan cheese

¼ cup frozen green peas

½ cup medium-dice cooked chorizo sausage

4 ounces medium-dice cooked chicken breast

Salt and freshly ground black pepper to taste

4 wild-caught salmon fillets (5 ounces each)

16 littleneck clams, washed well

¼ cup chopped parsley

Preheat the oven to 400°F. In a 2-quart saucepan, combine the cider, large-dice onion, celery, cinnamon, cloves, peppercorns, and salt and simmer for 5 minutes. Remove from the heat.

In a medium saucepan, bring the broth and saffron to a simmer. Melt the butter in another 2-quart saucepan over medium heat. Add the small-dice onion and cook until soft, about 2 minutes. Add the rice and stir to coat with butter. Add 1 cup hot broth and stir until mostly absorbed by the rice. Add ½ cup broth and stir. Continue to add the broth ½ cup at a time, stirring until the rice is tender, about 20 minutes. Stir in the sausage, chicken, peas, and cheese. Season with salt and pepper, then cover and remove from the heat.

Place the salmon and clams in a large ovenproof sauté pan. Pour in the cider mixture through a strainer and cover the pan. Transfer to the oven and cook until the clams have opened and the salmon is cooked to the desired doneness, 8 to 10 minutes.

Spoon a pile of risotto into the center of 4 large dinner plates or soup bowls. Using a spatula, carefully place the salmon on the rice. Place the opened clams around the outer edges of the plate (discard any unopened ones). Stir the parsley into the poaching liquid and, using a solid spoon or ladle, drizzle some of the liquid over the salmon and clams and serve immediately.

The Final Touch: Adding a spoonful of lemon or red pepper chutney to the salmon and serving with several lemon wedges are nice touches. You can find chutneys in the gourmet sections of most supermarkets and in specialty shops.

SUMMER PAN-SEARED SALMON
ON WILD MUSHROOM RAGOÛT

Serves 4

CHEF'S NOTE: This is the perfect salmon dish to serve during the height of mushroom season. While we recommend three different mushrooms that are usually available at local farmers' markets during the summer, you can try other mushrooms in other seasons, such as morels in the spring. The white truffle oil adds incredible flavor to this dish and can be found in many gourmet shops and online, but if you decide not to use it, the dish is fine without it.

2 leeks, washed well, halved, and cut into ½"-thick half-rounds (white and light green parts only)

3 tablespoons olive oil

1 tablespoon minced garlic

1 cup trimmed and cleaned chanterelle mushrooms

1 cup stemmed and quartered shiitake mushrooms

1 cup stemmed and quartered oyster mushrooms

1 cup heavy cream

Salt and freshly ground black pepper to taste

¼ teaspoon fresh lemon juice

4 wild-caught salmon fillets (6 ounces each)

2 tablespoons vegetable oil

2 tablespoons (¼ stick) butter

2 tablespoons chopped fresh parsley

4 drops white truffle oil

Preheat the oven to 375°F.

In a 2-quart saucepan over medium-high heat, cook the leeks in the olive oil until limp, about 2 minutes. Add the garlic and mushrooms and cook until tender, about 4 minutes. Add the cream and bring to a simmer. Reduce the heat to medium and cook until the cream begins to thicken, about 6 minutes. Add the lemon juice, season with salt and pepper, and remove from the heat.

Season the salmon with salt and pepper. Heat a 12-inch ovenproof sauté pan over medium-high heat, then add the vegetable oil. When the oil is hot, add the salmon skin-side up and cook until golden brown, 2 to 3 minutes. Turn the fillets, transfer to the oven, and cook for about 6 minutes.

Return the mushroom mixture to medium-high heat and whisk in the butter until melted. Add the parsley and stir.

Spoon the ragout onto 4 warmed plates. Using a spatula, carefully place the salmon on top. Using a teaspoon for each portion, drizzle the truffle oil onto the salmon and serve immediately.

❧ *The Final Touch:* Parmesan mashed potatoes and asparagus go very well with this dish. If you'd prefer a different green vegetable to brighten the plate, you can sprinkle around freshly sautéed English peas, sugar snap peas, or green beans.

SEARED SALMON WITH CREAMY DILL AND FETTUCCINI

Serves 4

CHEF'S NOTE: This is a great dish to serve to company because it looks elegant and can be prepped quickly well in advance. The sauce can be made 2 days ahead and refrigerated. Be sure to use fresh wild Pacific salmon, if available, and fresh dill. While plain fettuccini works well with this dish, spinach fettuccini is also a good choice, as is linguini.

½ cup mayonnaise

½ cup sour cream

1 tablespoon fresh lemon juice

1 teaspoon Worcestershire sauce

3 tablespoons chopped fresh dill

Salt and freshly ground black pepper to taste

3 teaspoons vegetable oil

4 wild-caught salmon fillets (6 ounces each)

8 ounces fettuccini, cooked

1 lemon, cut into 8 wedges

Preheat the oven to 400°F.

In a medium bowl, stir together the mayonnaise, sour cream, lemon juice, Worcestershire sauce, and dill. Season with salt and pepper.

Heat the vegetable oil in a 10-inch ovenproof sauté pan over medium-high heat. Season the salmon with salt and pepper, add to the pan skin-side up, and cook until golden brown, 2 minutes. Turn the fillets, transfer to the oven, and cook for about 8 minutes.

Bring 2 quarts water to a boil in a medium saucepan. Add the fettuccini and heat for 1 minute, then drain and transfer to a medium bowl. Add ½ cup dill sauce, season with salt and pepper, and toss, using tongs.

Place equal portions of pasta in the center of 4 warmed dinner plates. Using a spatula, place the salmon on top. Spoon the remaining sauce over the salmon and pasta, garnish with the lemon wedges, and serve immediately.

The Final Touch: A fresh dill garnish on top of the salmon and steamed baby carrots are easy ways to add an elegant touch to this dish.

BAKED STRIPED BASS

Serves 4

CHEF'S NOTE: One of the best times of the year for New England seafood lovers is when striped bass is in season during the middle of summer. This recipe doesn't cover up the flavor of the bass with sauce or distract your guests with unusual ingredients — the fish is the star of the show.

½ cup panko (Japanese) or plain bread crumbs

1 tablespoon minced garlic

2 tablespoons chopped fresh parsley

3 tablespoons olive oil

Salt and freshly ground black pepper to taste

4 striped bass fillets (6 ounces each)

Preheat the oven to 400°F. Lightly butter or oil a 10 x 10–inch baking pan.

In a medium bowl, stir together the bread crumbs, garlic, parsley, and oil. Season with salt and pepper.

Place the bass in the baking pan and lightly season with salt and pepper. Spoon equal amounts of the crumb mixture on each fillet and bake for 10 to 12 minutes (for 1-inch-thick fillets). Using a spatula, place the bass on 4 warmed plates.

The Final Touch: Place a couple of lemon wedges and a sprig of fresh parsley on each plate. Any seasonal vegetable, such as corn on the cob, and a green salad are good complements. If you'd like to serve a sauce with the bass, Lemon Butter Sauce (recipe on page 57) is quite nice.

GRILLED TROUT WITH ROASTED POTATOES AND A BUTTERED WINE SAUCE

Serves 4

CHEF'S NOTE: This elegant dish can be prepared very quickly. The key to grilling trout is to oil it properly, make sure the grill is very hot, and finish the trout in the oven (or on a baking sheet with the grill closed). If you can't find sugar snap peas, snow peas or green beans work well.

Potatoes

2 cups cubed (1") peeled Yukon Gold potatoes

2 tablespoons olive oil

Salt and freshly ground black pepper to taste

Trout

4 boneless trout fillets (5 ounces each)

2 tablespoons olive oil

Salt and freshly ground black pepper to taste

Peas

1 tablespoon butter

2 cups sugar snap peas, washed and stems removed

Salt and freshly ground black pepper to taste

Sauce

¼ cup white wine

¼ cup (½ stick) butter, cut into 1-tablespoon pieces and kept refrigerated

1 tablespoon chopped fresh parsley

Preheat the grill. Preheat the oven to 400°F.

To make the potatoes: Place the potatoes in a 10 x 10–inch baking pan. Add the oil, season with salt and pepper, and toss to coat. Bake for 12 minutes, then stir with a spatula. Bake until golden brown and tender, about 8 minutes. Remove from the oven and keep warm.

To make the trout: Lightly coat the trout with the oil and season with salt and pepper. Place on the grill skin-side up. After 1 minute, using a spatula, turn and cook for 40 seconds. Using a spatula, place skin-side down in a 12 x 12–inch pan, then transfer to the oven and bake for about 4 minutes. (You can grill the trout completely, but it may be difficult to remove in 1 piece. Another option is to transfer the trout to the pan and place on the grill, then turn off the heat, close the grill, and cook for 4 minutes.)

To make the peas: Heat a 10-inch sauté pan over medium-high heat, then add the butter and melt it. Add the peas and cook for 5 minutes, adding 2 tablespoons water to help keep them from browning too much. Season with salt and pepper.

To make the sauce: In a 1-quart nonreactive saucepan over medium-high heat, cook the wine until reduced to 1½ tablespoons (be careful not to let it burn). Remove from the heat and slowly whisk in the cold butter 1 piece at a time. When all the butter has melted, add the parsley and season with salt and pepper.

Place a trout fillet in the center of each plate and scatter the potatoes and peas around it. Drizzle the sauce over the trout and serve immediately.

◆ *The Final Touch:* A basket of freshly baked buttermilk biscuits and some honey butter round out this meal nicely.

CAMP-STYLE TROUT

Serves 4

CHEF'S NOTE: Whether you're camping and cooking up your day's catch or are at home looking for a nice way to cook trout, this recipe works well. The recipe calls for head-on boneless trout, but boneless headless trout works fine as well. Old Bay seasoning is available in most supermarkets. If you get it for this recipe and wonder how else you can use it, try it on oven-roasted potatoes or home-made french fries.

---

4 slices bacon, cut into ½" pieces

¼ cup medium-dice onion

1 tablespoon minced garlic

½ cup medium-dice cored seeded green bell peppers

½ cup medium-dice cored seeded red bell peppers

¼ cup medium-dice celery

2 cups clam juice

2 cups medium-dice Yukon Gold potatoes

2 teaspoons Old Bay seasoning

2 tablespoons chopped fresh parsley

Salt and freshly ground black pepper to taste

4 whole boneless trout, with heads (8 ounces each)

8 slices lemon

4 sprigs fresh thyme

¼ cup vegetable oil

Preheat the oven to 375°F.

In a 2-quart saucepan over medium heat, cook the bacon, stirring occasionally, until crisp. Add the onion, garlic, bell peppers, and celery and cook until tender, about 5 minutes. Add the clam juice, potatoes, and seasoning and simmer until the potatoes are tender. Add the parsley and season with salt and black pepper.

Season the cavity and outside of each fish with salt and pepper. Place 2 lemon slices and a sprig of thyme into the cavity and close. Heat the oil in a large ovenproof sauté pan over medium-high heat. Working in 2 batches if necessary, carefully place the trout in the pan and cook until golden brown, 2 minutes. Turn and cook on the other side for 2 minutes. Transfer to the oven and cook for about 5 minutes.

Using a solid spoon, divide the potato mixture equally among 4 warmed plates. Carefully remove the lemons and thyme from the fish and place the trout on the potatoes.

🍃 *The Final Touch:* Moist cornbread goes well with this hearty meal and complements the rustic theme.

LE SOMMELIER: The simple flavors in this dish call for a simple, straightforward beverage. To highlight the fresh, delicate flavor of the trout, look for a simple, subtle lager beer. Lagers tend to have lighter flavors than ales and offer crisp and flexible pairing options. Try this dish with Otter Creek's Vermont Lager after a day of fishing or camping.

SAUTÉED TROUT WITH CAPELLINI PASTA AND LEMON-CAPER BROWN BUTTER

Serves 4

CHEF'S NOTE: Boneless wild trout fillets cook incredibly fast, have great flavor, and go with many types of foods. Capellini pasta is very thin and can be found in most supermarkets. You can substitute thin spaghetti or linguini if you don't have capellini.

6 ounces capellini pasta, cooked and lightly oiled

¼ cup olive oil

1 cup small-dice plum tomato

2 tablespoons chopped fresh parsley

Salt and freshly ground black pepper to taste

¼ cup vegetable oil

4 boneless trout halves (5 ounces each), with skin

¼ cup (½ stick) butter

3 tablespoons fresh lemon juice

2 tablespoons fresh parsley, chopped

¼ cup capers, rinsed and drained

Preheat the oven to 375°F.

Bring 2 quarts water to a boil in a saucepan, add the pasta, and heat for 1 minute. Drain and place in a medium bowl. Add the olive oil, tomato, parsley, salt, and pepper. Cover and set aside.

Heat a large sauté pan over medium-high heat and add the vegetable oil. Season the trout with salt and pepper. Working in 2 batches if necessary, place the trout in the pan skin-side up and cook until golden brown, 2 minutes. Transfer to the oven and cook for about 4 minutes.

Using tongs, place equal portions of pasta on half of each plate. Using a spatula, place the trout skin-side down on the other half of the plate. Drain the oil from the pan and return it to medium-high heat. When the pan is very hot, add the butter and swirl the pan. As the butter foams, then begins to collapse and brown, add the lemon juice, parsley, and capers. Remove from the heat. Using a solid spoon, drizzle the butter over the trout.

❧ *The Final Touch:* Sautéed or steamed fresh green beans go great with this dish and add nice color. A lemon wedge and parsley sprig are a traditional garnish.

TROUT STUFFED WITH WILD RICE, PECANS, AND APPLES, WITH CIDER BUTTER SAUCE

Serves 4

CHEF'S NOTE: This is a nice fall dish. The recipe calls for head-on boneless trout, but you can use headless trout if you like. The basmati rice can be tricky to cook because of the starch content, but it's worth the effort. Soaking and rinsing the rice before cooking helps remove some of the starch.

Rice

2 tablespoons (¼ stick) butter

¼ cup small-dice onion

¼ cup small-dice carrot

⅔ cup basmati rice, soaked in cold water and drained 3 times

1 tablespoon chopped fresh thyme leaves

¼ cup wild rice, cooked

⅓ cup pecans, toasted and chopped

2 scallions, chopped

½ cup small-dice Granny Smith apple, tossed with 1 tablespoon cider vinegar

2 tablespoons brown sugar

Salt and freshly ground black pepper to taste

Trout

4 whole boneless trout, with heads (10 ounces each)

2 tablespoons olive oil

1 tablespoon minced garlic

¼ cup vegetable oil

Sauce

½ cup apple cider

2 tablespoons cider vinegar

1 tablespoon fresh lemon juice

1 tablespoon minced shallots

2 sprigs fresh thyme

5 black peppercorns

3 tablespoons heavy cream

¼ cup (½ stick) butter, cut into 1-tablespoon pieces and kept refrigerated

Preheat the oven to 400°F.

To make the rice: Melt the butter in a 2-quart saucepan over medium-low heat. Add the onion and carrot and cook until tender, approximately 3 minutes. Add the basmati rice and 1⅓ cups water and bring to a simmer. Cover the pan, reduce the heat to medium low, and cook for 10 minutes. Reduce the heat to low and cook for 12 minutes. Add the wild rice, pecans, scallions, apple, and brown sugar. Season with salt and pepper and remove from the heat.

To make the trout: Lightly coat the outside and inside of the trout with oil. Season the cavity with salt and pepper and rub with the garlic. Place the rice in the cavity and close.

Heat a 14-inch sauté pan over medium-high heat. Add the vegetable oil and heat it. Carefully place the trout in the pan and cook until golden brown, 2 minutes. Using a spatula, carefully turn and cook on the other side for 1 minute. Transfer to the oven and cook for about 6 minutes.

To make the sauce: Meanwhile, in a 1-quart stainless steel saucepan over medium-high heat, combine the cider, vinegar, lemon juice, shallots, thyme, and peppercorns. Cook until the liquid is reduced to a few tablespoons. Add the cream and cook until reduced by ½. Reduce the heat to low and slowly whisk in the cold butter 1 piece at a time. When all the butter has melted, remove from the heat and season with salt and pepper.

Place the trout in the center of 4 warmed plates and top with the sauce.

❧ *The Final Touch:* Roasted root vegetables and steamed green beans are great accompaniments to this dish. Garnish the rims of the plates with sliced apple or pear.

GRILLED BLUEFISH WITH CORN
AND SUMMER SQUASHES

Serves 4

CHEF'S NOTE: Bluefish is considered an oily fish with a limited shelf life, so many people who don't live near the coast avoid it. That's too bad, because few fish provide the flavor of fresh bluefish. If you can buy it fresh, grab it. If you can't, you may substitute tautog (blackfish).

---

1 zucchini

1 summer squash

½ cup extra-virgin olive oil

Salt and freshly ground pepper
   to taste

4 ears corn

2 ripe heirloom tomatoes

4 bluefish fillets (6 ounces each),
   skin removed, rinsed and dried

4 tablespoons Basil Baste (recipe
   on page 83)

Prepare a charcoal grill (hardwood charcoal or wood chips produce the best flavor). Wash the zucchini and summer squash, then halve them and remove the seeds. Cut lengthwise into ¾-inch-thick slices. Place in a medium bowl with 1 tablespoon oil and season with salt and pepper.

Grill the squashes and corn, turning the squashes when grill marks appear and turning the corn to cook all sides. Cooking time will depend on the temperature of the grill, but be careful not to overcook the squashes. Remove from the grill and let cool.

Cut the squash slices into ¾-inch squares and remove the corn kernels from the cobs (you should have about 1 cup kernels from each cob). In a large bowl, toss the vegetables with 2 tablespoons oil and season with salt and pepper.

Core the tomatoes and cut into ¼-inch-thick slices. Divide the squash and corn among four 12-inch-square sheets of heavy-duty foil. Season the fish well on both sides with salt and pepper and place a fillet on each of the foil sheets. Top each with 3 or 4 tomato slices. Fold the ends of the foil up around the fish, leaving a little hole at the top, then place on the grill and close the lid. Cook until the fish flakes easily when tested with a fork, 20 to 40 minutes, depending on the temperature of the grill.

When the fish is almost done, brush the top of each fillet with 1 tablespoon Basil Baste, being careful not to disturb the tomatoes. Remove the packets from the grill and let cool for 10 minutes. To serve, either place the packets directly on plates or remove the fish and vegetables from the foil.

BASIL BASTE

½ clove garlic, finely chopped
6 tablespoons olive oil
1½ cups packed basil leaves, washed and dried

1 tablespoon grated lemon zest
Pinch of salt
Ground white pepper to taste

In a food processor, combine the garlic, oil, basil, lemon zest, salt, and pepper and process with short pulses until combined (don't allow the processor to run, or it will produce an unattractive emulsion).

BEER-BATTERED SMELTS

Serves 4

CHEF'S NOTE: One secret of making crisp fried fish is oil temperature: The fish should sizzle gently as it enters the oil. Line-caught fish from a local ice fisherman on a cold winter's day will offer superb flavor. If you vacation in a winter ski area with freshwater lakes, consider stopping by local docks with a cooler and some ice before you head home. Otherwise, check the frozen fish section of your supermarket. Be sure to use flat Magic Hat beer. Our chefs have found that it makes a crisper crust than any of the other beers they tested.

---

1 free-range egg

½ bottle flat Magic Hat beer

1 cup all-purpose flour

1 teaspoon baking powder

2 tablespoons dry mustard

2 tablespoons cracked mustard
  seed

1 teaspoon salt

½ teaspoon garlic powder

Peanut oil

2 pounds smelts, cleaned

Lemon wedges

In a medium bowl, beat the egg slightly, then beat in the beer, flour, baking powder, mustard, mustard seed, salt, and garlic powder until smooth (do not overbeat). Let stand for 30 minutes.

In a large, heavy skillet over medium heat, heat ½ inch of oil to 375°F. Dip the smelts in the batter and drain off the excess. Working in batches, carefully place the smelts in the skillet and cook until golden brown, 2 minutes. Turn and cook for up to 4 minutes, transferring each batch to paper towels as they are done. Serve immediately.

> LE SOMMELIER: What else to drink with beer-battered fish but a fine, cold beer? Go with an India pale ale from any of Vermont's several microbreweries—Otter Creek, Long Trail, and Magic Hat are all good!

🥢 *The Final Touch:* Line a platter or basket with several sheets of the *Boston Globe* (yes, we mean the newspaper) and add homemade tartar sauce, vinaigrette coleslaw, and hand-cut homemade frites. Serve during halftime.

SKATE WITH TOMATOES, CAPERS, AND OLIVE OIL

Serves 4

CHEF'S NOTE: The skate is a member of the ray family. While its popularity is questionable, the texture and flavor of the meat are undeniably exceptional. The sweet flesh found between the cartilage of the wings has the texture of crab-meat and the sweetness of cod. If skate isn't available, you can substitute almost any other fish, such as fluke (summer flounder), Try some of the lesser-known varieties, such as tautog (blackfish), cusk, or pollack. Be careful when flipping flakier fish, as they tend to fall apart when cooked.

1½–2 pounds skate wing, skin removed

Salt and ground white pepper to taste

1 cup flour

3 tablespoons vegetable oil

3 cups Tomato Broth (recipe on page 86)

3 tablespoons finely chopped parsley

1½ tablespoons capers, rinsed

8 tablespoons extra-virgin olive oil

½ cup small-dice seeded ripe heirloom tomato

Cut the skate into 4 pieces and season with salt and pepper. Place the flour in a shallow dish and dredge the skate, shaking off the excess.

Heat 1½ tablespoons vegetable oil in a large sauté pan until it begins to smoke. Add 2 pieces of skate, shaking the pan slightly to prevent sticking. Reduce the heat and cook until golden brown, about 3 minutes. Turn and cook on the other side until cooked through, about 3 minutes. Test with a fork to be sure the skate is cooked through; it should be tender and soft to the touch. Transfer to a plate and keep warm. Add the remaining 1½ tablespoons vegetable oil to the pan and repeat with the remaining fish.

Bring the broth to a boil in a small saucepan. Add the parsley, capers, and 6 tablespoons olive oil. Remove from the heat, add the tomatoes, and season with salt and pepper.

Arrange the skate in 4 shallow bowls and divide the sauce among them, creating a pile in the center of each portion. Drizzle with the remaining 2 tablespoons olive oil.

TOMATO BROTH

Makes 3 cups

CHEF'S NOTE: Overripe tomatoes that have been puréed in a food processor will work for this recipe, as will a combination of tomato juice and tomato purée.

½ small onion, coarsely chopped
1 stalk celery, coarsely chopped
1 (4") piece carrot, peeled and coarsely chopped
1 clove garlic

1 bay leaf
¼ cup fresh parsley
1 quart tomato juice or purée
¾ cup free-range egg whites (about 6 eggs)

In a food processor, combine the onion, celery, carrot, garlic, bay leaf, and parsley and pulse until finely chopped.

Place the tomato juice in a small saucepan and whisk in the vegetables and egg whites. Bring to a simmer (do not boil) and cook for 20 minutes. Using a China cap or other cone strainer lined with a coffee filter, strain small amounts of the broth at a time into a bowl, pressing on the solids to force the liquid through (you may need to change the filter several times). The resulting liquid should be clear.

DANCING SHRIMP WITH CUCUMBER AND FRESH GREENS

Serves 4

CHEF'S NOTE: A New England twist on a classic Asian recipe. Once you have made the marinated shrimp in this dish, you have other serving options besides those in the recipe. For instance, you could serve the shrimp with steamed rice and stir-fried vegetables or as is, as an appetizer. Lemongrass is sold in the produce section of most supermarkets. If you can't find it, you can substitute 2 teaspoons minced lemon zest. Fish sauce and Sambal Oelek (a type of chili paste) can be found in the Asian foods section of most stores.

---

5 tablespoons Nam Pla fish sauce

¼ cup fresh lime juice

1 tablespoon minced garlic

½ tablespoon minced peeled fresh ginger

2 tablespoons Sambal Oelek

1 stalk lemongrass, finely minced

¼ cup thin strips red onion

4 scallions, thinly sliced

2 tablespoons chopped fresh basil

2 tablespoons chopped fresh mint

1 tablespoon sugar

2 tablespoons salt

1 pound large shrimp (21–25 per pound)

1 cup half rounds peeled seeded cucumber

⅔ cup julienned (⅛" x ⅛" x 2" strips) peeled carrot

⅔ cup julienned cored seeded red bell pepper

½ cup julienned peeled celery

3 tablespoons fresh lime juice

1 tablespoon soy sauce

1 tablespoon vegetable oil

1 teaspoon sesame oil

3 cups mixed local salad greens

In a medium bowl, stir together the fish sauce, lime juice, garlic, ginger, Sambal Oelek, lemongrass, onion, scallions, basil, mint, and sugar.

In a medium saucepan, bring 2 quarts water and the salt to a boil. Add the shrimp and cook until pink, 1 to 2 minutes. Drain and toss with the marinade. Cover and refrigerate until needed (it will keep for 2 days).

In a medium bowl, combine the shrimp, cucumber, carrot, bell pepper, and celery.

In another medium bowl, combine the lime juice, soy sauce, vegetable oil, and sesame oil. Add the greens and toss.

Divide the greens among 4 plates and spread out. Place the shrimp mixture in the center of the greens and serve immediately.

LE SOMMELIER: The slight spiciness and Asian influence in this dish make pairing it with wine a little more challenging than with other dishes. The aromatic, spicy notes of the Gewürztraminer grape form a natural complement to Asian cuisine, and New England produces some high-quality Gewürztraminers. Try the Gewürztraminer from Stonington Vineyards in Stonington, Connecticut, and see how well the flavors work together.

MUSSELS MARINIÈRE

Serves 4

CHEF'S NOTE: This recipe allows the flavor of the mussels to really come through. When preparing mussels, discard any that don't close when squeezed. Wash in cold water and discard any that float. Serving this dish in large bowls is a good idea because of the flavorful broth.

3 tablespoons butter

½ cup small-dice onion

2 tablespoons minced garlic

2 cups dry white wine

4 pounds mussels, washed well and beards removed

2 tablespoons chopped fresh thyme leaves

¼ cup chopped fresh parsley

Salt and freshly ground black pepper to taste

Melt the butter in a large saucepan over medium-high heat. Add the onion and garlic and cook for 45 seconds. Add the wine and mussels, cover, and steam until the mussels open, 2 to 3 minutes. Remove from the heat and transfer the mussels to serving bowls, discarding any unopened ones.

Return the broth to medium-high heat, add the thyme and parsley, and season with salt and pepper. Cook until reduced by ½, then pour over the mussels and serve immediately.

❧ *The Final Touch:* A big bowl of tossed salad and a basket of crusty bread are the only additions you need. Don't forget a bowl for the discarded mussel shells!

LE SOMMELIER: It's a good idea to use a crisp, dry white wine such as a Sauvignon Blanc in preparing this dish and then serve that wine with the dish to echo its flavors. Try the Sauvignon Blanc from Pindar Vineyards in Peconic, New York. The Long Island region is known for its seafood and increasingly for its wines, and this is a great example of why.

WINTER HOLIDAY OYSTERS ON THE HALF SHELL

Serves 4

CHEF'S NOTE: The bright red and green sauce in this recipe is very festive for the winter holidays, the time of year when oysters are traditionally at peak quality. It can be made a few hours ahead and refrigerated.

18–24 oysters, rinsed well, chilled or iced before opening

½ cup Tomato Broth (recipe on page 86)

2 tablespoons finely chopped seeded heirloom tomato

½ small shallot, minced

1 tablespoon minced fresh parsley

¼ teaspoon freshly ground black pepper

1 teaspoon prepared horseradish (optional)

Kosher salt

In large bowl, combine the oysters, broth, tomato, shallot, parsley, pepper, and horseradish (if using) and let stand for 15 minutes.

Spread some kosher salt on a platter, then open the oysters and arrange on the platter (the salt acts as a base to keep them from tipping). Top each with a teaspoon of sauce.

CLAM FRITTERS

Serves 4

CHEF'S NOTE: In parts of New England, these fritters are sometimes called cakes; in some recipes, the batter is thicker and almost cakelike. They are often served with red or white chowder. If you buy clams already minced or chopped, you'll need to chop them further since they can be a bit chewy.

½ pound fresh clams

1 cup all-purpose flour

3 tablespoons cornmeal

1 teaspoon baking powder

1 free-range egg

6 tablespoons milk

6 tablespoons clam juice

¾ cup minced onion

1 clove garlic, minced

¼ teaspoon freshly ground black pepper

¾ teaspoon salt

1½ quarts vegetable oil

Wash the clams, squeeze to remove excess moisture, and mince.

In a medium bowl, combine the flour, cornmeal, and baking powder. In a small bowl, combine the egg, milk, and clam juice. Add slowly to the dry ingredients and stir to form a batter. Fold in the onion, garlic, and clams and season with salt and pepper. The batter should be the consistency of very thick pancake batter. If it's too thick, thin with additional clam juice or milk; if it's too thin, add more flour or cornmeal.

Heat the oil to 360°F in a deep fryer. Drop a tablespoon of batter into the oil and cook until golden brown. Break open the fritter to see if it's cooked through; this will help you gauge cooking time. Repeat with the remaining batter. Season the fritters with salt while still hot.

❧ *The Final Touch:* Serve with the traditional lemon wedges and tartar sauce.

SEARED SEA SCALLOPS WITH FRESH BASIL

Serves 4

CHEF'S NOTE: The basil and tomatoes make this more of a summer dish, but it can be a nice midwinter treat when cherry tomatoes are available. Fresh basil is a must; it's available in most supermarkets year round.

---

8 tablespoons virgin olive oil

1 tablespoon balsamic vinegar

1 tablespoon white balsamic vinegar

1 clove garlic, minced

1 shallot, thinly sliced

Salt and freshly ground black pepper to taste

8 yellow teardrop tomatoes

8 red grape tomatoes

8 cherry tomatoes

½ cup fresh basil, stems removed

4 slices foccacia, country, or baguette bread

2 tablespoons vegetable oil

¾ pound sea scallops

1 tablespoon pine nuts, toasted

In a medium bowl, combine 4 tablespoons oil, the balsamic vinegars, and the garlic and shallot. Season with salt and pepper.

Cut all the tomatoes in half and add to the vinaigrette. Slice the basil into thin strips with a sharp knife or cut with scissors, add to the vinaigrette, and toss.

Heat the grill. Brush the bread slices with the remaining 4 tablespoons oil, then grill over medium heat for 2 minutes.

Heat a medium nonstick skillet and add the vegetable oil. Add the scallops without crowding, so they don't touch each other. Cook over high heat until a golden crust forms, 2 minutes. Season with salt, turn, and season with salt and pepper. Cook for 1 to 2 minutes.

Divide the scallops among 4 plates, add equal portions of tomato-basil salad, and garnish with the pine nuts. Serve the grilled bread on the side.

🍃 *The Final Touch:* Try blanched lemon zest sprinkled on the scallops to add color and a dramatic citrus taste. Or add diced cucumber and red onion for crunchy texture with the cherry tomatoes; the dish will taste more like a gazpacho.

SALMON-WRAPPED SCALLOPS

Serves 4

CHEF'S NOTE: A scallop has a small whitish muscle attached to its side. Since the muscle is tough and flavorless, be sure to peel it off when you wash the scallops.

¾ pound wild-caught salmon

12 large sea scallops, washed

2 tablespoons (¼ stick) butter

4 shallots, peeled and minced

6 cups spinach, cleaned and stems removed

Salt and freshly ground black pepper to taste

4 cups mashed potatoes

Cut the salmon into 12 thin slices and wrap 1 slice around each scallop, using toothpicks to secure them.

Melt 1 tablespoon butter in a medium nonstick skillet. Add the seafood rolls and sauté until golden brown, tender, and translucent. Transfer to a plate.

Melt the remaining 1 tablespoon butter in another medium skillet over low heat. Add the shallots and cook until translucent, then add the spinach and cook until tender. Season with salt and pepper.

Place equal portions of mashed potatoes in the center of 4 plates. Top with spinach and arrange the scallops on either side of the potatoes. Drizzle with the spinach cooking liquid.

SEARED SEA SCALLOPS IN A
LEMON-PARSLEY BROTH

Serves 4

CHEF'S NOTE: The mussels and clams used to make the shellfish stock can be combined with the scallops to create a mixed shellfish dish. Be sure to use little-neck clams when making the broth if you plan to serve them with the scallops. The larger quahogs are too tough to be served this way.

---

2 tablespoons canola oil

1½ pounds medium sea scallops (25–30 per pound)

Salt and ground white pepper to taste

2 cups Shellfish-Lemon Broth (recipe on page 95)

4 tablespoons minced parsley

4 small heirloom tomatoes, blanched, skin removed, and coarsely chopped

¼ cup (½ stick) cold butter, cubed

Heat the oil in a large nonstick sauté pan over high heat. Season the scallops with salt and pepper, add to the pan, and cook until browned, 1 to 1½ minutes per side. Transfer to a plate and keep warm.

Drain the fat from the pan and add the broth. Bring to a simmer, then add the parsley and tomatoes. Remove from the heat and swirl in the butter just until melted. Season with salt and pepper.

Divide the scallops among 4 shallow bowls, ladle ½ cup broth over each portion, and serve immediately.

❧ *The Final Touch:* Drop a single sprig of parsley in the center of each bowl.

SHELLFISH-LEMON BROTH

Serves 6 to 8

CHEF'S NOTE: Lemongrass has a subtle flavor. Experiment with it in other seafood dishes as well.

---

3 stalks lemongrass, washed and thinly sliced

1 quart Shellfish Stock (recipe on page 96)

2 sprigs lemon thyme or thyme

6 sprigs parsley, with stems

1 medium ripe heirloom tomato, cut into medium dice

1 clove garlic, crushed

1 bay leaf

In a medium saucepan, combine the lemongrass, stock, thyme, parsley, tomato, garlic, and bay leaf and simmer for 5 minutes. Remove from the heat and let stand for 15 minutes. Strain and refrigerate until needed.

SHELLFISH STOCK

CHEF'S NOTE: Since this recipe calls for adding enough water to cover the shellfish, the size of the saucepan is important. If it's too large, the stock will be watery. Keep to a medium-sized pot.

---

1 teaspoon vegetable oil

½ cup large-dice onion

¼ cup large-dice carrot

¼ cup large-dice celery

½ cup white wine

2 pounds quahogs or other clams, washed well

¼ pound mussels, washed and beards removed

1 bay leaf

2 sprigs fresh thyme

8 black peppercorns

Heat the oil in a medium saucepan over medium heat. Reduce the heat to low, add the carrot, onion, and celery, and cook for 10 minutes (do not brown). Add the wine and cook until the liquid is reduced by ½. Add the clams, mussels, bay leaf, thyme, peppercorns, and enough water to cover. Simmer for 30 minutes, then remove the clams and mussels, discarding any unopened ones, and refrigerate for another use (they will keep for 1 day). Strain the stock and refrigerate until needed.

MAINE LOBSTER SOUFFLÉ

Serves 4

CHEF'S NOTE: Soufflé is not as difficult to prepare as you might think. It's a nice dish that is impressive because of its appearance and its amazing texture in the mouth. It must be served quickly after being removed from the oven, or it will deflate, and the effect won't be as spectacular. But don't worry; your effort will be rewarded by the taste.

---

2 live lobsters (1½ pounds each)

½ cup vegetable oil

½ cup small-dice white onion

½ cup small-dice peeled carrot

½ cup small-dice celery

2 cloves garlic, minced

¼ cup brandy

2 cups white wine

1 teaspoon tomato paste

4 sprigs fresh tarragon

2 tablespoons unsalted butter

2 tablespoons all-purpose flour

½ cup heavy cream

6 free-range egg whites

2 pinches cream of tartar

1 pinch nutmeg

2 pinches cayenne pepper

Salt and freshly ground black pepper to taste

Butter four 10-ounce soufflé molds, dust with flour, and shake off the excess.

Bring a pot of water large enough to hold the lobsters to a boil. Carefully plunge the lobsters in the water and cook for 3 minutes. Remove from the pot and let cool, then cut into pieces.

Rinse the cooking pot and add the oil, onion, carrot, and celery. Cook over medium heat until soft, 10 minutes. Add the lobsters and brandy and ignite the liquid. Add the wine and tomato paste and cook until the liquid is reduced by ½. Add the tarragon and 3 quarts water and simmer for 10 minutes.

Transfer the lobster to a cutting board, let cool slightly, and remove the meat from the shells. Return the shells to the pot and simmer for 20 minutes. Cut the meat into ½-inch cubes.

Preheat the oven to 400°F. Strain the stock through a fine-mesh strainer into a bowl. Melt the butter in a 2-quart saucepan, then stir in the flour and cook over medium heat for 3 to 4 minutes. Whisk in the stock and simmer until reduced to 1 cup. Stir in the cream and cook until reduced to 1 cup. Remove from the heat and let cool.

In a small bowl, beat the egg whites with the cream of tartar until soft peaks form. Gently fold the egg whites and lobster meat into the stock. Add the nutmeg and cayenne and season with salt and black pepper.

Bring a large saucepan of water to a boil. Fill the molds to the top and smooth the surface. Place in a shallow pan large enough to hold all of them and carefully pour in boiling water until it reaches ⅓ of the way up the sides of the molds. Bake until the soufflés rise about ½ inch beyond the rim, 15 to 20 minutes or more. Serve immediately.

The Final Touch: Individual soufflés are a nice appetizer or can be served as an entrée accompanied by wilted greens or baby bok choy, sautéed mushrooms, slow-roasted heirloom tomatoes, and tender baby carrots. For a garnish, reserve some lobster legs to put around the molds.

LOBSTER POTPIE

Serves 4

CHEF'S NOTE: A New England classic: pricey but priceless. The lobster harvest has remained fairly consistent, and lobster can be considered sustainable seafood, albeit expensive. This recipe uses the whole lobster, and including potatoes and homemade biscuit crust makes the dish more affordable. You can add more lobster and use fewer potatoes, but that would not be as sustainable, nor would it represent the frugality of New England cuisine.

---

2 live lobsters (1¼ pounds each)

1 teaspoon salt

1 tablespoon tomato paste

2 cups medium-dice peeled potatoes

3 tablespoons butter

½ cup small-dice onion

½ cup small-dice celery

1 teaspoon minced fresh thyme

1 tablespoon brandy

6 tablespoons white wine

4 tablespoons flour

1 cup milk

¼ cup heavy cream

1½ tablespoons minced fresh parsley

Biscuit Crust (recipe on page 101)

1 free-range egg yolk mixed with 1 tablespoon milk

Bring water to a boil in a pot large enough to hold the lobsters. Add the lobsters head first, cover, and cook for 7 minutes. Transfer to a bowl of cold water for 5 minutes, then drain. Reserve the cooking liquid in the pot.

Dismember each lobster by holding it over the reserved liquid and twisting the head away from the tail. Add all juices from the body to the pot, including the roe (eggs) if any and the tomalley (green paste). Remove and discard the sacs behind the eye sockets and chop the head sections into 1-inch pieces.

Place the shells from the head in the reserved liquid with 2 cups water and the tomato paste. Simmer until reduced to 1¾ to 2 cups, about 30 minutes. Strain into a bowl and set aside.

Shell the tails, claws, and knuckles and remove the digestive tract from the tail sections. Cut the meat into 1-inch pieces.

Fill a medium saucepan with 1 quart water and add the salt and potatoes. Bring to a boil and cook until tender but not soft, 20 minutes. Drain and submerge in cold water for 2 minutes. Drain again and set aside.

Melt the butter in a medium saucepan over medium heat. Reduce the heat to low, add the onion and celery, and cook for 20 minutes (do not brown). Stir in the thyme, then add the brandy and wine and cook until the liquid is almost evaporated.

Stir in the flour and cook for 3 minutes. Add the milk, cream, and 1¾ cups reserved stock and simmer until thickened, 15 minutes. If the mixture is too thin, cook until further reduced; if it's too thick, add more stock or milk. Remove from the heat and let cool for 5 minutes. Add the potatoes, parsley, and lobster meat (you should have about 4 cups).

Pour into a baking dish or deep pie dish. There should be at least ½ inch of space at the top to allow room for the crust and minimize boilover.

Preheat the oven to 350°F. On a work surface, roll out the biscuit dough about ¼ inch thick, using a little flour to keep it from sticking. Cut the dough to fit just inside the baking dish; there may be a small a gap between the dough and the edge of the dish. Refrigerate or freeze the extra dough for another use.

Brush the top of the crust with the egg yolk and milk. Place the baking dish on a foil-lined baking sheet and bake until a wooden pick inserted in the crust comes out clean, 30 to 40 minutes. Serve hot in the baking dish.

❧ *The Final Touch:* A vegetable or crisp salad goes well with this dish.

BISCUIT CRUST

1¾ cups all-purpose flour

1½ tablespoons sugar

2 tablespoons baking powder

½ cup (1 stick) cold butter, cut into small cubes

2 tablespoons minced fresh parsley

1 tablespoon grated lemon zest

¾–1 cup milk

Sift the flour, sugar, and baking powder together into a medium bowl. Add the butter and toss to coat. Work in the butter with your hands until the mixture resembles coarse meal.

Add the parsley and lemon zest, then slowly add enough milk to form a dough.

Place the dough on a work surface and add more flour if necessary, being careful not to overmix; the dough should be slightly tacky. Sprinkle with flour and cover until ready to use.

MAINE LOBSTER AND RICOTTA SALAD

Serves 4

CHEF'S NOTE: This salad is perfect for lunch or a light summer dinner. Maine lobster is at its best from May to July. If you want to start with whole lobster, you'll need 1¼ to 1½ pounds per person. The ricotta adds creamy texture and zest to the salad.

½ cup small-dice peeled celery

½ cup small-dice red onion

½ cup ricotta cheese

3 tablespoons fresh lemon juice

Zest of 1 lemon, blanched and finely chopped

2 tablespoons chopped fresh tarragon

2 tablespoons chopped fresh chives

2 tablespoons capers, rinsed

1 pound cooked lobster meat, cut into small dice

Salt and freshly ground black pepper to taste

In a medium bowl, combine the celery, onion, cheese, lemon juice and zest, tarragon, chives, and capers. Carefully fold in the lobster. Taste the salad and season with salt and pepper, then refrigerate until chilled.

❧ *The Final Touch:* Garnish the salad with lemon wedges, watercress, or arugula leaves and sprinkle some paprika on top. Serve with baguette bread and crudités such as tomatoes, cucumbers, radishes, and fennel.

MAINE CRAB CAKES

Serves 4

CHEF'S NOTE: Not many things taste as good as a well-prepared crab cake. This recipe produces a nice light cake that lets the crab be the primary flavor.

---

1 pound fresh Maine crab-meat (all leg meat if available), picked through to remove shell fragments

⅓ cup small-dice red bell pepper

⅓ cup small-dice green bell pepper

⅓ cup small-dice celery

⅓ cup mayonnaise

1 tablespoon yellow mustard

Tabasco sauce to taste

2 tablespoons fresh lemon juice

2 tablespoons chopped fresh parsley

2⅔ cups bread crumbs

Salt and freshly ground black pepper to taste

½–1 cup vegetable oil

1 lemon, cut into 8 wedges

In a medium bowl, combine the crabmeat, bell peppers, celery, mayonnaise, mustard, Tabasco, lemon juice, parsley, and ⅔ cup bread crumbs and mix well. Taste and season with salt and pepper.

Divide the mixture into ¼-cup portions and form into cakes. Place on a plate lined with plastic wrap and refrigerate until firm.

Place the remaining 2 cups bread crumbs in a shallow dish, then add the crab cakes and turn to lightly coat all sides. Heat ½ cup oil in a 12-inch sauté pan over medium-high heat (you can add more oil as needed). Carefully add the crab cakes to the pan (they will start to sizzle immediately if the oil is hot enough) and cook until golden brown, about 1 minute. Carefully turn and cook the other side until golden brown and cooked through. Transfer to paper towels to drain. To serve, place 2 or 3 cakes on each plate and garnish with the lemon wedges.

✤ *The Final Touch:* To stay with the New England theme, homemade tartar sauce goes well with these crab cakes. If you want to do something different, try a savory or fruit salsa.

3

POULTRY AND EGGS

Misty Knoll Farm sits in the middle of grasslands and cornfields that stretch from the Green Mountains in the east all across the Champlain Valley to Lake Champlain in the west. And possibly because it's so innocuously tucked into the rural landscape, it's one of the best-kept secrets in Vermont.

The farm produces thousands of free-range chickens and turkeys every year and is a favorite supplier of those of us who teach at the New England Culinary Institute. The reason is taste. Because once you've tasted one of Misty Knoll's fresh, free-range chickens, we doubt you'll ever again buy poultry that has been tortured in life and shrink-wrapped in death.

Although chefs everywhere still debate the matter whenever the topic comes up, the fact is that free-range poultry raised without growth hormones and antibiotics has such a light, delicate flavor that it requires nothing more than a "pinch of sea salt to bring out the flavor," as Chef Michel always tells young chefs. So, guided by his wisdom, we've included some classic New England dishes rendered with a new simplicity that's designed to reveal the poultry's delicate flavor.

If you're not fortunate enough to be able to buy a fresh Misty Knoll chicken, ask around at your local farmers' market to see who might be producing free-range chickens and what day they bring fresh chicken to market. Buy the chicken that day, cook it that night, and you're in for a treat.

As for free-range eggs — and, yes, that's how they're referred to — not only do they have a more delicate flavor than eggs produced in confinement systems, but a recent study seems to indicate that a free-range egg has twice the amount of vitamin E, six times as much beta carotene, four times the amount of heart-healthy omega-3 fatty acids, and half the cholesterol as an egg produced in a confinement system.

One caveat: The term "cage-free" is not the same thing as "free-range." Check the egg carton's label to make sure you get the real deal.

FARMHOUSE SLOW-COOKED CHICKEN
WITH ROOT VEGETABLES

Serves 4

CHEF'S NOTE: This slow-cooked country classic is perfect for a blustery fall or winter day.

---

1 whole free-range chicken (3–4 pounds), cut into 8 pieces, with legs, thighs, wings, and halved breast on the bone

½ teaspoon kosher salt

Freshly ground black pepper to taste

3 tablespoons canola oil

4 slices bacon, cut into ½" pieces

6 cloves garlic, sliced

1 medium turnip, peeled and cut into large dice

1 parsnip, peeled and cut into large dice

1 carrot, peeled and cut into large dice

20 pearl onions, peeled, with a small "x" cut into root ends

8 medium button mushrooms, brushed clean and quartered

8 new red potatoes, quartered

3 cups chicken broth

¾ cup chopped canned plum tomatoes

3 tablespoons chopped fresh parsley

Preheat the oven to 350°F.

Heat a large Dutch oven over medium heat for about 3 minutes. Season the chicken with salt and pepper. Add the oil to the pan and heat. Working in 2 batches, add the chicken skin-side down and cook until golden brown, about 3 minutes, then turn and cook until golden brown on the other side. Transfer to a plate.

Reduce the heat to low, add the bacon, and cook until crisp, scraping the bottom of the pan occasionally. Add the garlic, turnip, parsnip, carrot, onions, and mushrooms and cook until lightly caramelized, adding more oil and adjusting the heat as necessary.

Return the chicken to the pan and add the potatoes, broth, and tomatoes. Bring to a

simmer, then cover and cook in the oven for 1 hour. Add the parsley and season with salt and pepper. Divide among 4 warmed plates and serve immediately.

❦ *The Final Touch:* Serve with your favorite crusty artisanal bread.

LE SOMMELIER: This is a fairly substantial chicken dish with an appealing mélange of flavors, from smoky bacon to sweet parsnips to earthy mushrooms. What's needed is a wine with substance, probably a red, but not one that's so full bodied and tannic that it overpowers the chicken and vegetables. It should also have complementary aromas and flavors and good acid levels to match the acidity of the tomatoes. Sound complicated? Fortunately, one varietal meets all these criteria: Pinot Noir. Oregon produces very attractive, restrained, earthy Pinot Noirs; Sokol Blosser, Firesteed, and Adelsheim wineries all make reliable, affordable versions.

ROASTED CHICKEN WITH APPLES, ONIONS, AND FINGERLING POTATOES

Serves 4

CHEF'S NOTE: Choose apples that stand up well to baking so they will still have some texture, such as Paula Reds. Fingerling potatoes are great for this recipe, but you can use red potatoes if fingerlings aren't available.

---

6 tablespoons unsalted butter, softened

1 tablespoon fresh thyme, stems removed

2 medium onions, sliced

¾ pound fingerling potatoes

3 Paula Red apples, peeled, cored, and cut into 6 wedges each

2 tablespoons canola oil

Kosher salt and freshly ground black pepper to taste

1 whole free-range chicken (3½–4 pounds), rinsed and patted dry

Preheat the oven to 425°F.

In a small bowl, combine the thyme and butter. In a large bowl, toss the onions, apples, and potatoes with the oil. Sprinkle with salt and pepper.

Loosen the skin of the chicken and spread the thyme butter under the skin of the breasts and legs. Season liberally with salt and pepper.

Place a rack in a roasting pan and arrange the vegetables around the sides of the pan. Place the chicken breast-side up on the rack and roast for about 20 minutes. Stir the vegetables, reduce the oven temperature to 375°F, and roast for 20 minutes. Stir the vegetables again, then roast until the internal temperature of the chicken reaches 165°F on a thermometer inserted in the thigh. Total cooking time may be 1 to 1½ hours, depending on the weight of the chicken.

Transfer the chicken to a cutting board, keep warm, and let stand for 15 minutes. Transfer the vegetables to a platter and cover with foil. Carve the chicken, transfer to the platter, and serve immediately.

The Final Touch: For a tasty addition, cook 1 quart apple cider in a small saucepan until reduced by about ½, then whisk in about 2 tablespoons cold butter and a splash of cider vinegar. Ladle over the chicken and vegetables before serving.

LE SOMMELIER: Instead of pairing this dish with a wine that contrasts with its fruitiness and sweetness, play them up with one that has similar characteristics. Wines that have great fruit and a delightful touch of sweetness are off-dry German Rieslings at the Kabinett level of ripeness, such as the estate Riesling from Vermont's Shelburne Vineyards.

BRAISED CHICKEN AND FALL SQUASH STEW

Serves 6

CHEF'S NOTE: The flavors of fresh free-range chicken, spices, and squash merge in this dish to offer the rich taste of fall. You may use pearl onions, button mushrooms, parsnips, carrots, and celery root as alternative fall vegetables.

2 tablespoons canola oil

6½ pounds bone-in chicken breasts, with skin

1 cup diced onions

4 cloves garlic, chopped

1 cup diced peeled celery

3 cups canned plum tomatoes, seeded and chopped

1 cup chicken broth or stock

1 cup dry white wine

¾ teaspoon kosher salt

¾ teaspoon freshly ground black pepper

1 teaspoon fresh thyme, stems removed

4 cups coarsely chopped, peeled and seeded butternut and acorn squash

Heat a 4½-quart Dutch oven over medium-high heat and add the oil. Add the chicken skin-side down and cook until browned, about 5 minutes, then turn and cook until browned on the other side. Transfer to a plate.

Reduce the heat to medium low, add the onions, garlic, and celery, and cook for about 5 minutes. Return the chicken to the pan. Add the tomatoes, broth, wine, salt, pepper, and thyme and bring to a gentle simmer. Cover and simmer for about 20 minutes.

Add the squash and simmer until tender, 15 minutes.

Divide the chicken among 6 plates and spoon the vegetables on top.

❧ *The Final Touch:* Add ¼ cup chopped parsley at the end of cooking for extra color and aroma. Serve over basmati rice or brown rice pilaf.

WINTERTIME BRAISED CHICKEN LEGS WITH DRIED FRUIT

Serves 4

CHEF'S NOTE: This is a lovely recipe for a late winter evening, when the fruit flavors will come as a delightful reminder of warmer evenings to come.

¼ cup dried currants
¼ cup dried apricots, sliced
¼ cup dried Maine cranberries
1 tablespoon canola oil
4 free-range chicken leg quarters (leg and thigh)

Salt and freshly ground black pepper to taste
½ yellow onion, cut into medium dice
1 quart chicken stock or broth
1 sprig fresh thyme
1 sprig fresh marjoram

Preheat the oven to 350°F.

Heat an ovenproof sauté pan over medium-high heat. Add the oil and heat until shimmering. Season the chicken with salt and pepper and place skin-side down in the pan. Cook until golden brown, about 3 minutes per side. Place the onion on top of the chicken, then add the fruit. Pour in the broth, add the thyme and marjoram, and bring to a simmer. Season with salt and pepper.

Cover the pan and bake for 1 hour, then uncover and check for doneness; you should be able to easily move a leg bone. If the chicken is fully cooked, check the sauce; it should be reduced by at least ½. If not, cook over low heat until it reaches the desired consistency. Season with additional salt and pepper if desired. Transfer the chicken to a platter and top with the sauce.

❧ *The Final Touch:* Serve with your choice of pasta, gnocchi, or risotto, or try roasted potatoes or bread stuffing.

LE SOMMELIER: The sauce for this dish offers a delightful combination of tart flavors (currants and cranberries) and sweet ones (apricots). In order not to clash, the wine you serve with it should have its own share of these two tastes. A fruity, slightly off-dry Riesling, such as that made by Glenora Winery in New York's Finger Lakes region, is a good choice. Another option is a soft, fruity Rosé that retains a touch of sugar. Be sure the wine is a very light pink because the deeper the color, the more tannins it contains, and bitter tannins will clash with the tart sauce. Sakonnet Winery of Rhode Island makes a really pretty Rosé—full of fruit, quite dry, and almost devoid of bitter tannins. Perfect!

EARLY FALL CHICKEN
WITH BUTTERNUT SQUASH AND CHARD

Serves 4

CHEF'S NOTE: This is a nice dish as the weather starts to turn cool. In the garden, the chard is growing well and the squash is just coming in. When making the sauce, be patient. Let it simmer, and be careful not to let it scorch.

---

2 tablespoons (¼ stick) butter

1 medium onion, cut into small dice

1 clove garlic, minced

½ cup all-purpose flour

2 cups chicken broth or stock

3 cups bite-size pieces cooked free-range chicken

1½ cups medium-dice roasted peeled butternut squash

4 cups coarsely chopped washed Swiss chard

2 teaspoons chopped fresh sage

Salt and freshly ground black pepper to taste

2 tablespoons finely chopped fresh parsley

Melt the butter in a deep 3-quart saucepan over medium heat. Add the onion and garlic and cook until the onion is translucent and tender. Sprinkle the flour over the vegetables, stir, and cook until lightly browned and smelling faintly of nuts.

Gradually add the broth ½ cup at a time, whisking constantly to avoid lumps. Keep the sauce at a simmer and check the consistency; it should be thick enough to coat the chicken. When it reaches the desired consistency, simmer for 5 to 6 minutes. Add the

LE SOMMELIER: This dish calls out for a nice Chardonnay. The rich earthiness of the chicken stock and the squash work perfectly with the creamy yet crisp texture of the estate Connecticut Chardonnay from Jonathan Edwards Winery. The specific climate at the winery favors growing traditional grapes such as Chardonnay, but the cool temperatures help preserve the grapes' acidity.

chicken, squash, chard, and sage, then season with salt and pepper and return to a simmer. Cook until the chard is tender, then add the parsley.

❧ *The Final Touch:* Serve over homemade biscuits.

WHOLE POACHED CHICKEN STOCK

Makes 8 cups

CHEF'S NOTE: This yields a light chicken stock, good for potpie gravy, and moist cooked meat for hot dishes and salads. To keep the stock clear, don't stir it as it cooks. Since the meat isn't seasoned, you may want to adjust the seasoning amounts in any recipes in which you use it.

---

1 whole roasting chicken (about 4 pounds)

2 carrots, peeled and cut into large dice

3 stalks celery, cut into large dice

1 large onion, cut into large dice

3 cloves garlic

2 bay leaves

1 tablespoon peppercorns

1 sprig fresh sage

1 sprig fresh rosemary

1 sprig fresh thyme

4 sprigs fresh parsley

In a large stockpot, combine the chicken, carrots, celery, onion, garlic, bay leaves, peppercorns, sage, rosemary, thyme, and parsley. Add enough water to cover. Simmer over low heat (do not boil) until the skin and tendons of the leg start to pull away from the end of the bone and the joints are loose, 1 to 1½ hours. Use a large spoon or a ladle to skim off any foam that forms on the surface during cooking.

Transfer the chicken to a plate to cool. Strain the stock into a container and let cool, then cover and refrigerate until needed. When the chicken is still warm but cool enough to handle, pick the meat off the bones in chunks, discarding any small bones and cartilage. Package and refrigerate until ready to use.

PAN-ROASTED CHICKEN BREASTS
WITH CHANTERELLES

Serves 4

CHEF'S NOTE: Chanterelle mushrooms can be foraged throughout late July and August in Vermont woods. They're also sometimes available at farmers' markets, along with other wild mushrooms, which you can substitute for the chanterelles if you like.

---

2 tablespoons canola oil

4 boneless free-range chicken breasts (8 ounces each), with skin

½ teaspoon kosher salt

½ teaspoon freshly ground black pepper

3 tablespoons unsalted butter

1¼ pounds chanterelle mushrooms, cut into uniform slices

¼ cup minced shallots

3 tablespoons chopped chives

Preheat the oven to 400°F.

Heat the oil in a large ovenproof sauté pan over medium-high heat. Add the chicken skin-side down and cook until browned, about 4 minutes. Turn the chicken, season with salt and pepper, and transfer the pan to the oven. Cook until the internal temperature reaches 165°F, about 12 minutes. Transfer to a warmed plate.

Drain the fat from the pan and add the butter. When it starts to foam, add the mushrooms and toss to coat. Cook until tender, about 5 minutes, and add the shallots. Season

LE SOMMELIER: The perfect wine for a chicken dish with mushrooms is Pinot Noir, a medium-bodied red with unfailingly earthy aromatics that nicely match the earthiness of the chanterelles. Many fine Pinot Noirs are made in California, especially in cooler regions like Carneros, Russian River Valley, and Santa Barbara.

with salt and pepper and add the chives. Divide among 4 warmed plates and place a chicken breast on top of the mushrooms.

❧ *The Final Touch:* Serve with roasted red potatoes and baby carrots.

GOAT CHEESE AND BACON-STUFFED FREE-RANGE CHICKEN BREAST

Serves 4

CHEF'S NOTE: This dish is the essence of Vermont flavors.

---

8 slices Vermont Smoke and Cure bacon, cut into ½" pieces

1 tablespoon butter

8 scallions, thinly sliced

3 leeks, washed well and thinly sliced

1½ cups coarsely chopped mushrooms

1 clove garlic, minced

1 cup heavy cream

½ cup panko (Japanese) bread crumbs

6 ounces Vermont Butter and Cheese goat cheese (chèvre)

4 Misty Knoll boneless skinless chicken breasts (8 ounces each)

2 tablespoons olive oil

In a medium skillet over low heat, cook the bacon until most of the fat has rendered, about 5 minutes. Add the butter, scallions, leeks, mushrooms, and garlic and cook until soft, about 5 minutes. Add the cream and cook until the liquid is reduced by about ½. Remove from the heat and add the bread crumbs and cheese.

Cut a deep slit in the thickest part of each chicken breast to make a narrow pocket and stuff with ¼ of the mixture.

Preheat the oven to 350°F. Lightly butter a baking dish.

Heat the oil in a large sauté pan over medium-high heat. Add the chicken and sear until golden brown, 5 to 6 minutes on each side. Transfer to the baking dish and bake until the internal temperature reaches 165°F, about 10 minutes. Let stand in a warm place for 10 minutes before serving.

❧ *The Final Touch:* Slice each chicken breast on the diagonal to display the stuffing. Serve with an autumn rice pilaf and mashed butternut squash for a colorful and seasonal dish.

HERB-MARINATED CHICKEN WITH MESCLUN

Serves 4

CHEF'S NOTE: Wonderful lettuces of all types arrive in the farmers' markets in early summer and are available through the fall. Don't limit yourself to mesclun; choose whatever appeals to you. This recipe is very adaptable.

---

2 boneless skinless free-range chicken breasts (8 ounces each), halved lengthwise

6 tablespoons extra-virgin olive oil

Kosher salt and freshly ground black pepper to taste

Grated zest of 1 lemon

¼ teaspoon chopped fresh thyme leaves

2 tablespoons chopped fresh chives

2 tablespoons chopped fresh parsley

2 tablespoons chopped fresh basil

8 ounces mesclun lettuce

Juice of 1 lemon

Preheat the grill.

In a large bowl, combine the chicken and 2 tablespoons oil. Season with salt and pepper, then add the lemon zest, thyme, chives, parsley, and basil. Refrigerate for up to 1 hour.

Grill the chicken breasts until the internal temperature reaches 165°F. Transfer to a plate and keep warm.

Divide the lettuce among 4 plates. Drizzle with the remaining 4 tablespoons oil and the lemon juice, then sprinkle with salt and pepper. Place a piece of chicken on each salad and serve.

❧ *The Final Touch:* This salad lends itself to a variety of summer vegetables. You could add heirloom tomatoes, cucumbers, olives, artichoke hearts, and red onion. Serve with crusty artisanal bread.

LE SOMMELIER: There are two ways to go with this salad, with its lemon zest and juice and summer vegetables. You could pick a wine that's similar to the dish, with green aromatics, citrus flavors, and zesty acids—a Sauvignon Blanc or Pinot Grigio, or maybe a Frascati from Italy. Or you could choose a wine that contrasts with the salad by being off-dry and fruity—a pleasant, clean Rosé, such as a Tavel from the Côtes du Rhône or a Rosado from Spain, or one of California's drier White Zinfandels.

GRILLED CHICKEN BLTS

Serves 4

CHEF'S NOTE: By utilizing the best of the summer season, you can create an incredible grilled chicken sandwich. Nothing could be easier. You can find wonderful heirloom tomatoes, fresh arugula, and artisanal bread at local farmers' markets and food co-ops. For great cob-smoked, maple-cured bacon, try Vermont Smoke and Cure. The Woodstock Water Buffalo Company in South Woodstock, Vermont, makes the best buffalo mozzarella.

---

8 slices crusty artisanal bread

8 slices (¼" thick) Vermont Smoke and Cure bacon

2 boneless, skinless free-range chicken breasts (8 ounces each), halved lengthwise

2 teaspoons canola oil

Kosher salt and freshly ground black pepper to taste

8 slices (¼" thick) heirloom tomato

8 slices (¼" thick) Woodstock Water Buffalo mozzarella

2 cups washed and dried baby arugula

¼ cup extra-virgin olive oil

Preheat the oven to 375°F. Preheat the grill. Lightly toast the bread and set aside.

Place the bacon on a baking sheet and cook in the oven until browned and crisp, 7 minutes. Transfer to paper towels.

Brush the chicken with the canola oil and season with salt and pepper. Grill until the internal temperature reaches 165°F. (You may refrigerate the chicken for later use, but it's better to make the sandwiches while the chicken is warm.)

Place a slice of toasted bread on a work surface and layer with a piece of chicken; 2 slices each of bacon, tomato, and cheese; and ¼ of the arugula. Drizzle with the olive oil, sprinkle with salt and pepper, and top with a second slice of bread. Repeat with the remaining ingredients.

CHICKEN SOUP WITH RAMPS, WILD RICE, AND MOREL MUSHROOMS

Serves 6 to 8

CHEF'S NOTE: Morel mushrooms and ramps can be foraged in the woods of Vermont during the late spring. If you can't harvest them yourself, look for them at farmers' markets. Ramps are similar to scallion-size leeks, and the wild rice lends an earthy flavor to the soup. For a vegetarian soup, use vegetable broth instead of chicken broth.

½ cup wild rice

3 tablespoons canola oil

1 medium onion, chopped

8–10 ramps, washed and cut into ½" pieces

1 medium carrot, peeled and diced

8 ounces morel mushrooms, brushed clean

2 quarts chicken broth

Kosher salt and freshly ground black pepper

¼ cup chopped fresh parsley

Place the rice and 1½ cups water in a small saucepan over medium heat. Bring to a gentle simmer, cover, and cook until tender, up to 1 hour.

Place the canola oil in a large saucepan over medium heat, then add the onion, ramps, carrot, and mushrooms. Cook until soft, 2 to 3 minutes. Add the broth and simmer for 20 minutes. Season with salt and pepper and garnish with the parsley. Ladle into warmed bowls and serve.

❧ *The Final Touch:* If you like, add cooked chicken. Fresh asparagus and fiddlehead ferns, both available during spring in Vermont, would also be welcome additions to this soup.

CHICKEN SOUP WITH EGG RIBBONS, RAMPS, FRESH PEAS, AND CRAB

Serves 4

CHEF'S NOTE: If using homemade chicken stock, be sure to season it with salt and pepper to taste while it is heating. Ramps (wild leeks) are wonderful members of the allium (onion) family; along with fresh peas, they can be found at farmers' markets in late spring.

Ice water

8 ramps, washed

¼ cup fresh or frozen peas

1½ quarts chicken broth or stock

Salt and freshly ground black
    pepper to taste

4 free-range eggs

1 cup lump crabmeat, cleaned

Pinch of ground nutmeg

2 teaspoons fresh basil

½ cup grated Parmesan cheese

Pour the ice water into a bowl. Place 1 quart water in a medium saucepan and salt lightly. Bring to a rapid simmer over medium heat, add the ramps and peas, and cook for 2 minutes. Transfer to the ice water for 2 minutes, then transfer to a plate.

In a medium saucepan over medium-high heat, season the broth with salt and pepper and bring to a rapid simmer. In a small bowl, beat the eggs until thoroughly mixed. Pour into the simmering broth in a thin stream, stirring with a fork or whisking to form egg ribbons.

Divide the crab and peas among 4 bowls. Ladle an equal amount of broth into each bowl and sprinkle with nutmeg. Add some basil and 2 ramps and sprinkle generously with cheese.

The Final Touch: To make this soup a standout, make or find the best chicken broth you can. Serve it with crusty artisanal bread.

VERMONT CHÈVRE AND CHIVES OMELET

Serves 2

CHEF'S NOTE: Based in the town of Websterville, Vermont, Vermont Butter and Cheese Company supports a network of more than 20 family farms providing milk that meets the highest standards of purity. The story of its famous goat's-milk chèvre started many years ago in Brittany, France, where cheesemaker Allison Hooper, working for room and board, learned the time-honored traditions of European artisanal cheesemaking. Vermont chèvre is characterized by its simple, mild, fresh, goat's-milk flavor. Enjoy it in this very basic egg dish.

---

6 free-range eggs
½ bunch chives, thinly sliced
1 pinch sea salt

¼ cup (½ stick) unsalted butter
3 ounces Vermont Butter and Cheese goat cheese (chèvre)

In a small stainless steel bowl, whisk the eggs, chives, and salt until blended.

Heat a medium nonstick skillet over high heat. Add 2 tablespoons butter and swirl the pan to coat. When the butter stops sizzling, pour ½ of the egg mixture into the pan and stir briskly with a fork. Push the cooked eggs toward the center and let the uncooked eggs settle toward the edge of the pan. When the eggs are firm and fully set, remove from the heat and place ½ of the cheese in the middle of the omelet. Using a fork, start at the side nearest the handle and fold in half over the cheese. Holding the pan by the handle, tilt it so the omelet slides out of the pan onto a warmed plate.

Wipe out the pan and repeat with the remaining butter, egg mixture, and cheese.

♣ *The Final Touch:* Make a slit in the top of the omelet and add more goat cheese and chives.

VERMONT APPLE, COB-SMOKED BACON, AND CHEDDAR CHEESE FRITTATA

Serves 10

CHEF'S NOTE: Harrington's of Richmond, Vermont, offers great cob-smoked bacon, and Vermont has an incredible selection of apples from which to choose. Visit one of our local farmers' markets in the fall or learn all about them at the Vermont apple Web site (www.vermontapples.org). If you like, you can substitute maple breakfast sausage for the bacon or omit the bacon for a vegetarian dish.

4 Vermont apples, peeled and sliced

7 strips cob-smoked bacon, baked and crumbled

1 tablespoon Vermont maple syrup

10 free-range eggs

¼ cup heavy cream

½ teaspoon salt

2 cups shredded Cabot cheddar cheese

Preheat the oven to 350°F.

In a medium bowl, combine the apples and bacon. Stir in the syrup, then transfer to a buttered 9 x 12–inch baking dish or a 12-inch cast-iron or nonstick skillet.

In another medium bowl, whisk together the eggs, cream, and salt. Pour over the apples and bacon, then sprinkle the cheese on top. Bake until a metal skewer inserted in the frittata comes out clean, about 15 minutes. Let stand for 10 minutes and serve warm.

The Final Touch: Serve with warm Vermont maple syrup.

HERBED-SMOKED SALMON QUICHE

Serves 6

CHEF'S NOTE: To determine doneness, look at the edges of the quiche crust, not the top, where the crème fraîche will be soft and not browned.

---

1 cup light cream

2 teaspoons finely chopped fresh tarragon

2 teaspoons finely chopped fresh chervil

2 teaspoons finely chopped fresh chives

2 teaspoons finely chopped fresh basil

½ recipe Multipurpose Pie Dough (recipe on page 257)

4 ounces thinly sliced smoked salmon

3 large free-range eggs

1 tablespoon chopped fresh parsley

Salt and freshly ground black pepper to taste

2 tablespoons Vermont Butter and Cheese crème fraîche

In a small saucepan over medium heat, bring the milk just to a simmer. Remove from the heat and add the tarragon, chervil, chives, and basil. Let stand for 1 hour.

Preheat the oven to 400°F. On a work surface, roll out the pastry dough, then place in a 9-inch pie pan. Arrange the salmon on the bottom of the crust.

Beat the eggs and parsley into the cream and season with salt and pepper. Pour over the salmon and top with the crème fraîche. Transfer to the lowest rack in the oven and

LE SOMMELIER: This creamy quiche with its delicate touch of smoked salmon needs a wine that is as similar to it as possible. Try a California Chardonnay, which is a bit creamy in texture and ripe in fruit flavors but still subtle; it also has hints of butter in the nose and just the right amount of toasty oak, reminiscent of the delicate smokiness of a fading campfire. Kistler Winery and Landmark Winery, both in Sonoma, have long been famous for their quality Chardonnays.

bake for 10 minutes. Reduce the oven temperature to 300°F, move the quiche to the middle rack, and bake until a metal skewer inserted in the quiche comes out clean, 30 minutes. Let stand for at least 15 minutes before cutting.

❧ *The Final Touch:* A salad of bitter greens dressed with a citrus vinaigrette is a nice accompaniment.

SUMMERTIME SCRAMBLED EGGS WITH
HEIRLOOM TOMATOES, BASIL, AND TARENTAISE

Serves 2

CHEF'S NOTE: This dish, made with perfect summertime ingredients from a farmers' market, including Thistle Hill Farm Tarentaise cheese, is a wonderful breakfast, lunch, or light dinner. Tarentaise is an aged alpine raw milk cheese handmade on the Putnam family farm in North Pomfret, Vermont, following the tradition of the Tarentaise Valley in the Savoie region of the French Alps. Its flavor has subtle nutty undertones and is excellent for melting.

4 or 5 free-range eggs

2 tablespoons milk

Kosher salt and ground white or cayenne pepper to taste

¾ cup coarsely chopped heirloom tomato

1 tablespoon unsalted butter

¼ cup grated Thistle Hill Farm Tarentaise cheese

2 tablespoons torn fresh basil

In a medium bowl, whisk the eggs with the milk, season with salt and pepper, and stir in the tomato.

Melt the butter in a nonstick sauté pan over medium heat. When it begins to foam, add the eggs and stir with a wooden spoon until soft set. Remove from the heat and stir in the cheese and basil. Divide between 2 warmed plates and serve immediately.

❧ *The Final Touch:* Add just a bit of freshly grated Tarentaise cheese right before plating the eggs. Serve with toasted whole wheat artisanal bread.

EGGS WITH COB-SMOKED HAM, SWEET POTATOES, AND CHEDDAR

Serves 2

CHEF'S NOTE: This dish is very versatile and a perfect fall or winter breakfast or brunch. You can make the eggs almost any way you like, such as scrambled, poached, or sunny-side up.

---

1 sweet potato

½ cup all-purpose flour

1 teaspoon ground cinnamon

Kosher salt and freshly ground black pepper to taste

5 tablespoons canola oil

4 slices (¼" thick) cob-smoked ham

4 free-range eggs

1⅓ tablespoons milk

¼ cup minced chives

¾ cup shredded Cabot cheddar cheese

Cut the sweet potato into eight ¼-inch-thick slices. In a small saucepan with enough water to cover, simmer over medium heat just until tender. Lightly coat each slice with flour, sprinkle with cinnamon, and season with salt and pepper.

Preheat the oven to 200°F. In a medium nonstick sauté pan over medium heat, cook the sweet potatoes in 2 tablespoons oil until browned, 2 minutes per side. Transfer to a baking dish and keep warm in the oven.

In another nonstick pan over medium heat, cook the ham until heated through, then transfer to the baking dish.

Separate the eggs, placing the yolks and whites in separate bowls. Stir the milk and chives into the whites. Heat 1½ tablespoons oil in a medium nonstick skillet over medium-high heat and add ¼ of the egg white mixture. Immediately drop in 1 yolk, then cook as you would a fried egg (over easy, medium, or hard). Repeat with the remaining ingredients, adding more oil if necessary.

Place 2 sweet potato slices on both sides of each plate, top with a slice of ham and an egg, and season with salt and pepper. Sprinkle each egg with cheese, then return to the oven until the cheese melts.

SUMMER EGGS, ARUGULA, AND BABY BEETS WITH A CITRUS VINAIGRETTE

Serves 4

CHEF'S NOTE: This light warm-weather salad includes fresh soft-boiled eggs coated with bread crumbs. If you'd rather not make your own bread crumbs, you can use store-bought (the panko type works nicely). You can also use hard-boiled eggs if you like.

---

3 slices stale white bread

12 fresh baby beets or 3 large beets

½ cup extra-virgin olive oil

Juice of 1 lemon

Grated zest of ½ lemon

Salt and freshly ground black pepper to taste

½ cup canola oil

1 quart ice water

6 free-range eggs

1 cup all-purpose flour

1 quart vegetable oil

8 ounces arugula

¼ cup chopped fresh parsley

Preheat the oven to 375°F. In a food processor, chop the bread into crumbs of the desired consistency. Set aside.

Rub the beets with ¼ cup olive oil, place in a baking pan, and roast until they can be pierced easily with a fork, 30 minutes (1 hour for large ones). Let stand until still warm but cool enough to handle, then peel off the skin (wear plastic gloves to avoid dyeing your hands). Refrigerate until ready to serve.

In a medium bowl, combine the lemon juice and zest, then season with salt and pepper. Whisk in the remaining ¼ cup olive oil and the canola oil.

Pour the ice water into a medium bowl. Place 4 eggs on the bottom of a medium saucepan in 1 layer and add enough water to cover to twice the depth of the eggs. Bring to a low simmer over medium-high heat, then turn off the heat, cover, and let stand for 3 minutes. Transfer to the water to cool.

Place the flour and reserved bread crumbs in 2 bowls. Place the remaining 2 eggs in another bowl and beat lightly. Carefully peel the cooked eggs, then roll in the flour, raw egg, and bread crumbs. Heat the vegetable oil to 350°F in a deep fryer or deep skillet. Add the eggs and cook until golden brown, 3 minutes. Transfer to paper towels.

In a medium bowl, gently toss the arugula with ⅓ of the dressing, then season with salt and pepper. Divide among 4 plates and arrange the beets around the rims. (If using large beets, either slice thinly or cut into small cubes and mix into the salad.) Top each salad with egg, drizzle with dressing, and garnish with chopped parsley.

CREAMY SCRAMBLED EGGS WITH COBB HILL FARM CHEDDAR CHEESE AND CHIVES

Serves 4

CHEF'S NOTE: The cheese in this recipe is produced by Cobb Hill Farm in Hartland, Vermont. It's brined and aged for more than three months. If you like, you can substitute scallion greens or fresh basil for the chives.

---

8 free-range eggs

6 tablespoons milk

2 tablespoons minced chives

¼ teaspoon kosher salt

Pinch of freshly ground black pepper

1 tablespoon unsalted butter

¾ cup shredded Cobb Hill Farm Four Corners cheddar cheese

In a medium bowl, whisk the eggs, milk, chives, salt, and pepper just until blended.

Melt the butter in a 12-inch nonstick sauté pan over medium-low heat. When it begins to bubble, add the egg mixture and stir gently with a wooden spoon until soft and fluffy, about 3 minutes. Add the cheese and continue to stir until melted and blended into the eggs. Divide the eggs among 4 plates and serve hot.

❧ *The Final Touch:* Organic multigrain bread that has been lightly toasted and buttered is a wonderful accompaniment for these scrambled eggs.

SOFT-BOILED EGGS AND WILD MUSHROOMS WITH GRILLED ASPARAGUS

Serves 4

CHEF'S NOTE: This is a great, simple dish that highlights the freshness of locally grown produce. It can be served at any time but works best at breakfast or brunch. The freshness of the tomatoes really makes the difference between "good" and "great"; look for Brandywine, Missouri Pink Love Apples, or Moskovich. The recipe also works well with poached eggs.

---

3 medium heirloom tomatoes

4 tablespoons olive oil

Coarse sea salt and freshly ground black pepper to taste

16 medium spears asparagus, woody ends removed

4 jumbo free-range eggs

8 shiitake, black trumpet, or morel mushrooms, sliced

1 tablespoon butter

Cut the tomatoes into ⅓-inch-thick slices and arrange equal amounts in the center of 4 plates. Drizzle the asparagus lightly with 3 tablespoons oil and season with salt and pepper. Grill or cook in a very hot cast-iron pan until tender, 4 minutes (do not let it become limp). Lay 4 spears neatly across the tomatoes on each plate.

Place the eggs in a medium saucepan with enough water to cover to twice the depth of the eggs. Bring to a boil over high heat, then turn off the heat, cover, and let stand for 3 to 4 minutes. Transfer to a plate.

In a small sauté pan, cook the mushrooms in the remaining 1 tablespoon oil until soft. Remove from the heat, add the butter, and stir to melt and coat the mushrooms. Carefully peel the eggs and place on the asparagus and tomatoes. Top with the mushrooms and sprinkle with salt.

🍃 *The Final Touch:* If you like, you can puncture the eggs to let the yolk spill onto the asparagus and tomatoes.

SOFT-BOILED EGGS WITH ASPARAGUS
AND SMOKED SALMON

Serves 6

CHEF'S NOTE: This is a perfect dish for Sunday breakfast in the spring, when asparagus is abundant in local farmers' markets.

---

18 spears asparagus, woody ends removed, peeled 2–3" from the ends

6 free-range eggs

12 slices cold smoked salmon

Sea salt and freshly ground black pepper

In a medium saucepan, bring 1 quart lightly salted water to a boil over medium-high heat. Place the eggs in another medium saucepan with 1 quart water, bring to a simmer over medium heat, and cook for 4 minutes.

Add the asparagus to the boiling water and cook until tender, about 4 minutes. Drain and keep warm.

When the eggs are cooked, remove from the pan, slice off the tops (the yolks should still be liquid), and place in 4 egg cups. Place 3 asparagus spears, 1 egg, and 2 slices salmon on 4 warmed plates. Season with salt and pepper and serve immediately.

◆ *The Final Touch:* Lightly buttered whole wheat toast provides a nice textural contrast, and if you like, you can make a small breakfast sandwich with the egg, salmon, and asparagus.

4

MEAT

Looking out over the steers grazing along a fence line in north central Vermont, the pastoral scene is peaceful and far removed from the scenes on farms where animals are never let out of the barn. Here, animals graze on lush, nutrient-dense grass, and they have enough room to spread out and return their food to its source without causing an environmental disaster that can pollute local streams and wells.

It's a far cry from the typical factory farm system in which calves are stuffed into small crates until slaughtered for veal, and steers are fed corn, growth hormones, antibiotics, and — if news reports are true — stale candy and other oddities.

Fortunately, a new generation of farmers is turning away from these unhealthful practices and the genetically modified animals bred to withstand them. Instead, these practical men and women are returning to the heritage breeds of years past to produce a healthier, arguably more flavorful beef and veal. The same trend is emerging among lamb and pork producers as well — with the resulting gains in animal health and product flavor.

These changes also have a more beneficial effect on *our* health. Recent studies indicate that pasture-fed animals produce meat that has higher levels of heart-healthy omega-3 fatty acids and higher levels of conjugated linoleic acid, a substance that reduces the risk of cancer.

To find a farmer near you who produces pasture-fed meat, check with farmers at your local farmers' market, or go to www.eatwild.com.

GRILLED BEEF TENDERLOIN WITH
MIXED MUSHROOM TAPENADE

Serves 4

CHEF'S NOTE: You can buy pasture-fed beef tenderloin cleanly trimmed and ready to cook. Buy from a local farmer/producer if possible. The flavor of grass-fed beef is far superior to that of the meat most supermarkets carry, and you'll be supporting your neighbors as they bring food production closer to home. Since this beef is leaner than the kinds usually found in the meat case, it cooks more quickly and will be dry if you cook it beyond medium rare.

---

1 medium russet potato

¼ cup vegetable oil

4 pasture-fed beef tenderloins (5 ounces each)

Salt and freshly ground black pepper

4 cups warm Purple Fingerling Potato Salad (recipe on page 11)

2 cups Mixed Mushroom Tapenade (recipe on page 131)

Preheat the grill.

Cut the potato into julienne strips. Heat the oil in a medium skillet, add the potatoes, and cook until browned and crisp. Season with salt, transfer to paper towels, and keep warm.

When the grill is quite hot, season the steaks with salt and pepper and grill until the internal temperature reaches 110°F (for medium rare; see Chef's Note). Let stand for about 5 minutes before serving.

Spoon the potato salad into the center of each plate and place the steak on top, nesting it into the salad. Top with some tapenade and the potatoes. (Be sure to have extra tapenade on the table; it goes fast.)

MIXED MUSHROOM TAPENADE

Makes 1 cup

CHEF'S NOTE: This tapenade is best made one or two days ahead to allow the flavors to blend. Store in a container in the refrigerator.

---

2 ounces portobello mushrooms, gills removed

2 ounces shiitake mushrooms, stems removed

2 ounces oyster mushrooms, stems removed

2 ounces white mushrooms, stems removed

1 ounce sun-dried tomatoes, soaked and minced

1 tablespoon minced shallots

2 teaspoons chopped garlic

1 tablespoon chopped capers

2 teaspoons white truffle oil

1½ anchovy fillets, mashed

1 tablespoon Asiago cheese

1 teaspoon chopped fresh parsley

1 teaspoon chopped fresh rosemary

1 teaspoon chopped fresh thyme

¾ cup extra-virgin olive oil

Salt and freshly ground black pepper to taste

Grill or broil the mushrooms until tender, then refrigerate until chilled. Pulse in a food processor until finely chopped, being careful not to purée them.

Transfer to a medium bowl and combine with the shallots, garlic, capers, truffle oil, anchovies, cheese, parsley, rosemary, thyme, and olive oil. Season with salt and pepper.

LE SOMMELIER: This dish is perfectly served by the rich, fruity flavors of a delicious Merlot. Pindar Vineyards in Peconic, New York, is one of a growing number of wineries on Long Island that take advantage of the moderating influence of the Atlantic Ocean to help achieve the perfect climate to ripen grapes. Try this dish with Pindar Vineyards Reserve Merlot to see for yourself the potential of Long Island wineries.

YANKEE POT ROAST

Serves 8

CHEF'S NOTE: A cold winter day calls for a classic New England roast that warms the heart as well as the stomach. This simple dish fits the bill perfectly.

I sprig fresh thyme

I bay leaf

2 cloves garlic, thinly sliced

2 leeks

7 pounds pasture-fed beef chuck roast, trimmed and tied

Salt and freshly ground black pepper

3 tablespoons canola oil

2 cups small-dice onion

I cup small-dice celery

I cup small-dice carrot

¼ cup flour

2 cups red wine

I can (12 ounces) crushed tomatoes

4 cups beef broth or water

I cup pearl onions

3 medium potatoes, cut into large dice

I carrot, peeled and cut into medium dice

Make a bouquet garni by tying the thyme, bay leaf, garlic, and leeks in a piece of cheesecloth. Season the roast with salt and pepper.

Heat a deep, heavy-bottomed pot (the roast should fit snugly, with enough room for a lid) over medium-high heat, then add enough oil to cover the bottom. When it begins to ripple, add the roast and cook until browned on all sides. Add the diced onion, celery, and carrot and cook until they begin to brown. Add the flour and stir until combined.

Add the wine and tomatoes and stir until a thick red sauce begins to form. Add the bouquet garni and broth. Cover, bring to a simmer, and cook until the roast is tender and separates easily when tested with a fork, about 2 hours. Transfer to a plate.

Cook the liquid in the pot until reduced by ⅓, then strain into a bowl. Pour back into the pot, add the pearl onions, potatoes, and carrots, and simmer until the carrots are tender, about 15 minutes. Slice the roast and serve with the sauce and vegetables.

The Final Touch: Sprinkle with sea salt and garnish with parsley. Serve with horse-radish.

LE SOMMELIER: This hearty dish calls for an equally hearty beverage. Bluefin Stout, brewed by Shipyard Brewing Company in Portland, Maine, is a classic Irish stout that will work perfectly with this classic Yankee dish.

BARBECUED BEEF SHORT RIBS

Serves 6

CHEF'S NOTE: Beef short ribs are a nice combination of meat, fat, and bone that offers wonderful flavor and texture when treated with care and patience. Take your time with this recipe, and you'll be rewarded with a great meal.

2 teaspoons ground cumin

2 teaspoons ground coriander

1 teaspoon freshly ground black pepper

2 teaspoons dried thyme

1 tablespoon minced garlic

1 medium onion, minced

6 pasture-fed beef short ribs (about 3" long), trimmed of large pieces of fat

4 tablespoons bacon fat or canola oil

Salt to taste

¼ cup cider vinegar

1 cup New England Barbecue Sauce (recipe on page 134)

In a small bowl, combine the cumin, coriander, pepper, thyme, garlic, and onion. Coat the ribs with the mixture, wrap tightly, and refrigerate for at least 24 hours.

Melt the bacon fat in a large heavy-bottomed saucepan over medium-high heat. Season the ribs with salt, add to the pan, and cook until browned. Add 2 cups water and the barbecue sauce and bring to a simmer over low heat. Cover and cook, turning occasionally, until tender, about 2 hours, adding more water if needed to keep the meat from scorching. Divide into individual portions and serve with the sauce.

🍃 *The Final Touch:* To add smoky flavor to the ribs, finish them by brushing with fresh barbecue sauce and grilling gently over a slow hardwood charcoal fire for 5 to 10 minutes.

NEW ENGLAND BARBECUE SAUCE

Makes 8 cups

CHEF'S NOTE: Ancho chiles are dried mild peppers with a roasted, earthy flavor. Chipotles are jalapeño peppers that have been dried and smoked. These peppers are spicy, so it's a good idea to wear plastic gloves when handling them.

---

1 medium onion, cut into small dice

8 cloves garlic, minced

2 tablespoons mustard

¼ cup soy sauce

2 cups ketchup

3 cups canned diced tomatoes

2 cups orange juice

¾ cup molasses

2 bay leaves

½ cup cider vinegar

2 Ancho chile peppers, stems removed, seeded

2 canned chipotle chile peppers

Salt and freshly ground black pepper to taste

In a heavy-bottomed 2-quart saucepan over medium heat, sauté the onion and garlic until the onion is tender and translucent. Add the mustard, soy sauce, ketchup, tomatoes, orange juice, molasses, bay leaves, vinegar, and chile peppers and simmer for 1 hour. Season with salt and pepper, then remove from the heat and let cool.

Pour into a blender and process until smooth. Transfer to a container and refrigerate until needed. The sauce will keep for about 2 weeks refrigerated and can be frozen in smaller containers.

SEARED FLANK STEAK WITH APPLE AND ROSEMARY SAUCE

Serves 4

CHEF'S NOTE: Flank steak is the traditional cut used for London broil. For this recipe, any lean, long-muscled cut will do. Hanger steak and flap are becoming popular, and bottom round cut into slabs will also work. Pasture-fed beef holds up well to grilling and the flavorful sauce.

---

2 pasture-fed beef flank steaks (about 1 pound each), trimmed of fat and silver skin

Marinade

1 McIntosh apple, cored and chopped

2 shallots, minced

3 cloves garlic, minced

1 tablespoon chopped fresh thyme

1 tablespoon chopped fresh rosemary

3 tablespoons chopped fresh parsley

¼ cup canola oil

½ tablespoon freshly ground black pepper

Sauce

1 shallot, minced

1 bay leaf

1 teaspoon black peppercorns

1½ cups apple cider

1 sprig fresh rosemary

2 McIntosh apples, cored and diced

Salt and freshly ground black pepper

Place the steaks in a rectangular glass or ceramic pan.

To make the marinade: In a medium bowl, combine the apple, shallots, garlic, thyme, rosemary, parsley, oil, and pepper. Pour over the steaks and turn to coat. Cover with plastic wrap and refrigerate overnight.

Preheat the grill.

To make the sauce: In a heavy-bottomed 1- or 2-quart saucepan over high heat, combine the shallot, bay leaf, peppercorns, cider, and rosemary. Bring to a boil, then reduce the heat and simmer until the liquid is reduced by about 80 percent. When the sauce reaches the consistency of syrup, add the apples and cook until tender. Season with salt and pepper and keep warm over low heat.

Remove the steaks from the marinade and wipe off any solids. Discard the marinade. Grill the steaks for about 8 minutes per side (for medium rare). Transfer to a cutting board and let stand for 5 minutes. Slice thinly across the grain, arrange on individual plates or a platter, and add a generous amount of sauce.

NEW YORK STRIPLOIN WITH SUMMER VEGETABLES AND PORCINI MUSHROOM SAUCE

Serves 2

CHEF'S NOTE: This flavorful summer dish of grilled steak and fresh vegetables is perfect after a day of swimming in Lake Champlain.

8 fingerling potatoes, bias-cut into ¼"-inch-thick slices

7 tablespoons olive oil

Salt and freshly ground black pepper to taste

2 cups sliced fresh vegetables, such as summer squash, bell peppers, onions, and eggplant

1 shallot, chopped

1 cup fresh, frozen, or dried porcini mushrooms

2 cups heavy cream

2 pasture-fed New York striploin steaks (10 ounces each)

Preheat the oven to 400°F.

In a medium bowl, toss the potatoes with 3 tablespoons oil. Transfer to a baking sheet and season with salt and pepper. Bake until golden brown, about 20 minutes. Set aside.

Heat 2 tablespoons oil in a medium sauté pan, then add the vegetables and cook until heated through. Add the potatoes and toss to combine. Remove from the heat and keep warm.

In a medium saucepan over medium heat, cook the shallot in the remaining 2 tablespoons oil until translucent, about 2 minutes. Add the mushrooms and cook for about 2 minutes. Deglaze the pan with the cream and simmer for about 15 minutes.

Meanwhile, grill the steaks to the desired doneness, 5 to 7 minutes per side (for medium rare). Transfer to 2 plates, cover, and keep warm in the oven if necessary.

Purée the sauce with a hand blender, then strain. Season with salt and pepper. Top the steaks with the vegetables and potatoes and drizzle with sauce.

MAIN STREET MEAT LOAF

Serves 6

CHEF'S NOTE: This is one of our most popular menu items at NECI's Main Street Grill in Montpelier. Every time we try to replace it with something "more modern," the protests from the diners are deafening, even in summer. Use leftovers the next day for a sandwich on a hearty bread with pickles, onions, and mustard.

---

2 tablespoons canola oil

1 medium onion, cut into small dice

1 large carrot, cut into small dice

4 cloves garlic, minced

3 pounds pasture-fed ground beef

2 pounds pasture-fed ground pork

⅔ cup bread crumbs

4–6 tablespoons tomato juice

3 free-range eggs, beaten

1 tablespoon salt

½ tablespoon freshly ground black pepper

½ cup chopped fresh parsley

Preheat the oven to 350°F.

Heat the oil in a medium sauté pan over medium heat. Add the onion, carrot, and garlic and cook until tender, 5 to 10 minutes. Remove from the heat and let cool completely.

In a large bowl, combine the vegetables, beef, pork, bread crumbs, tomato juice, eggs, salt, pepper, and parsley and mix well. (If using an electric mixer, use the paddle attachment.)

Transfer to 2 loaf pans or roll into 2 logs 4 to 5 inches in diameter and place on a baking sheet. Bake until the internal temperature reaches 155°F. Let stand for 10 to 15 minutes before slicing.

✥ *The Final Touch:* For added color and flavor, coat the top of the loaf with ketchup before baking.

VEAL MEDALLIONS WITH PORTOBELLO AND SHIITAKE MUSHROOMS

Serves 4

CHEF'S NOTE: This dish is very quick once you get started. The key to success is having all the ingredients prepared before you heat up the pan. Use a good wine, not "cooking wine," which is usually lower in quality and has added salt, making it harder to control the seasoning.

---

8 pasture-fed Applecheek Farms veal loin medallions (3 ounces each)

Salt and freshly ground black pepper to taste

2 tablespoons canola oil

2 tablespoons (¼ stick) butter

1 tablespoon minced shallots

1 clove garlic, minced

8 ounces portobello mushrooms, stems and gills removed, sliced

8 ounces shiitake mushrooms, stems removed, sliced

¼ cup Madeira wine

¼ cup low-sodium beef stock

6 tablespoons (¾ stick) cold butter, cubed

1 teaspoon chopped fresh sage

1 teaspoon chopped fresh parsley

Season the veal with salt and pepper. Heat a heavy-bottomed sauté pan over medium-high heat and add the oil. Add the veal and sear on both sides for 30 seconds to 1 minute. Transfer to a plate and keep warm.

Add the 2 tablespoons butter to the pan. When it foams, add the shallots and garlic and cook until tender (do not let them brown or burn). Add the mushrooms and cook until softened and lightly browned, 2 to 3 minutes. Add the wine carefully, being careful not to ignite it, and cook until reduced by ¾. Add the stock and cook until all the liquid begins to thicken. Add the cubed butter a few pieces at a time, whisking after each addition. Season with salt and pepper and add the sage and parsley.

Place 2 medallions on each plate with equal portions of mushrooms. Ladle on the sauce and serve immediately.

🍀 *The Final Touch:* Place a simple sprig of sage on each plate.

BAKED HAM WITH MAPLE-MUSTARD GLAZE

Serves 4

1½–2 pounds cob-smoked ham   2 cups Maple Mustard (recipe on
                                          page 13)

Preheat the oven to 325°F. In a small roasting pan with a rack, bake the ham for 20 minutes. Remove from the oven and increase the temperature to 425°F.

With a sharp knife, score the skin in a crosshatch pattern. Pour 1 cup maple mustard into a small bowl, then use a pastry brush to coat the ham liberally.

Return the ham to the oven and bake, basting occasionally, until it reaches an internal temperature of 155°F. Transfer to a platter, cover with foil, and let stand for 10 minutes. Slice thinly and serve with the remaining glaze on the side.

> LE SOMMELIER: The sweet maple notes of the glaze and the richness of the ham call for a rich beer. Harpoon Brewery in Windsor, Vermont, produces an excellent brown ale called Harpoon Brown Session Ale. The slight sweetness of the malts and the richer body of the ale make a great backdrop for the ham.

ROASTED PORK LOIN STUFFED WITH FETA, SUN-DRIED TOMATO, AND SPINACH

Serves 6

CHEF'S NOTE: Make sure that the pork is cooked to an internal temperature of 140°F on an instant-read meat thermometer. Artichokes make a nice side with this dish.

Stuffing

6 ounces fresh spinach, stems removed

1 tablespoon olive oil

½ cup minced onion

3 cloves garlic, minced

1 tablespoon chopped fresh thyme

4 ounces sun-dried tomatoes, soaked and chopped

3 ounces bread crumbs

1 free-range egg, beaten

2 ounces feta cheese

Salt to taste

Pork

1½ pounds pasture-fed pork loin

2 tablespoons olive oil

1 carrot, peeled and cut into medium dice

1 stalk celery, peeled and cut into medium dice

1 medium onion, diced

Salt and freshly ground pepper to taste

Sauce

1 tablespoon butter

2 cloves garlic, minced

1 shallot, minced

Salt and freshly ground black pepper

¼ cup dry white wine

2 cups veal stock

1 tablespoon chopped fresh rosemary

To make the stuffing: In a sauté pan over medium heat, cook the onion and garlic in the oil until tender but not browned. Add the spinach and cook until wilted. Transfer to a cutting board until cool, then chop. In a medium bowl, combine the onion, garlic, spinach, thyme, tomatoes, bread crumbs, egg, and cheese. Mix well and season with salt.

To make the pork: Preheat the oven to 325°F. Slice the pork loin lengthwise about ¾ through the diameter of the loin, making a pocket. Spoon the stuffing into the pocket, being careful not to overfill. Tie gently but firmly with kitchen twine about every 2 inches along the loin to close the pocket. Season the outside with salt and pepper.

Heat the oil in a large heavy-bottomed skillet over medium-high heat. Add the pork and cook until browned, 2 to 3 minutes per side. Place the carrot, celery, and onion in the bottom of a roasting pan and place the pork on top. Roast until the internal temperature reaches 140°F, about 1 hour. Transfer to a warmed platter and let stand for about 5 minutes before slicing.

To make the sauce: Melt the butter in a nonreactive saucepan over medium heat. Add the garlic, shallots, and a pinch of pepper and cook until soft but not browned. Add the wine and cook until reduced by 90 percent. Add the stock and simmer until reduced by ½. Season with salt and pepper.

Transfer the pork to a cutting board. Add ¼ to ½ cup water to the pan, swirl it around, and add to the sauce. Cook until reduced to about ½ cup, skimming off any fat that rises to the surface, then add the rosemary and more salt and pepper if desired.

Using a very sharp knife, slice the pork into 2-slice portions and moisten with sauce.

❧ *The Final Touch:* A sprig of rosemary is a nice garnish for color and fragrance.

BRATTLEBORO PORK LOIN

Serves 4

CHEF'S NOTE: Marinating is great, but you have to be careful when using acidic ingredients, since they can start to "cook" the proteins, affecting the tenderness of the meat. Overmarinating makes meat mushy.

¼ cup orange juice

2 tablespoons lime juice

2 tablespoons dark rum

2 tablespoons olive oil

½ red onion, minced

1 clove garlic, minced

½ teaspoon cumin seed, toasted and ground

½ teaspoon dried oregano

¼ teaspoon cayenne pepper

1 teaspoon freshly ground black pepper

4 pasture-fed pork loin medallions (6 ounces each)

1 tablespoon chopped fresh cilantro

Zest of 1 lime, minced

¼ teaspoon ground cinnamon

3 oranges

Salt to taste

In a small stainless steel bowl, combine the orange juice, lime juice, rum, oil, onion, garlic, cumin, oregano, cayenne, and ½ teaspoon black pepper. Rub the pork with the mixture and let stand for 2 to 3 hours.

Preheat the grill to medium high.

In a medium bowl, combine the cilantro, lime zest, cinnamon, and the remaining ½ teaspoon black pepper. Peel the oranges with a knife, cut the segments from the membrane, and add to the bowl (along with the juice squeezed from the pieces left after cutting the segments). Season with salt and stir to combine.

Drain any excess marinade from the pork and grill until the internal temperature reaches 140°F, 2 to 3 minutes per side. (The pork will cook quickly, so be careful to turn it before sugars in the marinade caramelize too much and burn.) Serve with the orange relish.

RABBIT BLANQUETTE

Serves 4

CHEF'S NOTE: When the entire house is filled with the fragrance of this rabbit stew, you'll understand why it's a fall favorite in Vermont.

---

2 rabbits, each cut into 6 pieces

1 cup (2 sticks) + 2 tablespoons (¼ stick) butter

½ cup flour

1½ quarts chicken stock or bouillon

2 cloves garlic, finely chopped

2 tablespoons fresh thyme

1 teaspoon black peppercorns

1 bay leaf

2 tablespoons fresh parsley

Ground nutmeg to taste

Cayenne pepper to taste

Salt and freshly ground black pepper to taste

2 pounds pearl onions

2 pounds button mushrooms

Juice and zest of 1 lemon

4 cups heavy cream

Preheat the oven to 325°F.

Heat a heavy-bottomed ovenproof skillet over medium heat and add ½ cup butter. When it starts to foam, add the rabbit and cook until very lightly browned, 1 to 2 minutes per side. Transfer to a plate.

Wipe the skillet with a paper towel, add another ½ cup butter and the flour, and stir to make a roux. Add the stock, garlic, thyme, peppercorns, bay leaf, parsley, nutmeg, cayenne, salt, and black pepper and bring to a simmer. Return the rabbit to the pan and bake until tender, about 1 hour. Add the onions to the pan and bake until the rabbit meat pulls easily from the bone, about 45 minutes.

Meanwhile, in another skillet, cook the mushrooms with 2 tablespoons butter until soft, about 5 minutes. Stir in the lemon juice and remove from the heat.

Transfer the rabbit and onions to a deep serving dish. Strain the sauce into a saucepan and bring to a simmer over medium heat, then add the cream and lemon zest and cook

until thick enough to coat the back of a spoon. Add the mushrooms to the serving dish and ladle the sauce over the rabbit and vegetables.

◆⁄ *The Final Touch:* Garnish with chopped parsley and serve over wild rice or wide egg noodles.

LE SOMMELIER: This dish offers a variety of flavors and calls for a relatively complex wine. Jonathan Edwards Winery in Connecticut produces a delicious and complex Cabernet Franc that offers rich fruit and a slightly herbal undertone that would match the flavors of this dish very well.

GUINNESS-BRAISED LAMB STEW

Serves 4

CHEF'S NOTE: If you prefer not to make your own stock, you can buy prepared broth and stock at supermarkets and natural food stores. If you want to avoid excess salt, look for low-sodium versions. You can also simply keep a container of vegetable stock powder on hand to substitute for any stock and to fortify soups and sauces. Don't be afraid to increase the seasonings if you like, and you can add parsnips as a nice variation. Like all stews, this one is often better the second day.

1½ pounds lamb shoulder, diced

¾ cup flour

½ teaspoon salt

1½ teaspoons freshly ground black pepper

3 tablespoons vegetable oil

1 carrot, cut into medium dice

2 stalks celery, cut into medium dice

1 large onion, cut into medium dice

2 tablespoons chopped garlic

6 ounces Guinness stout

3 cups chicken broth or stock

2 tablespoons tomato paste

1 tablespoon chopped fresh rosemary

2 teaspoons paprika

2 teaspoons ground cumin

2 teaspoons curry powder

Salt to taste

Heat a heavy-bottomed pot large enough to hold 4 quarts comfortably. Place ½ cup flour in a shallow bowl and add ½ teaspoon each salt and black pepper. Dredge the lamb in the flour and shake off the excess.

Add the oil to the pot, then add the lamb and cook over medium heat until browned, 1 to 2 minutes per side, being careful not to scorch. Add the carrot, onion, celery, and garlic, stirring to keep them from burning. Add the stout and bring to a simmer.

Place the remaining ¼ cup flour in a small bowl and stir in enough broth to give the mixture the consistency of heavy cream.

Add the remaining broth and the tomato paste to the pot and bring to a simmer. Add the rosemary, cumin, curry powder, and the remaining 1 teaspoon pepper. Stir the flour mixture and slowly add to the stew, stirring constantly. Simmer gently until the meat and vegetables are tender, about 30 minutes, stirring frequently to avoid scorching. Season with salt if desired.

❧ *The Final Touch:* To brighten both the appearance and the flavor of the dish, add chopped fresh herbs such as parsley, thyme, rosemary, chives, or sage just before serving.

LE SOMMELIER: Lamb simmered in highly seasoned stout (a dark top-fermented ale) is best served with a beer, preferably a dark, highly seasoned ale. Harpoon Brewery makes a terrific ale called Harpoon Munich Dark, which would be perfect with this dish. If you prefer wine, try a spicy red Zinfandel from California or a Malbec from Argentina.

Vermont Apple, Cob-Smoked Bacon, and Cheddar Cheese Frittata

Lavender-Roasted Venison with Sherry

Rack of Lamb with Aged Balsamic

Sage-Cured Duck Breast with Hard Cider Sauce

Root Vegetable Medley in Savoy Cabbage Leaves with Beurre Monté and Tomatoes

Goat Cheese and Smoked Chicken Ravioli

Shrimp in Spicy Carrot Sauce with Linguine

Wintertime Braised Chicken Legs with Dried Fruit

VERMONT SPRING LAMB WITH NATURAL JUICES

Serves 4

CHEF'S NOTE: This dish is a fresh take on an old favorite.

---

2 eggplants

3 tablespoons olive oil

2 heirloom tomatoes, sliced

½ cup grated Swiss cheese

½ cup grated Parmesan cheese

8 pounds lamb leg, trimmed of
    excess fat

1 teaspoon mixed chopped fresh
    herbs, such as parsley, sage,
    chives, and rosemary

1 red onion, thinly sliced

1 cup spinach

½ cup finely chopped garlic

Pinch of freshly grated nutmeg

Salt and freshly ground black
    pepper to taste

Preheat the oven to 375°F.

Using a vegetable peeler, peel alternating strips of skin from the eggplants and slice thinly. In a large nonstick skillet over medium heat, cook the eggplant in 1 tablespoon oil until golden brown, 1 to 2 minutes. Transfer to a baking pan, top with the tomatoes, Swiss, and Parmesan, and bake for 20 minutes. Let stand until cool.

Cut the lamb into 6-ounce portions. In a medium ovenproof skillet over medium heat, cook the lamb in another 1 tablespoon oil until browned, 1 to 2 minutes per side. Transfer to the oven and bake until pink, up to 5 minutes depending on thickness. Let stand for 3 to 5 minutes before slicing.

In a medium skillet over medium heat, cook the onion in the remaining 1 tablespoon oil until soft. Add the spinach, a few drops of water, and the garlic, nutmeg, herbs, salt, and pepper. As soon as the spinach is wilted, place in the center of a platter and add the eggplant and tomatoes. Slice the lamb very thinly and arrange on top of the vegetables.

❧ *The Final Touch:* Reserve some of the cooking liquid from the eggplant, whisk with 1 teaspoon butter, and splash around the meat and vegetables on the plate.

RACK OF LAMB WITH AGED BALSAMIC

Serves 4

CHEF'S NOTE: Use a good balsamic vinegar, preferably one aged 10 years.

½ cup balsamic vinegar

½ cup chives

2 cloves garlic, chopped

½ cup + 2 tablespoons canola oil

2 racks of lamb (about 1 pound each), frenched by a butcher

6 plum tomatoes, halved

6 white potatoes, peeled and quartered

½ cup (1 stick) butter

½ cup milk

2 teaspoons finely chopped rosemary

Salt and freshly ground black pepper to taste

In a small saucepan over medium heat, bring the vinegar to a simmer and cook until reduced to 2 tablespoons. Remove from the heat.

Bring a small saucepan of salted water to a boil, then add the chives and steep for 10 seconds. Immediately place in a bowl of ice water for about a minute, then pat dry and chop. In a blender, combine the chives, garlic, and ½ cup oil and process until smooth. Season with salt and pepper.

Preheat the oven to 375°F. Heat 2 tablespoons oil in a sauté pan, then add the lamb and brown on all sides. Transfer to a roasting pan and roast until the internal temperature reaches 130°F (for medium rare), about 1½ hours, adding the tomatoes halfway through cooking. Remove from the oven and let stand for 5 minutes. Transfer the lamb to a platter or cutting board and slice between the bones, forming either single or double chops.

Place the potatoes in a large saucepan with enough salted water to cover. Bring to a boil over medium heat and cook until tender, 15 to 20 minutes. Drain and mash with the butter, milk, and rosemary. Season with salt and pepper.

Divide the lamb, tomatoes, and potatoes among 4 plates. Drizzle with the balsamic vinegar and chive oil.

LAMB CUTLETS IN A GREEN MOUNTAIN ROASTERS COFFEE SAUCE

Serves 4

CHEF'S NOTE: East meets West in this imaginative mingling of traditional Middle Eastern flavors and fresh Vermont lamb.

¼ cup (½ stick) butter

⅓ cup strong-brewed Green Mountain Roasters coffee

⅓ cup honey

2 tablespoons Worcestershire sauce

¼ teaspoon grated mace

¼ teaspoon ground cardamom

½ teaspoon ground cinnamon

¼ teaspoon ground cloves

½ teaspoon ground allspice

½ teaspoon salt

¼ cup fresh orange juice

1 cup all-purpose flour

2 tablespoons clarified butter or oil

8 lamb cutlets (4 ounces each)

Salt and freshly ground black pepper

16 Medjool dates, pitted

Melt the butter in a medium saucepan over low heat. Add the coffee, honey, Worcestershire sauce, mace, cardamom, cinnamon, cloves, allspice, salt, and orange juice. Bring to a simmer and stir, then cover and remove from the heat.

Preheat the oven to 120°F. Place the flour in a shallow bowl. Heat the clarified butter

LE SOMMELIER: This complex, exotic dish, with its strongly bitter tones from the coffee, calls for a deeply complex, tannic red wine, itself full of bitterness thanks to the tannins. Be sure it also has ripe berrylike fruit flavors and toasty oakiness to match the hint of sweetness in the sauce from the honey and dates. One wine that easily fits the bill is the reserve Merlot from Wolffer Estate Vineyard on Long Island's North Fork.

The other obvious beverage choice is a cup of strong, steaming coffee—from Vermont's own Green Mountain Coffee Roasters, of course!

in a large skillet until bubbling. Season the lamb with salt and pepper, dredge lightly in the flour, and pat to remove any excess. Add to the skillet and cook until golden brown, 1 to 2 minutes per side. Transfer to a baking sheet lined with paper towels and keep warm in the oven.

Return the sauce to the heat and bring to a simmer. Strain into another saucepan and add the dates. Remove from the heat.

Divide the lamb and dates among 4 plates and spoon the sauce over the cutlets.

The Final Touch: Serve with couscous and garnish with fresh greens.

SAGE-CURED DUCK BREAST
WITH HARD CIDER SAUCE

Serves 8

CHEF'S NOTE: The elegant presentation of this dish makes the extra effort it requires worth every second. It's perfect for fall.

Duck

½ cup fresh sage, stems removed and reserved

¼ cup sea salt

3 tablespoons black peppercorns

4 duck breasts, fat trimmed to ¼" and trimmed fat reserved

Sauce

1 cup diced Spanish onion

1 cup diced, peeled, and cored Granny Smith apples

3 cups apple cider

3 quarts chicken broth or stock

Salt and freshly ground black pepper to taste

Relish

1 butternut squash, peeled and cut into small dice

3 cups diced, peeled, and cored Granny Smith apples

¼ cup tart cherries

¼ cup sugar

2 teaspoons fresh lemon juice

1 cinnamon stick

¼ teaspoon ground allspice

1 bunch Swiss chard, washed and chopped

2 tablespoons (¼ stick) butter

To prepare the duck: In a spice grinder, pulverize the sage, salt, and pepper into a fine powder. Carefully rub the mixture into the fat of the duck, then refrigerate on a rack for 3 hours.

To make the sauce: In a heavy saucepan over medium heat, combine the onion and apples and cook until the onion is translucent, 3 to 4 minutes. Add the cider and cook until thickened to the consistency of syrup, 10 to 15 minutes. Add the broth and simmer for 1 hour. Strain through a mesh strainer into another saucepan, then return to the heat, add the reserved sage stems, and simmer until thickened to sauce consistency. Strain again and season with salt and pepper.

To make the relish: Melt the reserved duck fat in a sauté pan over medium-high heat. Add the squash and cook until browned, then reduce the heat and cook until tender, 15 minutes.

In a small saucepan over medium-low heat, combine the apples, cherries, sugar, lemon juice, allspice, and cinnamon stick. Cover and simmer until the mixture resembles coarse applesauce. Add to the squash and set aside.

Remove any excess sage mixture from the duck. Place the duck fat-side down in a large sauté pan over medium-low heat and cook, draining off excess fat frequently, until the skin is very crisp and deep brown, 5 to 10 minutes. Increase the heat to high, turn the duck, and cook until evenly browned and reddish-pink inside, 2 to 3 minutes. Transfer to a rack in a warm place and let stand for a few minutes.

Return the relish and sauce to the stove and heat through. Add more salt and pepper to the sauce if desired.

Transfer the duck to a cutting board and slice thinly against the grain.

❧ *The Final Touch:* Mound some relish on one side of each plate. Place some of the duck slices on top of the mound, then fan the rest away from the relish. Lean 4 or 5 lightly steamed green beans against the other side of the mound. Spoon sauce over the duck and allow it to circle the plate, and garnish with chopped fresh parsley.

LAVENDER-ROASTED VENISON WITH SHERRY

Serves 4

CHEF'S NOTE: We generally think of venison as an autumn meat, and serving it with fall vegetables accentuates this quality. Modern farmed venison is lean and mild and is available year round from local sources nationwide, so try it with lighter vegetable preparations and sauces at any time of year. Lavender flowers are available at herbal tea shops that deal in bulk ingredients. They are very aromatic, so if you're not sure about the flavor, use less.

⅓ ounce dried lavender flowers

4 teaspoons salt

1 tablespoon freshly ground black pepper

1½ pounds boneless venison loin, trimmed of silver skin

¾ cup sugar

6 tablespoons sherry vinegar

1½ teaspoons chopped fresh thyme

2 tablespoons vegetable oil

In a spice mill, combine the lavender, salt, and pepper and pulse to incorporate. Coat the venison with the mixture and refrigerate for at least 3 hours.

In a heavy-bottomed 2-quart nonreactive saucepan over medium-high heat, combine the sugar and 6 tablespoons water. Simmer for 15 to 20 minutes, keeping the sides of the pan clean with a wet brush. Be careful not to let the mixture begin to crystallize. When the mixture is a medium brown caramel color, remove from the heat, add the vinegar, and whisk in the thyme.

Preheat the oven to 400°F. Heat a large cast-iron skillet over medium-high heat, then add the oil and venison and cook until golden brown, 1 to 2 minutes per side. Transfer to a medium roasting pan with a rack and roast until the internal temperature reaches 110 to 115°F (for medium rare), about 20 minutes.

Meanwhile, return the skillet to medium-high heat, add ¼ cup water, and dissolve the pan drippings, scraping with a wooden spoon. Cook until reduced to the consistency of syrup, then strain through a fine-mesh strainer into the sugar water mixture.

Remove the venison from the oven, cover with foil, and let stand for 10 minutes. Transfer to a cutting board and slice ¼ inch thick. Divide among 4 warmed plates and drizzle with the sugar water and drippings mix.

❧ *The Final Touch:* Sweet Potato–Celeriac Purée (page 181) and Sautéed Swiss Chard (page 175) are nice accompaniments to this dish.

FALL VENISON WITH SQUASH AND PUMPKIN-TARRAGON SAUCE

Serves 4

CHEF'S NOTE: This recipe is quite involved, but it's definitely worth the effort to make a great autumn meal. You can use any combination of seasonal vegetables as a garnish; just look for bright colors and flavors that complement the squash.

Squash

1 spaghetti squash

Salt and freshly ground black pepper to taste

½ cup (1 stick) butter

2 teaspoons maple syrup

Sauce

1 cup cooked diced pumpkin

2 cups vegetable stock

2 tablespoons fresh lemon juice

½ cup heavy cream

2 teaspoons butter

1 teaspoon chopped fresh tarragon

Salt and freshly ground black pepper to taste

Garnish

1 cup all-purpose flour

Salt and freshly ground black pepper to taste

2 cups canola oil

1 onion, halved and sliced very thinly

1 cup snow peas, trimmed, blanched, and diced

1 cup cooked corn kernels

1 tablespoon butter

Venison

1 pound venison loin

1 tablespoon olive oil

Salt and freshly ground black pepper to taste

To make the squash: Preheat the oven to 350°F. Lightly oil a baking sheet. Split and seed the squash and season with salt and pepper. Place on the baking sheet and roast until soft, about 20 minutes. Let stand until cool enough to handle, then scoop the pulp into a medium bowl and add the butter and syrup. Season with salt and pepper and mash with a fork or potato masher until smooth. Set aside and keep warm. Leave the oven set at 350°F.

To make the sauce: In a blender, combine the pumpkin and ⅓ of the stock. Start the motor, and as the squash begins to purée, add the lemon juice, cream, butter, tarragon, and salt and pepper to taste. Blend until smooth, adding more stock as needed, and add more seasoning if desired.

To make the garnish: Place the flour in a shallow dish and season with salt and pepper. Toss the onion in the flour and shake off any excess. Heat the oil in a deep medium skillet, then add the onions and fry until browned and crisp, being careful not to burn. Transfer to paper towels.

Melt the butter in a medium sauté pan over medium heat, then add the corn and snow peas and cook until tender. Remove from the heat and keep warm.

To make the venison: Cut the loin into 4 equal pieces and season with salt and pepper. In a heavy-bottomed ovenproof skillet over medium-high heat, sear the venison in the oil until browned, 1 to 2 minutes per side. Transfer to the oven and roast until the internal temperature reaches 110 to 115°F, about 15 minutes (for medium rare). Let stand for about 5 minutes before slicing.

Place a mound of squash in the center of a platter and make a well in the center to form a doughnut (savarin) shape. Thinly slice the venison and overlap the slices around the top of the squash. Ladle the sauce around the squash and garnish with the peas, corn, and onions.

PEPPER-CRUSTED VENISON MEDALLIONS WITH CIDER BRANDY

Serves 4

CHEF'S NOTE: This is an adaptation of a classic beef dish. The spiciness of the pepper goes very nicely with the sweetness of the cider, and if you use bacon fat, it adds a nice smoky touch. Making the dish with more thin medallions instead of fewer thick ones cuts the cooking time because you don't have to finish the meat in the oven.

---

8 venison loin medallions (3 ounces each)

Salt to taste

¼ cup cracked black pepper

3 tablespoons vegetable oil or bacon fat

1 tablespoon minced sweet onion or shallot

1 Granny Smith apple, cored and cut into small dice

½ cup brandy

1½ cups apple cider

2 teaspoons finely chopped fresh sage

Lightly salt the venison. Place the pepper in a pie plate or similar flat-bottomed pan and press each piece of venison into the pepper, coating both sides evenly.

Heat 2 tablespoons oil in a heavy cast-iron skillet over medium-high heat. (Test with a drop of water; if it spits and pops as it's dropped in, the oil is hot enough.) Working in batches and being careful not to overfill the skillet, cook the venison until browned, 30 seconds per side. Transfer to a plate.

When all the venison has been browned, wipe the skillet with a paper towel, add the remaining 1 tablespoon oil, and reduce the heat to medium. Add the onion and cook until tender and translucent, 2 minutes. Add the apple and cook, stirring, until beginning to soften, 2 to 3 minutes. Remove from the heat and add the brandy, then return to the heat and cook until reduced by about 90 percent. Add the cider and sage, bring to a simmer, and cook until the liquid thickens to the consistency of syrup. Season with salt and serve over the medallions.

❧ *The Final Touch:* Serve with red-skin potatoes roasted with garlic, roasted winter squash, or fried beet chips.

5

VEGETABLES

Fresh vegetables just pulled from the earth, gently washed, and expertly prepared are expected on the table for at least eight months of the year in the cities and towns surrounding the New England Culinary Institute.

In a rural state, where there's a kitchen garden in every backyard, a truck garden on every farm, and pots of herbs on every windowsill, we know what fresh vegetables taste like. And although many of us are unwilling to use millions of gallons of oil to transport veggies from warmer climes, *none* of us are willing to give them up because the ground is frozen.

That Yankee stubbornness is one of the things that's saving small-scale family farming in Vermont. To meet our passion for fresh vegetables, a new generation of farmers is putting up acre after acre of greenhouses so that when the ground's covered with snow — as it is five months of the year around here — we're still eating just-picked arugula and heirloom tomatoes.

That's not to say that we aren't partial to the more easily stored root vegetables, squashes, and the like. We are. It's just that we're greedy. We want both.

OVEN-DRIED TOMATOES WITH ASPARAGUS, FRISÉE, ASIAGO, AND BASIL OIL

Serves 4

CHEF'S NOTE: Oven drying is an age-old food preservation technique, but in this recipe it's used to concentrate the flavor of fresh tomatoes. You can prepare the basil oil and tomatoes a day ahead.

---

2 cups fresh basil, stems removed

1 cup fresh Italian parsley, stems removed

1 cup corn oil

3 heirloom tomatoes

2 tablespoons olive oil

1 tablespoon sugar

Salt and freshly ground black pepper

2 teaspoons chopped thyme, parsley, and basil

1 bunch asparagus

1 bunch frisée lettuce, washed and ends removed

1 cup shaved Asiago cheese

Bring 1 quart water to a boil in a medium saucepan. Blanch the basil and parsley by placing them in a small strainer and plunging it into the boiling water for 20 seconds. Immediately transfer to a bowl of ice water to cool quickly, then squeeze out any excess water. Place the herbs and corn oil in a blender and purée for 1 minute. Pour into a container and let stand at room temperature for 2 hours or refrigerate overnight, then strain twice through a strainer lined with cheesecloth to remove any herb particles. The oil should be bright green with no sediment. (The infused oil may be refrigerated for up to a week.)

Cut the core from each tomato with a paring knife and cut a small "x" in the bottom. Blanch the tomatoes in boiling water for 10 seconds, then transfer to an ice bath until cool. Peel off the skins with the tip of the paring knife, then quarter the tomatoes, remove the seeds, and drain off the juice.

Preheat the oven to 250°F. Place the tomatoes on a rack in a shallow baking pan and drizzle with the olive oil, sprinkle with the sugar, and season with salt and pepper. Bake for 1 hour, then turn and bake for another hour. Let cool for 15 minutes, then dice.

Transfer to a medium bowl and toss with just enough basil oil to coat. Add the chopped thyme, basil, and parsley.

Break the asparagus spears near the bottom of the stalks and trim the ends. Peel off the skin with a vegetable peeler. Blanch in boiling water until tender, 3 to 5 minutes, then transfer to a medium bowl and toss with basil oil to coat. Season with salt and pepper and keep warm.

Place the tomatoes near the center of a platter. Overlap the asparagus spears on the tomatoes and arrange the lettuce on top. Place the cheese on top of the greens and drizzle the entire platter with basil oil.

❧ *The Final Touch:* This dish is beautiful when presented family style, but it's also nice in single "stacked" servings, with the asparagus laid over the tomatoes in a triangle shape, the lettuce and cheese on top, and the basil oil drizzled on the plates. Crusty French bread is a wonderful accompaniment.

OVEN-DRIED TOMATO TART

Serves 4

CHEF'S NOTE: Since drying the tomatoes in the oven takes several hours, do it the day before you make this recipe.

Tomatoes

3 tablespoons olive oil

2½ cups sliced plum tomatoes

2 tablespoons sugar

Salt and freshly ground black pepper

Garlic

1 head garlic

1 tablespoon olive oil

Tart

2 cups pearl onions or shallots

½ cup (1 stick) butter, cut into small cubes

½ cup sugar

5 teaspoons chopped fresh thyme

2 teaspoons chopped fresh parsley

1 sheet thawed frozen puff pastry dough

To make the tomatoes: Preheat the oven to 150°F. Brush a baking sheet with 1½ tablespoons oil and add the tomatoes cut-side up. Sprinkle with sugar, salt, and pepper and drizzle with the remaining 1½ tablespoons oil. Bake for 8 to 9 hours. Let cool and refrigerate until ready to use.

To make the garlic: Preheat the oven to 375°F. Cut ¼ inch off the top of the garlic head. Rub the garlic with the oil and place on a piece of foil, then fold to close. Bake until golden brown, about 40 minutes. Let cool for about 10 minutes, then gently squeeze the cloves to extrude the garlic.

To make the tart: Preheat the oven to 350°F. In an ovenproof sauté pan over medium-high heat, combine the onions, butter, sugar, 4 tablespoons thyme, 1 tablespoon parsley, and ¼ cup water. Bring to a boil, cover with a piece of parchment paper, and cook until all the water has evaporated and the onions are cooked through, about 20 minutes. Remove the parchment and cook until golden brown, 15 minutes.

Add the tomatoes and garlic to the pan. Top with the pastry dough, trim from around the sides of the pan, and make a small hole in the center. Bake until the pastry is golden brown, about 20 minutes. Place a round platter on top of the tart and invert. Sprinkle with the remaining thyme and parsley and serve immediately.

HERBED SUMMER SUCCOTASH

Serves 4

CHEF'S NOTE: This succotash is a northern adaptation of a southern specialty.

---

6 ears corn

¼ cup canola oil

½ small onion, cut into small dice

1 clove garlic, minced

¼ cup sherry vinegar

1 cup fresh or frozen baby lima beans

¼ cup finely chopped fresh basil leaves

1 tablespoon finely chopped fresh parsley

1 cup spinach, stems removed

Salt and freshly ground black pepper to taste

Remove the kernels from the corn. In a 12-inch sauté pan over medium heat, cook the onion in the oil, stirring until soft and translucent. Add the garlic and cook, stirring, for 1 minute. Add the corn kernels and vinegar and cook for 3 minutes. Stir in the lima beans, basil, parsley, and spinach and cook until warmed through and the spinach is slightly wilted. Season with salt and pepper and serve warm.

FRESH SUMMER CORN, SMOKED BACON, AND SCALLION HASH

Serves 4

CHEF'S NOTE: This is a perfect side dish full of summer flavors.

---

4 slices smoked bacon, cut into small dice

½ Vidalia or Spanish onion, cut into small dice

4 cups fresh or frozen corn kernels

1 small red bell pepper, cored, seeded, and cut into small dice

½ cup beef broth

1 tablespoon butter

1 scallion, thinly sliced

Salt and freshly ground black pepper to taste

In a 10-inch sauté pan over medium heat, cook the bacon until the fat begins to liquefy and the bacon begins to brown. Add the onion, reduce the heat to medium low, and cook until fragrant but not browned, 7 minutes. Stir in the corn and bell pepper, increase the heat to medium high, and cook for 4 minutes. Add the broth and cook until almost all of the liquid has evaporated. Remove from the heat and stir in the butter and scallion until the butter is melted and the scallion is translucent, 4 to 5 minutes. Season with salt and pepper and serve hot.

GRATIN OF ZUCCHINI

Serves 4

CHEF'S NOTE: Typically, a gratin is a dish that's baked, topped with bread crumbs or cheese, and browned. Choose uniformly sized zucchini for even cooking. This dish is an excellent accompaniment to any meal, but it can also be an entrée. You can try substituting different cheeses, such as aged cheddar or gouda, for different flavor and texture.

---

3 medium zucchini

Salt and freshly ground black pepper to taste

2 cloves garlic, chopped

2 teaspoons chopped thyme, parsley, and basil

1 Spanish onion

2 tablespoons olive oil

¾ cup heavy cream

1 cup shredded Swiss cheese

5 teaspoons grated Parmesan cheese

Wash 2 zucchinis and halve lengthwise. Using a spoon, remove the flesh, making a boat-like shape, with the sides about 1 inch thick and the bottom about ½ inch thick. Roughly chop the flesh and set aside in a medium bowl.

Wash the remaining zucchini and quarter lengthwise. Cut into thin triangles and add to the bowl. Season with salt and pepper and add the garlic, herbs, and 1 tablespoon olive oil.

Preheat the oven to 375°F.

In a medium skillet, cook the onions in the remaining 1 tablespoon oil until soft but not browned, 3 minutes. Add the zucchini mixture and cook until tender, 5 minutes. Add the cream and cook until thickened and somewhat dry, 5 minutes. Remove from the heat and fold in the cheese. Add more salt and pepper if desired.

Line a baking sheet with parchment paper or foil and brush lightly with oil. Place the zucchini "boats" on the baking sheet and season with salt and pepper. Spoon in the zucchini mixture, then sprinkle with the cheese. Bake until tender and golden brown on top, 20 minutes.

SUMMER GRATIN OF EGGPLANT, TOMATO. AND BASIL

Serves 4

CHEF'S NOTE: A dish that celebrates the garden.

Sauce

1 Spanish onion, chopped

1 tablespoon olive oil

6 heirloom tomatoes, diced

3 cloves garlic, minced

½ cup chopped basil

Salt and freshly ground black
    pepper

Gratin

1 eggplant

½ cup olive oil

2 heirloom tomatoes, cut into
    ⅛"-thick slices

Salt and freshly ground black
    pepper to taste

8 ounces fresh mozzarella cheese,
    cut into ⅛"-thick slices, or
    2 cups shredded mozzarella

To make the sauce: In a medium skillet over low heat, cook the onion in the oil until soft but not browned, about 3 minutes. Add the tomatoes, cover, and simmer for 20 minutes. Add the garlic and basil and simmer for 3 minutes. Season with salt and pepper and remove from the heat.

To make the gratin: Cut off the stem and bottom ends of the eggplant. Using a vegetable peeler, remove the peel, then halve the eggplant lengthwise. Lay each half flat-side down and cut into ¼-inch-thick half moons.

Preheat the oven to 350°F.

Heat the oil in a medium sauté pan over medium-high heat. Working in batches, add the eggplant, being careful not to overcrowd the pan. Cook until browned, 20 minutes per side, then transfer to paper towels. Season with salt and pepper while still hot.

Place a few tablespoons of sauce on the bottom of a 9 x 9–inch baking dish. Add a layer of eggplant, a layer of tomatoes, and another layer of eggplant. Top with sauce and a layer of mozzarella. Bake until bubbling, 30 minutes.

❧ *The Final Touch:* Serve with additional sauce on the side and garlic bread.

VEGAN SPINACH GRATIN

Serves 6 to 8

CHEF'S NOTE: This dish offers an amazing blend of earthy spring flavors.

---

5 ounces unsalted raw cashews

¼ cup rice wine or white wine vinegar

Salt and freshly ground black pepper to taste

¼ cup olive oil

1 onion, finely chopped

3 cloves garlic, finely chopped

1 pound Tweed Farm mushrooms (shiitakes and oysters, or portobellos), thinly sliced

1 can (16 ounces) artichokes, rinsed and drained, thinly sliced

2 roasted red peppers, cut into strips

1 pound Screamin' Ridge Farm spinach, stems removed, coarsely chopped

1 cup seasoned bread crumbs

In a blender, combine the cashews, vinegar, and 1 cup cold water and purée until smooth. Season with salt and pepper (it should taste like salted cashews). Strain into a bowl through a fine-mesh strainer, pressing out all the moisture. Discard the dry nut pulp.

Heat a large brazier or sauté pan and add the oil. When it shimmers, add the onion and garlic and cook until translucent, adjusting the heat as necessary so they don't brown. Add the mushrooms and cook until heated through and all moisture has been absorbed.

Preheat the oven to 350°F. Lightly oil a 9 x 13–inch baking dish.

Add the artichokes and peppers and toss to coat with oil. Add the spinach; cook just until beginning to wilt. Remove from the heat and season with salt and pepper. If the mixture seems too watery, drain in a colander for a minute or two.

Stir in enough of the cashew cream to moisten. Transfer to the baking dish and top with the bread crumbs. Bake until heated through, 30 to 40 minutes.

HERB AND SPINACH CASSEROLE

Serves 4 to 6

CHEF'S NOTE: This is a great summer dish that features fresh herbs and can be served warm or cold. You can substitute Swiss chard or kale for the spinach.

---

10 ounces fresh spinach, washed and stems trimmed

1 large onion, chopped

2 cloves garlic

2 stalks celery, peeled and chopped

1 cup chopped fresh parsley, basil, thyme, and oregano (or other complementary herbs of your choice)

½ cup olive oil

2 free-range eggs

1 cup grated Jarlsberg or sharp cheddar cheese

Salt and freshly ground black pepper to taste

1 cup bread crumbs

½ cup grated Parmesan cheese

2 tablespoons olive oil

Fresh parsley, basil, thyme, and oregano leaves

Preheat the oven to 300°F.

Bring 1 cup water to a boil in a medium saucepan, then add the spinach and cook until tender, about 40 seconds. Drain, reserving ½ cup cooking liquid.

Heat the oil in a sauté pan over medium heat. Add the onion, garlic, and celery and cook until tender, 5 minutes. Transfer to a food processor, add the spinach, cooking liquid, and herbs, and blend until smooth.

Add the eggs and blend for 20 seconds, then add the Jarlsberg and pulse quickly. Season with salt and pepper.

Spread the mixture evenly in a 9 x 13–inch baking pan. Sprinkle with the bread crumbs and Parmesan and drizzle with the oil. Bake until the top is crisp and the center is cooked through, 30 to 40 minutes. Cut into squares and serve on a platter garnished with fresh herbs.

SUMMER FLOWERS

Serves 4

CHEF'S NOTE: An easy and whimsical offering from your garden.

Stuffing

4 baby zucchini, with blossoms

4 patty pan squash, with blossoms

1 large zucchini

2 teaspoons olive oil

½ red onion

2 plum tomatoes

Salt and freshly ground black
pepper to taste

½ head garlic, chopped

½ cup chopped fresh parsley

2 teaspoons chopped fresh
herbs, such as thyme, basil, and
oregano

½ cup vegetable stock

Sauce

4 heirloom tomatoes, diced

½ head garlic, chopped

1 bunch basil, chopped

Salt and freshly ground black
pepper to taste

2 tablespoons olive oil

To make the stuffing: Slice the baby zucchinis and patty pans, leaving ½ inch still attached to the blossoms. Dice the onion and large zucchini.

Heat the oil in a medium skillet. When it begins to smoke, add the onion and cook until golden brown. Add the diced zucchini and tomatoes and season with salt and pepper. Cook for 3 minutes, then stir in the garlic, parsley, and herbs. Transfer to a bowl and refrigerate until chilled.

Preheat the oven to 375°F. Fill the squash blossoms with stuffing, using a pastry bag if possible, and twist to close the ends. Place the squash in a shallow baking pan with the stock, then cover and bake for 10 minutes.

To make the sauce: Process the tomatoes in a blender, then add the garlic and basil. Season with salt and pepper, add the oil, and process for 30 seconds. Spoon onto a plate, arrange the squash on top, and serve immediately.

SPICED PUMPKIN AND MAPLE PURÉE

Serves 4

CHEF'S NOTE: Pumpkin or winter squash purée is great with pork, chicken, or meat dishes; its sweetness helps balance bitter or rich flavors from the other dishes in the meal. To peel the squash, simply use a serrated knife to cut off the top and bottom ends. Place the squash flat-side down on a cutting board and use the knife to peel from the top down in small strips.

---

4 cups pumpkin or winter squash, peeled, seeded, and cut into large dice

1 cup Cold Hollow Vermont apple cider

1 tablespoon butter

3 tablespoons maple syrup

¼ teaspoon ground cloves

1 teaspoon ground cinnamon

1 teaspoon salt

In a 2½- to 3-quart saucepan over medium heat, combine the pumpkin and cider. Cover and cook at a steady simmer until tender, about 20 minutes. Add the butter, syrup, cloves, and cinnamon and stir to combine. Add the salt and remove from the heat. Using an immersion blender, food processor, or blender, purée until smooth (the pumpkin should be moister than mashed potato, but not soupy). Because the starch level of winter squashes varies, the consistency of the finished product will be slightly different with any substitution, but this can be remedied by ladling off excess liquid before puréeing, or adding additional liquid to adjust a mixture that appears too thick.

❧ *The Final Touch:* If serving family style in a bowl, garnish the top with a pinch of ground cinnamon.

SUMMER VEGETABLE RAGOÛT

Serves 4

CHEF'S NOTE: Fresh fava beans, available in spring and early summer, brighten both the color and the flavor of this dish, which can be served as a side dish with fish or poultry or as a vegetarian main dish. While the beans are somewhat labor intensive, their brilliant green color and flavor are worth it. If favas are unavailable, substitute 1 cup fresh or frozen lima beans. And though we would never open a bottle of champagne for cooking, this is a good use for the remains of a bottle.

½ pound red bliss potatoes, with skins

1½ pounds whole fava beans

¼ cup (½ stick) butter

1 cup sugar snap peas or snow peas, stems and strings removed

1 medium summer squash, quartered lengthwise and cut into ¼" wedges

2 medium plum tomatoes, cored and diced

¼ cup champagne or Chardonnay

¼ cup heavy cream

Salt and freshly ground black pepper to taste

1 tablespoon chopped fresh chervil or ½ tablespoon chopped fresh tarragon

1 tablespoon chopped fresh parsley

Cook the potatoes in boiling water until tender, 20 to 25 minutes. Drain and let cool, then halve lengthwise and cut into ¼-inch wedges.

Shell the beans. Bring a saucepan of salted water to a boil, add the beans, and cook until tender, 2 minutes. Drain and rinse with cold running water to stop cooking and set the color. Peel off the thin opaque skin by pinching with your fingers.

Melt the butter in a large sauté pan over medium-high heat. When it foams, add the squash and peas and cook until the peas are bright green and the squash is tender, 3 minutes. Add the potatoes, beans, and tomatoes and cook until heated through, 4 minutes. Add the wine, increase the heat to high, and cook until reduced by ½. Add the cream and cook until slightly thickened. Season with salt and pepper.

CREAMED LEEKS WITH BACON, TOMATO, AND TARRAGON

Serves 4

CHEF'S NOTE: This dish is wonderful with pork chops or roasted pork loin and is especially delicious with fresh tomatoes and tarragon from your home garden. When using fresh herbs, it's very important not to cut them too fine. Coarsely chopping or tearing herbs releases aroma and flavor into the dish without bruising the leaves, which can happen when they're chopped aggressively. Also, the sharper your knife, the less bruising. If you don't have homemade chicken stock, substitute a low-sodium, natural product.

---

4 slices lean bacon, finely chopped

4 leeks, halved lengthwise and rinsed well, then thinly sliced

Salt and freshly ground black pepper to taste

½ cup small-dice heirloom tomatoes

2 tablespoons coarsely chopped fresh tarragon

⅓ cup heavy cream

⅓ cup chicken stock or broth

Cook the bacon in a 2-quart saucepan over low heat until crisp. Using a slotted spoon, transfer to paper towels.

Add the leeks to the bacon fat and cook gently for 2 minutes. Season with salt, cover the pan, and cook for about 8 minutes. Stir in the tomatoes, tarragon, cream, and stock and simmer until the cream thickens, about 10 minutes. Stir in the bacon and season with salt and pepper.

WINTER BRUSSELS SPROUTS WITH
BROWNED BUTTER AND WALNUTS

Serves 4

CHEF'S NOTES: Brussels sprouts are fantastic fall and winter vegetables and a great accompaniment to many dishes, including poultry and pork, and they're hearty enough to be part of a complete meal when combined with other vegetable sides. In this recipe, butter is cooked to a light brown color, also known as beurre noisette. Cooking it until it colors develops its nutty flavor, which pairs nicely with the walnuts. Other nuts, such as pecans, almonds, or pine nuts, may be substituted.

---

1 pound brussels sprouts, washed

1 tablespoon + ½ teaspoon salt

¼ cup (½ stick) butter

1 cup walnuts, coarsely chopped

½ teaspoon freshly ground black pepper

1 tablespoon coarsely chopped fresh thyme

Cut a ⅛-inch-deep "x" in the bottom of each brussels sprout. Partially fill a medium bowl with cold water and ice.

In a 2-quart saucepan, bring 1½ quarts of water to a boil and add 1 tablespoon salt. Add the sprouts and cook until tender when pierced with a paring knife, 5 minutes. Drain and quickly plunge into the ice bath until cool. Halve the sprouts and set aside.

Melt the butter in a 10-inch sauté pan over medium heat. When it begins to brown slightly, add the walnuts and cook, stirring, until they begin to darken slightly, about 3 minutes (be careful not to burn the butter or nuts). Add the sprouts, season with the pepper and remaining ½ teaspoon salt, and stir in the thyme.

BRAISED FALL GREENS

Serves 4

CHEF'S NOTE: Wilted fresh greens are the perfect accompaniment to grilled or roasted poultry, meat, or fish and can even be served cold the next day as a lunch treat.

Be sure to use local greens for this dish. Remove the Swiss chard ribs by holding the base of the stem with one hand and tugging the greens away from the stem toward the tip.

---

3 tablespoons olive oil

2 cloves garlic, minced

2 shallots, minced

1 head Swiss chard, ribs removed, chopped into 1" squares, and washed

1 head escarole, cored, chopped into 1" squares, and washed

½ cup vegetable broth

2 teaspoons salt

1 teaspoon freshly ground black pepper

Heat a braising pan or wide-bottomed 4-quart saucepan over medium heat, then slowly add the oil. Stir in the garlic and shallots and cook for 1 minute, reducing the heat if they start to color. Add the chard, escarole, and broth and increase the heat to medium high. Cover and cook for 2 minutes. Uncover and add the salt and pepper, then reduce the heat to medium low, stir, and cook until tender, about 10 minutes.

BRAISED CABBAGE WITH APPLES AND BACON

Serves 4

CHEF'S NOTE: This recipe is a fantastic way to incorporate local apples and cider into a savory dish (Cortlands work beautifully, but any local apples will do), and it's wonderful with any fall or winter meal, especially one that includes pork. Try using the cabbage as a bed for sliced pork loin and adding a garnish of chopped fresh thyme.

---

4 slices bacon, cut into small dice

1 red onion, cut into ⅛"-thick slices

1 head green or red cabbage, cored, quartered, and cut into ⅛"-thick slices

1 teaspoon salt

2 Cortland apples, quartered, cored, and cut into ⅛"-thick slices

2 tablespoons cider vinegar

2 tablespoons light brown sugar

2 tablespoons Cold Hollow Vermont apple cider

Salt and freshly ground black pepper to taste

In a 4-quart stainless steel saucepan, cook the bacon until crisp, 4 minutes. Add the onions, cover the pan, and cook until soft but not browned. Add the cabbage and salt and cook, covered, until it begins to wilt, about 2 minutes. Stir in the apple. Add the vinegar, sugar, and cider, then cover and cook for 5 to 10 minutes. Season with salt and pepper and cook until the cabbage is tender but the apples still retain their shape, 8 to 12 minutes.

SAUTÉED SWISS CHARD

Serves 4

CHEF'S NOTE: With a firmer texture than spinach and a hearty flavor, Swiss chard stands up well as an accompaniment to game, red meats, and seafood. Multicolored varieties such as Bright Lights add color to dishes.

¼ cup (½ stick) unsalted butter

2 pounds Swiss chard, cleaned, stems removed, and cut into 1" ribbons

Salt and freshly ground black pepper to taste

Melt the butter in a large sauté pan over medium-high heat. When it begins to foam, add the leaves and toss until bright green, 2 minutes. Add about 2 tablespoons water, cover, and cook until softened, 6 to 8 minutes. Season with salt and pepper and transfer to a plate with a slotted spoon.

⤞ *The Final Touch:* For additional color and texture, especially if using multicolored varieties of chard, include the stems. Julienne or bias cut medium and small stems and sauté until partially softened before adding the leaves.

BOURBON-GLAZED CARROTS

Serves 4

CHEF'S NOTE: This is an attractive dish with great flavor.

---

2 pounds carrots, peeled and
  cut into ¼"-thick strips about
  2" long

¼ cup light brown sugar

⅛ cup bourbon

2 tablespoons (¼ stick) unsalted
  butter

1 teaspoon salt

¼ teaspoon freshly ground black
  pepper

In a 4-quart saucepan over medium heat, combine the carrots, sugar, and 2 cups water. Simmer until the carrots are tender and almost all of the water has evaporated, about 20 minutes. Stir in the bourbon and cook for 1 minute. Add the butter and stir to incorporate, then add the salt and pepper. (The carrots should be very shiny; if they look dull, add a bit more butter.)

FIDDLEHEADS AND CARROTS FINES HERBES

Serves 4

CHEF'S NOTE: Fiddleheads are the unopened fronds of the ostrich fern and can be foraged in early spring in Vermont and the rest of northern New England. They resemble the neck of a fiddle and are often available at local stores and farm stands; choose ones that are tightly coiled. Fines herbes is a classic combination of chopped fresh parsley, chervil, tarragon, and cut chives that goes well with vegetables, fish, and eggs. If chervil isn't available, use a bit more tarragon and parsley.

---

2 cups fiddleheads

1 cup julienned carrots

1 tablespoon butter, softened

4 teaspoons chopped fresh parsley

1 teaspoon chopped fresh chervil

1 teaspoon chopped fresh tarragon

1 teaspoon cut chives

Salt and freshly ground black pepper to taste

Cut the fiddlehead stems to about 1½ inches. If the skins are dry, rub off the excess, then fill a large bucket with cold water, add the fiddleheads, and agitate the water with the coarse spray of a garden hose. Remove the fiddleheads from the water, leaving the skins and dirt behind. If the skins are initially wet or the fiddleheads are very dirty, you may need to repeat the process in another bucket of water.

Before cooking, blanch the fiddleheads to eliminate enzymes and remove impurities. Bring a 2-quart saucepan of water to a boil. Prepare an ice bath by placing water and ice in a large bowl. When the water in the pan is boiling rapidly, add the fiddleheads and cook until crisp-tender, about 5 minutes. Using a slotted spoon, transfer to the ice bath until cool. Drain well in a colander.

Bring a small saucepan of water to a boil, add the carrots, and cook until tender, 3 minutes. Transfer to a plate and let cool.

Bring another 2-quart saucepan of salted water to a boil over medium-high heat. Add the fiddleheads and carrots and cook until tender, about 1 minute. Drain all but 1 tablespoon of water from the pan. Add the butter, parsley, chervil, tarragon, and chives, season with salt and pepper, and toss to combine.

ROASTED ROOT VEGETABLES

Serves 6

CHEF'S NOTE: The secrets of perfect roasting are vegetables cut to a uniform size, a hot oven, and a pan large enough to hold the vegetables without crowding. This ensures crispness and even browning.

---

1 rutabaga, peeled and cut into strips 2" long and ½" thick

8 parsnips, peeled and cut into strips 2" long and ½" thick

2 turnips, peeled and cut into strips 2" long and ½" thick

8 carrots, peeled and cut into strips 2" long and ½" thick

2 celeriac roots, peeled and cut into strips 2" long and ½" thick

6 large beets, peeled and cut into strips 2" long and ½" thick (keep separate from the other vegetables)

2 cups olive oil

Salt and freshly ground black pepper to taste

Preheat the oven to 400°F.

Place the oil in a large bowl. Working in batches, add the rutabaga, parsnips, turnips, carrots, and celeriac and toss to coat, then toss the beets. Spread on a baking sheet and roast until lightly browned. Season with salt and pepper and serve hot or refrigerate to serve cold.

❧ *The Final Touch:* Toss the vegetables with 2 tablespoons Autumn Spice Rub (page 182) for a different taste.

BRAISED WINTER ROOT VEGETABLES

Serves 6

CHEF'S NOTE: Root vegetables serve to anchor those of us who live under snow four or five months of the year. Their warm, nourishing scent reminds us that, yes, we can eat well even through the long winter darkness.

---

2 large parsnips (about 1 pound total)

2 large leeks (white and light green parts only)

2 small fennel bulbs

1 medium celeriac

¼ cup (½ stick) unsalted butter

2 large cloves garlic, crushed

¼ teaspoon fresh thyme leaves

Pinch of sugar

⅓ cup dry white wine

Peel the parsnips and cut into 3 x ¼–inch pieces. Halve the leeks and cut into 3-inch lengths. Trim the stalks of fennel flush with the bulbs and cut each bulb lengthwise into 8 wedges. Peel the celeriac and cut into 8 wedges.

Preheat the oven to 325°F.

Melt 3 tablespoons butter in a heavy saucepan over medium heat. Add the parsnips, leeks, fennel, celeriac, and garlic, then stir to coat with butter and cook for 5 minutes. Add the thyme and sugar and season with salt and pepper. Add the wine and simmer for a few minutes. Cover and roast, stirring occasionally, until tender, 30 to 45 minutes. Stir in the remaining 1 tablespoon butter, season with salt and pepper, and serve immediately.

ROOT VEGETABLE MEDLEY IN SAVOY CABBAGE LEAVES WITH BEURRE MONTÉ AND TOMATOES

Serves 4

CHEF'S NOTE: This is an elegant presentation of earthy vegetables.

---

3 carrots, peeled and cut into small dice

1 small rutabaga, peeled and cut into small dice

2 turnips, peeled and cut into small dice

2 tablespoons (¼ stick) butter

Salt to taste

1 cup frozen green peas

4 leaves Savoy cabbage

½ cup (1 stick) butter

2 ripe heirloom tomatoes, peeled, seeded, and diced

In a medium saucepan over medium heat, combine the carrots, rutabaga, turnips, butter, and 1 cup water. Season with salt, cover, and cook until tender, 15 to 20 minutes. Add the peas and cook for 1 minute.

Meanwhile, bring a small saucepan of salted water to a boil. Add the cabbage and cook for 3 minutes. Transfer to a plate and refrigerate.

Line a coffee cup with plastic wrap so the wrap hangs over the sides, then line with the cabbage leaves. Fill with the vegetables and fold the leaves over the top. Remove by lifting out the wrap, then twist to close the wrap tightly, forming a ball.

Partially fill a medium saucepan with water and insert a vegetable steamer. Bring to a boil, add the wrapped ball, and steam for 10 minutes. Remove the plastic wrap and cut the ball into 4 wedges.

Bring ⅓ cup water to a boil in a small saucepan. Add the butter and whisk until foamy. Place each cabbage wedge on a serving plate, drizzle some butter mixture around the wedge, and top with the tomatoes.

SWEET POTATO–CELERIAC PURÉE

Serves 4

CHEF'S NOTE: Celeriac, or celery root, has a strong celery flavor and pairs well with sweet potato in this recipe. You can prepare the purée ahead and refrigerate for three to five days, then reheat when ready to use.

---

3 medium sweet potatoes

1 large celeriac root

Juice of 1 lemon

3 tablespoons unsalted butter

Salt and freshly ground black pepper

Preheat the oven to 400°F.

Place the sweet potatoes in a pie plate or small roasting pan and roast until very soft, about 45 minutes. Let cool, then peel with a paring knife.

Meanwhile, peel and dice the celeriac. Place in a medium saucepan over medium heat with 2 quarts salted water and simmer until very tender, 20 minutes. Drain well.

In a food processor, combine the celeriac, sweet potatoes, lemon juice, and butter and process until smooth. Season with salt and pepper. Keep warm until ready to serve or let cool and reheat later (it will keep at room temperature for up to 2 hours).

❧ *The Final Touch:* For a more elegant presentation, transfer the warm purée to a pastry bag with a large star tip and pipe it onto the plates in rosettes or spirals.

AUTUMN SPICE RUB

Makes 3 cups

CHEF'S NOTE: This is a wonderful rub for roasted vegetables.

---

1 cup fennel seeds

¼ cup allspice berries

¼ cup cumin seeds

1 tablespoon whole cloves

½ cup star anise

6 cinnamon sticks

½ cup paprika

Preheat the oven to 400°F. Place the fennel, allspice, cumin, cloves, anise, and cinnamon on a baking sheet and toast, stirring every 2 minutes, until the spices begin to release their aroma, 10 to 15 minutes. Transfer to a cool baking sheet, stir, and let cool. Place in a spice grinder or clean coffee grinder and grind until fine. (If you use a coffee grinder, be sure to clean it well afterward.) Transfer to a container with a lid and stir in the paprika. Store in a cool, dry place; for best flavor, use within 1 month.

CELERIAC AND PARSNIP PURÉE

Serves 4 to 6

CHEF'S NOTE: First cultivated in the Mediterranean region, celeriac (celery root) was introduced to England in the eighteenth century and to America not long afterward. Although available year round, it's best in spring and fall. Look for firm, heavy roots.

I pound celeriac (about 2 medium), peeled and cut into small dice

I pound parsnips, peeled and cut into small dice

¼ cup (½ stick) unsalted butter

½ cup chicken broth

½ cup heavy cream

Salt and ground white pepper to taste

I tablespoon chopped fresh parsley

In a large saucepan over medium-high heat, combine the celeriac, parsnips, butter, and broth. Bring to a boil, then reduce the heat and cook until the vegetables are tender and the liquid has evaporated, about 20 to 25 minutes. Heat the cream in a small saucepan over low heat. Transfer the vegetables and cream to a food processor and process until smooth. Season to taste with salt and white pepper, then transfer to a serving bowl and garnish with parsley.

❧ *The Final Touch:* For a spicy accent, add a tablespoon of horseradish.

SPICE-DUSTED PARSNIP CHIPS

Serves 4 to 6

CHEF'S NOTE: Experiment with different root vegetables for this recipe; beets, turnips, and carrots work equally well. The organic canola oil adds depth.

---

3 cups organic canola oil

1 pound organic parsnips, peeled

2 tablespoons kosher salt

½ teaspoon ground white pepper

½ teaspoon smoked paprika

½ teaspoon ground cumin

Heat the oil to 375°F in a medium saucepan.

Cut shavings from the parsnips using a swivel-blade peeler, approximately ⅛ inch thick. In a small bowl, combine the salt, pepper, paprika, and cumin.

Add ½ to ¾ cup parsnip shavings to the oil and cook, stirring frequently, until golden brown. Remove from the hot oil with a slotted spoon, drain well, and transfer to paper towels. Repeat with the remaining parsnips. Season immediately so the spices stick to the crisps.

◦ *The Final Touch:* Serve in baskets to accompany sandwiches or your favorite dip.

MASHED RUTABAGA

Serves 4 to 6

CHEF'S NOTE: Rutabagas, which are becoming more popular in the United States, are like giant yellow turnips and can be eaten raw or cooked. Raw, they're sweet and similar to mild radishes; the longer they sit on the shelf, the more turnip-like they become. Choose unwaxed rutabagas since waxing can cover up blemishes in the skin.

---

2 medium rutabagas, peeled and cut into large dice

¾ cup plain yogurt

2 tablespoons unsalted butter

1 teaspoon ground nutmeg

Salt and freshly ground black pepper to taste

Bring a medium saucepan of water to a boil and insert a steaming basket. Add the rutabagas and cook until tender, about 30 minutes, adding more water as necessary. Transfer to a medium bowl, add the yogurt, butter, and nutmeg, and mash with a fork or potato masher until smooth. Season with salt and pepper.

6

PASTA

Fresh pasta is one of the most versatile elements in cooking. Dried, it stands up to heavier sauces of meat and vegetables; fresh, its delicate flavors call for the lightest of sauces and herbs.

Unfortunately, most of the commercially available dried product is pretty tasteless. So if you can find fresh pasta in a local market — especially a pasta made from rich, artisanal flours — snap it up, and cook it that same day. And if you can actually take a long Saturday or Sunday afternoon to make the pasta yourself — fabulous! Either way, the following recipes will help bring out the delicacy of pasta's true nature.

SUMMER EGGPLANT AND GOAT CHEESE LASAGNA

Serves 9

CHEF'S NOTE: This recipe calls for fresh pasta, but you can substitute frozen lasagna sheets.

Noodles

¼ cup flour

1 recipe Basic Pasta Dough
(recipe on page 209)

Sauce

¼ cup olive oil

½ cup small-dice onion

2 tablespoons minced garlic

4 cups canned chopped tomatoes
in heavy sauce

2 tablespoons chopped fresh basil

2 tablespoons chopped fresh
oregano

2 teaspoons chopped fresh thyme

½ cup red wine

Salt and freshly ground black
pepper to taste

Eggplant and Filling

1 cup flour

4 free-range eggs

½ cup milk

2 cups bread crumbs

1 eggplant, cut into ¼"-thick
slices

1–2 cups olive oil

1 cup Vermont Butter and
Cheese goat cheese (chèvre)

2 cups ricotta cheese

1 tablespoon minced garlic

2 tablespoons chopped fresh
parsley

2 free-range eggs

Salt and freshly ground black
pepper to taste

Assembly

2 tablespoons oil

½ cup Parmesan Reggiano cheese

To make the noodles: Lightly flour a baking pan. Using a pasta machine on the second thinnest setting, roll the dough into 9 long sheets, then cut the noodles to fit your lasagna pan (13 inches long by about 3 inches wide). Transfer to the floured pan in layers, placing parchment paper between the layers. Wrap the whole pan in plastic wrap and refrigerate until needed. (You can make the pasta 1 day ahead as long as you wrap it properly and refrigerate it.)

To make the sauce: Pour the oil into a 2-quart saucepan over medium-high heat. Add the onion and garlic and cook for 45 seconds. Add the tomatoes, basil, oregano, thyme, and wine and bring to a simmer. Reduce the heat to medium-low and cook for 45 minutes. Purée with an immersion blender or put through a food mill and season with salt and pepper.

To make the eggplant and filling: Place the flour in a medium bowl. Break the eggs into another medium bowl, add the milk, and whisk together. Place the bread crumbs in a 10 x 10–inch pan. Bread the eggplant by dredging each slice in the flour, the egg mixture, and finally the bread crumbs, pressing firmly so the crumbs adhere. Transfer to a baking sheet.

Heat a large sauté pan over medium-high heat, then add 1 cup oil and heat. Fill the bottom of the pan with 1 layer of eggplant and season with salt and pepper. Cook until golden brown, about 2 minutes per side. Using tongs, transfer to a clean baking sheet. Repeat with the remaining eggplant, adding more oil as necessary.

In a medium bowl, combine the goat cheese, ricotta, garlic, parsley, and eggs. Season with salt and pepper.

To assemble: Preheat the oven to 400°F. In a large saucepan, bring 5 quarts salted water to a boil. Add the noodles and cook for about 4 minutes. Drain in a colander, then lightly oil the noodles.

Spoon a small amount of sauce into the bottom of a 9 x 13–inch baking pan. Add a layer of noodles and top with ½ of the cheese mixture. Arrange ½ of the eggplant on top of the cheese and spread with a little sauce. Add another layer of pasta, the remaining cheese mixture and eggplant, and more sauce. Finish with a layer of noodles and a generous amount of sauce. Cover the pan with parchment paper and a sheet of foil and bake until hot, approximately 45 minutes. Remove the foil and parchment, sprinkle with the Parmesan, and return to the oven until the cheese melts, about 5 minutes. Let stand for about 10 minutes before cutting.

❧ *The Final Touch:* Spread a few tablespoons of sauce on each plate before serving. Serve with a tossed green salad and crusty bread.

LE SOMMELIER: This cheese-filled lasagna with herby tomato sauce calls for a complex but not too tannic red wine, and Merlot is perfect. Try the very attractive, oak-aged Merlot made by Shelburne Vineyards in Vermont from grapes grown on the North Fork of Long Island.

LEMON-THYME LINGUINE WITH ROASTED RATATOUILLE

Serves 4

CHEF'S NOTE: This is a nice summer and fall pasta dish because it uses many fresh seasonal vegetables; roasting them brings out their natural sugars. You can substitute locally made fresh linguine (1 pound) or dry linguine (¾ pound) for the homemade pasta. Look for fresh fennel in the produce department of most supermarkets and lemon oil in the baking or spice aisle. If you don't have enough baking sheets to roast the vegetables separately, you can combine them, except for the tomatoes. Be careful not to overcrowd them, or they will steam and not caramelize properly.

Noodles

¼ cup flour

1 recipe Basic Pasta Dough (recipe on page 209); replace 1 tablespoon olive oil with 1 teaspoon lemon oil, 2 teaspoons olive oil, and 1 tablespoon finely minced fresh thyme leaves

Ratatouille

1 cup medium-dice cored fennel bulb

1 cup medium-dice onion

1 cup olive oil

Salt and freshly ground black pepper to taste

1 cup medium-dice cored and seeded green bell pepper

1 cup medium-dice cored and seeded red bell pepper

1 cup medium-dice zucchini

1 cup medium-dice yellow squash

1 cup medium-dice eggplant

1 cup coarsely chopped mushrooms

2 cups halved cherry tomatoes

2 tablespoons minced garlic

2 tablespoons chopped fresh thyme leaves

2 tablespoons chopped fresh parsley

2 tablespoons chopped fresh basil

Assembly

2 tablespoons oil

1 cup grated Parmesan cheese

Preheat the oven to 400°F.

To make the noodles: Lightly flour a baking pan. Using a pasta machine on the second thinnest setting, roll the dough into sheets. Cut to the desired length and roll through the linguine cutter. Place the pasta on the floured pan, wrap the whole pan with plastic wrap, and refrigerate until needed. (You can make the pasta 1 day ahead as long as you wrap it properly and refrigerate.)

To make the ratatouille: In a medium bowl, combine the fennel and onion. Add 2 tablespoons oil and a pinch of salt and pepper and toss to combine. Transfer to a small baking sheet. Add the bell peppers, zucchini, squash, another 2 tablespoons oil, and salt and pepper to the bowl and mix well. Transfer to a second small baking sheet. Add the eggplant and mushrooms, another 2 tablespoons oil, and salt and pepper to the bowl and mix well. Transfer to a third small baking sheet. Add the tomatoes, another 2 tablespoons oil, and salt and pepper to the bowl and mix well. Transfer to a fourth small baking sheet. Working in batches if necessary, roast the vegetables until very browned and soft, 20 to 30 minutes.

Heat a 4-quart saucepan over medium-high heat. Add ⅓ cup oil and the garlic and cook for 30 seconds, being careful not to let it brown or burn. Add the roasted vegetables and stir, then stir in the thyme, parsley, and basil. Season with salt and pepper, reduce the heat to low, and cook for 5 minutes.

To assemble: In a large saucepan, bring 4 quarts salted water to a boil. Add the linguine and cook for about 4 minutes. Drain, then transfer to a medium bowl and toss with the oil. Divide among 4 serving bowls, top with the ratatouille, and sprinkle with the cheese.

❧ *The Final Touch:* Garlic bread or fresh Italian bread adds a nice touch to this dish.

LE SOMMELIER: Choosing a wine for this dish is a bit tricky: Do you need a dry white with hints of citrus to match the lemon flavors or an off-dry white whose touch of sweetness matches the sweetness of the caramelized vegetables? How about one that can do both? The White Cayuga from Shelburne Vineyards in Vermont is slightly off-dry and has crisp acidity and a hint of citrus aroma and flavors. A Riesling from the Finger Lakes of New York or from Germany is another possibility.

LITTLENECKS IN RIESLING

Serves 4

CHEF'S NOTE: Riesling is a white wine that originated in Germany but is now produced in other countries, including the United States. For this recipe, choose a dry Riesling rather than a sweeter one.

---

2 tablespoons (¼ stick) butter

2 tablespoons minced shallots

2 cups Riesling wine

24 littleneck clams, washed well

1 cup heavy cream

3 tablespoons chopped fresh parsley

Salt and freshly ground black pepper to taste

¾ pound linguine, cooked and lightly oiled

Melt 2 tablespoons butter in a 3-quart saucepan over medium-high heat. Add the shallots and cook for 30 seconds. Add the wine, ½ cup water, and the clams. Cover and cook until the clams have opened, 4 to 5 minutes, stirring after 3 minutes. Using tongs or a skimmer, transfer the clams to a bowl, discarding any unopened ones, and keep warm.

Add the cream to the pan and bring to a simmer. Whisk into the clam broth and bring back to a simmer. Reduce the heat to low, add the parsley, and season with salt and pepper. Add the linguine and cook until heated through.

Meanwhile, remove the top halves of the clam shells. Using tongs, pile equal amounts of linguine in the center of 4 serving bowls. Arrange the clams around the linguine, pour on the broth, and serve immediately.

SHRIMP IN SPICY CARROT SAUCE
WITH LINGUINE

Serves 4

CHEF'S NOTE: A very simple, very colorful, and very unexpected dish.

---

1 pound fresh linguine

2 cups carrot juice

1 cup (1 stick) butter

¼ teaspoon cayenne pepper

¼ teaspoon ground cinnamon

Nutmeg to taste

Sea salt to taste

20 medium shrimp, peeled and
  deveined

In a large saucepan of salted water (it should taste like seawater), cook the linguine according to package directions. Drain but do not rinse.

In another large saucepan over medium heat, bring the carrot juice to a simmer. Stir in the butter, cayenne, cinnamon, and nutmeg, then add the linguine and toss.

Lightly oil a nonstick sauté pan. Add the shrimp and cook over medium heat until pink and curled, about 2 minutes. Season with salt.

Divide the linguine among 4 bowls and arrange 5 shrimp on each portion.

LINGUINE WITH LITTLENECK CLAM SAUCE

Serves 4

CHEF'S NOTE: This traditional Italian dish is perfect to serve when local little-neck clams (small quahogs) from the New England coast are available. Although you can substitute canned clams and clam juice, freshly shucked clams make this dish much more special and flavorful.

---

24 littleneck clams

¾ cup olive oil

½ cup small-dice onion

¼ cup minced garlic

½ cup white wine

½ teaspoon crushed red pepper

2 teaspoons chopped fresh thyme leaves

3 tablespoons chopped fresh parsley

2 tablespoons chopped fresh oregano leaves

2 tablespoons (¼ stick) butter

¾ pound linguine, cooked and lightly oiled

Salt and freshly ground black pepper to taste

½ cup shredded Parmesan cheese

Wash the clams well and shuck them, draining the juice into a bowl. On a cutting board, coarsely chop the clams. Strain the juice into another bowl.

Place the oil in a 2-quart saucepan over medium-high heat. Add the onion and garlic and cook for 30 seconds. Add the clam juice, wine, and red pepper and simmer for 3 minutes. Add the clams, 1 teaspoon thyme, 1½ tablespoons parsley, and 1 tablespoon oregano and return to a simmer. Sir in the butter until melted, then add the linguine and stir to combine. Season with salt and pepper. Using tongs, divide the linguine among 4 serving bowls. Pour on the broth, then sprinkle with the cheese and the remaining thyme, parsley, and oregano.

❧ *The Final Touch:* For a heartier presentation, you can serve a few whole steamed clams in their shells with the pasta. To make red clam sauce, follow the same procedure as above but add 1½ cups marinara sauce at the same time you add the clam juice and cook it to a thicker consistency before adding the clams.

TOMATO AND FRESH MOZZARELLA SUMMER PASTA

Serves 4

CHEF'S NOTE: This is the perfect lunch or dinner entrée for a hot summer day, especially if you grow your own tomatoes and basil. Although the recipe calls for regular red tomatoes, any type is fine. You can find fresh mozzarella in the specialty cheese department at most supermarkets; it's best to leave it in the brine until shortly before using. If you buy smaller balls of mozzarella, you may want to halve them instead of dicing.

2½ cups medium-dice ripe red heirloom tomatoes

1 tablespoon finely minced garlic

3 tablespoons ½"-long, very thin strips fresh basil

1 cup medium-dice fresh mozzarella

½ cup extra-virgin olive oil

Salt and freshly ground black pepper to taste

¾ pound fresh linguine or thin spaghetti

In a large bowl, combine the tomatoes, garlic, basil, mozzarella, and oil. Season with salt and pepper, stir well, and set aside.

In a large saucepan, bring 4 quarts salted water to a boil. Add the pasta and cook according to package directions until al dente, then drain but do not rinse. Add to the tomato mixture and, using tongs or a large fork, stir to combine. Let stand at room temperature for about 30 minutes. Season with salt and pepper if necessary; then, using tongs, divide the pasta among 4 plates.

❧ *The Final Touch:* To make this meal a little more substantial, add sliced grilled chicken or shrimp to the tomato mixture. Grilled bruschetta or Italian bread goes well with this pasta.

SWEET PEA RAVIOLI WITH CARROT BUTTER SAUCE

Serves 4

CHEF'S NOTE: Your family and friends will love this unique dish. Carrot juice is available at many supermarkets, or you can make it fresh if you have a juice extractor. If you prefer, you can use round wonton skins in place of fresh pasta. Look for mascarpone cheese in the specialty cheese section of most supermarkets.

Filling

2 cups fresh peas

3 tablespoons mascarpone cheese

1 tablespoon chopped fresh tarragon leaves

3 tablespoons fresh lemon juice

Salt and freshly ground black pepper to taste

Pasta

1 recipe Basic Pasta Dough (recipe on page 209)

1 free-range egg beaten with 2 tablespoons cold water

Sauce

3 cups carrot juice

1 cup apple cider

⅓ cup heavy cream

6 tablespoons (¾ stick) butter, cut into 1-tablespoon pieces and kept refrigerated

Salt and freshly ground black pepper to taste

To make the filling: Place the peas in a medium saucepan with enough water to cover. Bring to a boil and cook until tender, 1 minute, then transfer to an ice bath for about 2 minutes.

In a food processor, combine the peas, cheese, tarragon, 1 tablespoon lemon juice, and salt and pepper. Process for 20 seconds, then turn off the motor and use a rubber spatula to scrape the sides of the container. Continue to process, stopping to scrape the sides occasionally, until fairly smooth. Season with salt and pepper if necessary, then use the spatula to transfer to a small bowl.

To make the pasta: Line a baking sheet with parchment paper. Using a pasta machine on the second thinnest setting, roll the dough into 6 rectangular sheets 2 to 3 feet long. On 1 sheet, place a tablespoon of filling every 2 to 3 inches apart, depending on the desired size of the raviolis. Brush lightly with egg wash between the spoonfuls of filling and on the edges of the pasta. Cover with another sheet of pasta and gently press around the filling to remove any air. Using a ravioli cutter, cut the squares, transfer to the baking sheet. Repeat with the remaining filling.

To make the sauce: In a 2-quart saucepan over medium-high heat, combine the carrot juice, cider, and the remaining 2 tablespoons lemon juice. Bring to a boil and cook until reduced to ⅓ cup. Add the cream and cook until reduced by ½. Reduce the heat to low and whisk in the cold butter 1 piece at a time. Remove from the heat and season with salt and pepper. Cover and keep warm.

In a large saucepan, bring 4 quarts salted water to a boil, then add 10 raviolis and cook for 3 to 4 minutes. Using a slotted spoon, transfer to a plate and cover with foil. Repeat with the remaining raviolis.

Ladle some of the sauce onto 4 plates, place the raviolis on top, and serve immediately.

❧ *The Final Touch:* Serve with grilled chicken breast or grilled vegetables.

SEAFOOD RAVIOLI WITH TOMATO BROTH

Serves 4

CHEF'S NOTE: You can make a lot of ravioli with very little seafood. The recipe calls for fresh pasta dough, but you can use round wonton skins if you prefer. While fresh tomatoes are wonderful in this recipe, canned diced tomatoes work fine, especially in the cold-weather months.

Filling

5 ounces cod, cubed

5 ounces scallops, muscle removed

5 ounces shrimp, peeled and deveined

2 teaspoons salt

1 teaspoon ground white pepper

½ teaspoon finely chopped fennel seed

¼ cup heavy cream

1 free-range egg white

1 tablespoon minced capers

1 teaspoon finely chopped lemon zest

1 tablespoon fresh lemon juice

Pasta

1 recipe Basic Pasta Dough (recipe on page 209)

1 free-range egg beaten with 2 tablespoons cold water

Broth

2 tablespoons olive oil

2 tablespoons minced garlic

3 cups small-dice cored and seeded heirloom tomatoes

½ cup white wine

2 tablespoons chopped fresh parsley

2 tablespoons chopped fresh basil

Salt and freshly ground black pepper to taste

3 tablespoons butter

To make the filling: In a food processor, combine the cod, scallops, and shrimp and process for 20 seconds. Turn off the motor and stir with a rubber spatula, then process for 20 seconds. Add the salt, pepper, fennel, cream, and egg white. Process, stopping to stir occasionally, until smooth, then use the spatula to transfer to a medium bowl. Stir in the capers and lemon zest and juice, then cover and refrigerate until needed. (The filling can be made 1 day ahead as long as it is refrigerated.)

To make the pasta: Line a baking sheet with parchment paper. Using a pasta machine on the second thinnest setting, roll the dough into 6 rectangular sheets 2 to 3 feet long. On 1 sheet, place a tablespoon of filling every 2 to 3 inches apart, depending the desired size of the raviolis. Brush lightly with egg wash between the spoonfuls of filling and on the edges of the pasta. Cover with another sheet of pasta and gently press around the filling to remove any air. Using a ravioli cutter, cut the squares, then transfer to the baking sheet. Repeat with the remaining filling.

To make the broth: Place the oil in a 2-quart saucepan over low heat, then add the garlic and cook for 45 seconds. Add the tomatoes, increase the heat to medium high, and cook for 3 minutes. Add the wine and cook until the liquid is reduced by ½. Add ½ cup water and the parsley and basil. Reduce the heat to medium and cook for 5 minutes. Season with salt and pepper and remove from the heat.

In a large saucepan, bring 4 quarts salted water to a boil, then add 10 raviolis and cook for 3 to 4 minutes. Using a slotted spoon, transfer to a plate and cover with foil. Repeat with the remaining raviolis.

Return the broth to medium-high heat and bring to a simmer, then stir in the butter until melted. Ladle some of the broth onto 4 plates, place the raviolis on the broth, and top each ravioli with a small spoonful of tomato. Serve immediately.

❧ *The Final Touch:* Sauté some fresh spinach and place a small pile in the center of each plate, then surround with the raviolis. Serve with some crusty bread.

OPEN RAVIOLI WITH ROASTED CHICKEN, PEAS, MUSHROOMS, AND TOMATOES

Serves 4

CHEF'S NOTE: Open ravioli is a layered pasta dish assembled right in the serving bowl. This recipe is a great way to use leftover roasted chicken, and the carcass is an important ingredient in the nicely flavored sauce. If you prefer, you can use lasagna sheets instead of fresh pasta. The recipe calls for fresh peas, but if you use frozen, add them just before serving.

Sauce

1 chicken carcass, cleaned of meat and skin

1 cup large-dice onion

½ cup large-dice peeled carrot

½ cup large-dice peeled celery

1 bay leaf

2 sprigs fresh thyme

2 sprigs fresh parsley

2 tablespoons (¼ stick) butter, softened

3 tablespoons all-purpose flour

Salt and ground white or cayenne pepper to taste

Filling

2 tablespoons (¼ stick) butter

2 tablespoons minced shallots

2 cups sliced mushrooms

2 cups medium-dice peeled and seeded heirloom tomatoes

3 tablespoons white wine

1 tablespoon fresh lemon juice

2 cups shredded skinless roasted chicken

1 cup fresh green peas

2 tablespoons chopped fresh parsley

2 tablespoons chopped fresh thyme leaves

Salt and freshly ground black pepper to taste

Noodles

1 recipe Basic Pasta Dough (recipe on page 209)

To make the sauce: Place the chicken carcass in a 4-quart soup pot with the onion, carrot, celery, bay leaf, thyme, and parsley. Add enough cold water to cover by 2 inches and bring to a low simmer over medium-high heat. Reduce the heat to medium and simmer for about 1½ hours, occasionally skimming off any foam that forms on the surface. Strain through a fine-mesh strainer into a saucepan and return to medium-high heat, then bring to a simmer and cook until reduced to 3 cups.

In a small bowl, combine the butter and flour. Whisk into the stock, return to a simmer, and season with salt and pepper. The sauce should be thick enough to coat the back of a spoon. If it's too thin, combine a little more butter and flour and whisk it in. If it's too thick, add a little water.

To make the filling: Melt the butter in a 12-inch sauté pan over medium-high heat. Add the shallots and cook for about 45 seconds. Add the mushrooms and cook until tender, about 2 minutes. Add the tomatoes, wine, and lemon juice and cook until reduced by ½. Add the chicken, peas, parsley, and thyme and cook until heated through. Season with salt and pepper, then add 1 cup sauce and stir to combine.

To make the noodles: Using a pasta machine on the second thinnest setting, roll the pasta dough into 3 sheets the width of the pasta roller and about 12 inches long. Cut into 4-inch pieces. In a large saucepan, bring 5 quarts salted water to a boil. Add the pasta and cook until al dente, about 4 minutes. Drain well.

Place 1 noodle flat in the bottom of each serving bowl. Divide ½ of the filling evenly among the bowls, then top with another noodle. Evenly spoon the remaining filling on top (it's fine if it falls out of the pasta and into the bowl), then add another noodle. Ladle the sauce over the ravioli and around the sides of the bowl.

◆ *The Final Touch:* Spoon a small pile of tomato from the bowl on top of the ravioli and sprinkle with a little chopped parsley and grated Parmesan.

GOAT CHEESE AND SMOKED CHICKEN RAVIOLI

Serves 4

CHEF'S NOTE: This challenging recipe is one your children will pass down for generations.

Filling

1 cup Vermont Butter and Cheese goat cheese (chèvre)

1 cup cream cheese

1 cup smoked chicken, cut into small cubes

¼ cup chopped fresh parsley

6 cloves garlic, minced

Salt and freshly ground black pepper to taste

Sauce

1 onion, minced

4 cloves garlic, minced

2 tablespoons olive oil

3 heirloom tomatoes, diced

3 tablespoons chopped parsley

¾ cup white wine

6 tablespoons (¾ stick) butter

Salt and freshly ground black pepper to taste

Tomatoes

1½ cups bread crumbs

6 cloves garlic, minced

3 tablespoons minced parsley

¼ cup grated Parmesan cheese

6 tablespoons butter, melted

Salt and freshly ground black pepper to taste

6 heirloom tomatoes, cored and seeded but kept whole

Pasta

4 cups flour

3 tablespoons kosher salt

4 free-range eggs

3 tablespoons olive oil

1 free-range egg beaten with 2 tablespoons cold water

To make the filling: In a large bowl, combine the goat cheese, cream cheese, chicken, parsley and garlic. Season with salt and pepper and refrigerate.

To make the sauce: In a medium saucepan over low heat, cook the onion and garlic in the oil until tender, 5 minutes. Add the tomatoes and parsley and cook for 2 minutes. Add the wine and cook until reduced by ½. Whisk in the butter until incorporated. Season with salt and pepper and remove from the heat.

To make the tomatoes: Preheat the oven to 375°F. In a medium bowl, combine the bread crumbs, parsley, garlic, and cheese. Add the butter and toss to combine, then season with salt and pepper. Place the tomatoes in a baking pan and spoon in the filling. Bake until golden brown and tender, about 5 minutes.

To make the pasta: In a food processor, combine the flour and salt. With the motor running, add the eggs 1 at a time. Add the oil and blend until the dough begins to form a ball, then transfer to a work surface and knead until smooth. Let stand for 15 minutes.

Line a baking sheet with parchment paper. Using a pasta machine set on the second thinnest setting, roll the dough into 6 rectangular sheets 2 to 3 feet long. On 1 sheet, place a tablespoon of filling every 2 to 3 inches apart, depending on the desired size of the raviolis. Brush lightly with egg wash between the spoonfuls of filling and on the edges of the pasta. Cover with another sheet of pasta and gently press around the filling to remove any air. Using a ravioli cutter, cut the squares, then transfer to the baking sheet. Repeat with the remaining filling.

In a large saucepan, bring 4 quarts salted water to a boil, then add 10 raviolis and cook for 3 to 4 minutes. Drain and toss with the sauce. Place a tomato and an equal portion of ravioli on each plate.

FALL BUTTERNUT SQUASH RAVIOLI
WITH SAGE CREAM

Serves 4

CHEF'S NOTE: This is a nice ravioli dish to make in the cold months. Roasting the squash instead of boiling it keeps the raviolis from getting soggy. If you prefer not to make fresh pasta, you can use round wonton skins. (Brush the edges with egg wash, add a tablespoon of filling, fold to make a half moon, and crimp the edges closed with a fork.) You can make and assemble the raviolis up to 2 days ahead if you wrap them well and keep refrigerated.

Filling

1 butternut squash, halved
   lengthwise and seeded

2 tablespoons olive oil

1 tablespoon chopped fresh
   thyme

1 tablespoon chopped fresh
   parsley

2 teaspoons chopped fresh sage

¼ cup grated Parmesan cheese

Salt and freshly ground black
   pepper to taste

Pasta

1 recipe Basic Pasta Dough
   (recipe on page 209)

1 egg beaten with 2 tablespoons
   cold water

Sauce

2 tablespoons (¼ stick) butter

1 tablespoon minced shallots

1 tablespoon minced garlic

1½ cups heavy cream

⅓ cup grated Parmesan cheese

1 tablespoon fresh sage, chopped

Salt and ground white pepper
   to taste

To make the filling: Preheat the oven to 400°F. Place the squash in a 10 x 10–inch baking pan and lightly oil the cut sides. Roast until tender when pierced with a knife, 30 to 40 minutes. Let cool for 10 minutes.

Using a large spoon, scoop the squash flesh into a container (discard the skins). Measure out 2 cups and refrigerate the remainder for another use.

In a food processor, combine the squash, thyme, parsley, sage, and cheese and process until smooth. (Alternatively, use a fork or potato masher.) Season with salt and pepper.

To make the pasta: Line a baking sheet with parchment paper. Using a pasta machine on the second thinnest setting, roll the dough into 6 rectangular sheets 2 to 3 feet long. On 1 sheet, place a tablespoon of filling every 2 to 3 inches apart, depending on the desired size of the raviolis. Brush lightly with egg wash between the spoonfuls of filling and on the edges of the pasta. Cover with another sheet of pasta and gently press around the filling to remove any air. Using a ravioli cutter, cut the squares, then transfer to the baking sheet. Repeat with the remaining filling.

To make the sauce: Place the butter in a 1-quart saucepan over medium-high heat, then add the shallots and garlic and cook for 45 seconds. Add the cream and bring to a simmer. Reduce the heat to medium low and whisk in the cheese and sage. Season with salt and pepper.

In a large saucepan, bring 4 quarts salted water to a boil, then add 10 raviolis and cook for 3 to 4 minutes. Using a slotted spoon, transfer to a plate and cover with foil. Repeat with the remaining raviolis.

Divide the raviolis among 4 plates, top with sauce, and serve immediately.

The Final Touch: Sauté some sliced zucchini, place a pile in the center of each plate, and surround with ravioli. Serve with crusty bread.

SEAFOOD LOVER'S PASTA PLATE

Serves 4

CHEF'S NOTE: The great thing about this dish is that there are very few pans to wash since almost everything is cooked in one large pot. As with any combination dish, it's difficult to cook many types of seafood together and have everything properly cooked, but the resulting flavors are unbeatable.

¼ cup olive oil

½ cup medium-dice cored and seeded yellow or red bell pepper

2 tablespoons minced garlic

12 large shrimp, peeled and deveined

24 mussels, beards removed and washed well

½ cup medium-dice heirloom tomato

⅔ cup white wine

1 teaspoon crushed red pepper

12 ounces calamari, sliced into rings and tentacles

12 ounces haddock, cut into 1" cubes

½ cup heavy cream

1 tablespoon chopped fresh parsley

1 tablespoon chopped fresh oregano

1 tablespoon chopped fresh basil

¾ pound penne pasta, cooked and lightly oiled

Salt and freshly ground black pepper to taste

1 cup shredded Parmesan cheese

Place the oil in a 3-quart saucepan over medium-high heat. Add the peppers and garlic and cook for 30 seconds, being careful not to burn the garlic. Add the shrimp and cook for 40 seconds. Add the mussels, tomato, wine, and red pepper, then cover and steam the mussels for 1 minute. Add the calamari and haddock and cook, covered, for 1 minute. Stir in the cream, parsley, oregano, and basil and cook until heated through. Stir in the pasta, season with salt and pepper, and cook until heated through, about 1 minute. Using a large slotted spoon, divide the seafood and pasta among 4 deep bowls, adding as little broth as possible. Return the broth to medium-high heat and cook until thickened enough to coat the back of a spoon. Season with salt and pepper, ladle over the pasta, and top with the cheese.

❧ *The Final Touch:* Grilled bruschetta or garlic bread is excellent with this dish.

PAPPARDELLE WITH VERMONT-FORAGED CHANTERELLES

Serves 4

CHEF'S NOTE: Each year from July through early September, New England chanterelles make their brief appearance in Vermont's wooded areas. Many local stores, especially those that pride themselves on carrying local and gourmet foods, sell harvested chanterelles. You can use rehydrated dried chanterelles instead of fresh, but the quality and flavor won't be as good. Pappardelle are wide egg noodles that are available in the imported pasta section of many supermarkets. If you want to make your own, use the Basic Pasta Dough recipe on page 209, roll the dough into thin sheets, and cut into 1/2-inch-wide strips.

---

2 tablespoons (¼ stick) butter

2 tablespoons olive oil

3 tablespoons minced shallots

1 tablespoon minced garlic

3 cups chanterelles, cleaned and stems removed

2 tablespoons fresh lemon juice

⅓ cup white wine

¼ cup chopped fresh parsley

Salt and freshly ground black pepper to taste

1 pound pappardelle pasta, cooked and lightly oiled

1 cup Parmesan Reggiano cheese, shaved into wide, thin strips

Melt the butter with the oil in a large sauté pan over medium heat. Add the shallots and garlic and cook until soft, 20 seconds, being careful not to burn the garlic. Increase the heat to medium high and add the chanterelles. Toss to coat with butter and cook for 3 to 4 minutes. Add the lemon juice and cook for 30 seconds. Add the wine and cook until almost all of the liquid has evaporated. Add the parsley and season with salt and pepper.

Add the pappardelle and toss until heated through, then season with salt and pepper if desired. Divide the pasta among 4 plates, top with the cheese, and serve immediately.

❧ *The Final Touch:* Although this pasta is delicious as is, sliced asparagus and grilled chicken add more substance. Serve fresh crusty bread so your guests can enjoy the last tasty pieces on their plates.

GARGANELLI WITH ASPARAGUS AND PANCETTA IN LEMON CREAM SAUCE

Serves 4

CHEF'S NOTE: This is a nice baked pasta dish to serve during the spring and early summer asparagus season. It's great by itself, but you can also serve it with roasted chicken, grilled pork chops, or other meat dishes. Garganelli is egg pasta shaped into small, ridged tubes; look for it in the imported pasta section. Penne pasta is a good substitute if you can't find garganelli. Pancetta is a rolled, salt-cured Italian bacon that can be found in the meat section of some high-end supermarkets. If you can't get it, you can use prosciutto by just adding it to the bowl instead of crisping it; you can also substitute mild local bacon.

2½ cups heavy cream

1 tablespoon finely chopped lemon zest

½ cup grated Pecorino Romano cheese

½ cup grated Parmesan Reggiano cheese

¼ cup Vermont Butter and Cheese fromage blanc cheese or ricotta cheese

1 tablespoon salt

2 tablespoons olive oil

1 cup thin strips pancetta

12 spears asparagus, trimmed and bias cut into thin slices

¾ pound garganelli pasta, cooked al dente and lightly oiled

Preheat the oven to 400°F. Lightly oil four 1½- to 2-cup baking dishes.

In a medium bowl, combine the cream, lemon zest, Romano, Parmesan, and salt and stir well.

Place the oil in a 12-inch sauté pan over medium-high heat. Add the pancetta and cook until crisp, 4 to 5 minutes. Using a slotted spoon, transfer to a plate lined with paper towels. Add the asparagus to the pan and cook for 45 seconds. Using a slotted spoon, transfer to a small dish.

Add the cooled pancetta and the garganelli to the cheese mixture and stir well. Divide among the baking dishes and top with the asparagus. Bake until the liquid bubbles and the asparagus begins to brown, 12 to 15 minutes.

BASIC PASTA DOUGH

Makes 1½ pounds

CHEF'S NOTE: The easiest way to make this pasta dough is in a food processor, but you can also do it by hand. Free-range eggs generally have brighter yolks and give the dough wonderful color and texture.

1 pound all-purpose flour
4 free-range eggs
1 free-range egg yolk

1 tablespoon olive oil
1 teaspoon salt

Food processor method: Combine the flour, eggs, egg yolk, oil, and salt and pulse until the mixture reaches the consistency of cornmeal. Take a handful and squeeze it to see if it holds together. If it crumbles, add a tablespoon of cold water to the mixture and mix with short pulses. Transfer to a cutting board and knead into a smooth ball, then flatten into a disk. Wrap in plastic wrap and refrigerate for at least 1 hour.

Hand method: In a medium bowl, combine the flour and salt, then place in a mound on a clean work surface. Make a well in the center and add the eggs, egg yolk, and oil. Using a small fork or your fingers, stir the egg mixture in a circular motion, gradually incorporating the flour from the sides. Continue as described above.

Rolling and cooking: Set up a pasta machine with the rollers at the widest setting. Divide the dough into 4 to 6 pieces, flatten by hand, and lightly dust with flour. Roll each piece through the machine, then fold in thirds and roll again, repeating 6 to 8 times, until smooth and satiny. Unfold the sheets and roll again, narrowing the setting each time and lightly dusting with flour if the dough is sticky. After rolling each sheet through the second thinnest setting, transfer to a very lightly floured work surface or baking sheets lined with parchment paper. If the sheets are too long to handle, cut them in half, then cut to the desired shape, cover, and refrigerate until ready to use.

To cook, use at least 1 gallon of boiling water per pound of dough, adding 1½ tablespoons salt per gallon.

❧ *The Final Touch:* Using this recipe as a base, you can create a number of colorful and flavorful doughs. Variations with moist ingredients may require more flour if the dough is sticky and are best made in a food processor.

Herb pasta: Add 3 to 4 tablespoons chopped fresh herbs or 1 to 2 tablespoons dried herbs.

Beet pasta: Use only 3 eggs and add ¼ cup cooked beet purée.

Spinach pasta: Use only 3 eggs and add ⅔ cup cooked spinach, well drained and puréed.

Carrot pasta: Reduce the oil to 1½ teaspoons and add ¼ cup fresh carrot juice and 1 tablespoon milk.

Tomato pasta: Use only 3 eggs and add 5 tablespoons tomato paste.

AUTUMN

Looking out over Vermont's kaleidoscopically colorful mountains from the 4,300-foot peak of Mt. Mansfield, the view is breathtaking.

The explosion of color across our mountains at this time of year—the bold oranges, muted russets, deep reds, and muffled golds—snatches away the ennui of everyone from the IBM executives in Essex Junction to the seventh-generation farmers in Starksboro. It energizes our spirits and renews our connection to the land.

Down slope, an early morning frost crystallizes meadows overflowing with spiky milkweed, exuberant goldenrod, and gone-to-seed Queen Anne's lace. Black and white cows dot the green of distant pastures. Lake Champlain sparkles farther on—backed by the Adirondack Mountains, and edged by cornfields packed with thousands of migrating Canada geese. A whisper of wood smoke from a kitchen fire in the valley rides an errant draft up above the timberline. And everywhere, from north to south and east to west, the birches, maples, cherry, and alder have torched the hills with color, while piles of roadside leaves swirl into bits of maple fire.

Autumn is a special time in Vermont. For those of us who live here, it's harvest time in the land of milk and honey. In front of every barn, huge baskets of apples—McIntosh,

Macoun, Honeycrisp, Gingergold, and the remaining Paula Reds — are stacked in front of homemade farm stands, while huge wooden wagons next to them are piled high with every shape and size of squash — butter cup, butternut, delicata, carnival, hubbards, and sweet dumplings, framed by what must be tons of the all-American carving pumpkin.

Inside the stands, farmers and assorted members of their families — children in miniature Wellies, grandmothers in heavy, hand-knit wool sweaters, wives, husbands, and partners in University of Vermont sweats — stoke the woodstove and keep wooden shelves lined with preserves made from local blueberries and raspberries harvested over the summer, plus jars of honey from the local beekeeper.

Racks of carefully crafted local wines from Charlotte Village Winery, Boyden Valley, and Snow Farm Vineyard tower over tables of homemade breads and pies, while, along the back wall, gallons of freshly made apple cider, pints of Ben and Jerry's decadent ice cream, and wheels of Vermont's award-winning artisanal cheeses — an aged cheddar from Shelburne Farms, Vermont Brie from Blythedale Farm, Bayley Hazen blue from Jasper Hill Farm, a mozzarella from Woodstock Water Buffalo Creamery, and maple-smoked gouda from the Taylor Farm — fill coolers and freezers. Dried wildflowers — lavender, coreopsis, delphs, monkshood, and the like — hang from rafters overhead.

It's no wonder that an amazing number of "flatlanders" — those whose families have not been privileged to live in Vermont for at least two generations — come to visit us during the fall. And although we may grumble about the number of cars at the local farmers' market on Saturday afternoon, or the number of folks who crowd into our favorite diner for breakfast on Sunday morning, the truth is that we understand why they've come.

We understand that in a manic world of simmering passions and 24/7 electronic availability, taking a moment to simply sit quietly by the woodstove in a country store can offer the space in which to reconnect with who you really are.

Here, where you can take a breath of crisp clean air, munch a juicy just-picked apple, and eat cheese made from the herd of sweet cows just over the hill, it's hard to be anything else.

7

POTATOES, GRAINS, AND BEANS

Potatoes, grains, and beans are the workhorses of any home kitchen. They're at the top of every nutritionist's recommended foods list for their ability to prevent and manage a host of diseases and conditions, and their storage capabilities make them perfect for those cold Vermont winters in which getting to the market after a snowstorm can require the assistance of the town plow.

Unfortunately, too many unimaginative recipes floating through the culinary world have discouraged the home cook from exploring the wide range of tastes and flavors these foods make available. So, on the following pages, we've tried to give you a sampling of what these foods are capable of.

To get the best possible flavor, we suggest you buy heirloom varieties wherever possible. And since a study by the USDA in 2006 found that 81 percent of potatoes contained pesticides even after extensive washing and peeling, we also suggest that any potatoes you buy be certified organic.

DILLED ORGANIC NEW POTATOES

Serves 4

CHEF'S NOTE: Real new potatoes are harvested from the plant's trailing underground root system while the plant is still growing. They tend to be very small, and their skin is flaky and thin. They have a delicate flavor, and there's nothing better than new potatoes straight from the ground. Wash them gently to remove any dirt, but don't scrub, because you don't want to wash away the important nutrients in the skin.

---

24 tiny new potatoes
½ cup (1 stick) butter

Salt and freshly ground black pepper to taste
5 tablespoons chopped fresh dill

Wash the potatoes and dry with a paper towel. Melt the butter in a large cast-iron skillet over medium heat. Add the potatoes, season with salt and pepper, and stir to coat with butter. Reduce the heat to low, cover, and cook until fork tender, about 30 minutes, shaking the skillet occasionally. Toss with the dill.

🐝 *The Final Touch:* Serve with grilled fish for a simple — and simply delicious — meal.

BAYLEY HAZEN BLUE FINGERLING POTATO GRATIN

Serves 6

CHEF'S NOTE: Bayley Hazen blue, a creamy natural-rind, blue-veined, raw-milk cheese, is the perfect complement to the earthy fingerling potatoes in this rich, decadently delicious dish. For a vegetarian entrée, serve with a sauté of wild mushrooms.

5 ounces Bayley Hazen blue cheese

2½ cups half-and-half

Salt to taste

½ teaspoon freshly ground white pepper

1 teaspoon chopped fresh thyme or ½ teaspoon dried thyme

2 pounds local fingerling potatoes, washed and cut into ¼"-thick slices

Preheat the oven to 400°F. Butter a 9 x 13–inch baking dish.

In a medium stainless steel bowl, mash the cheese and ½ cup half-and-half with a fork to form a smooth paste. Add the remaining 2 cups half-and-half and stir to combine.

Place ¼ of the potatoes in the baking dish and top with ¼ of the cheese mixture. Continue alternating layers of potatoes and cheese, ending with the cheese. Cover the pan with parchment paper and a sheet of foil and bake for 30 minutes. Uncover and bake until the potatoes are tender and golden brown, 20 to 30 minutes. Let stand for 10 minutes before serving.

❧ *The Final Touch:* Garnish with chopped fresh chives and serve with warm, crusty multigrain bread.

BUTTERMILK MASHED POTATOES

Serves 4 to 6

CHEF'S NOTE: This simple dish is made unforgettable by the buttermilk.

---

2 pounds russet or Yukon gold potatoes, peeled and cut into 2" cubes

3 tablespoons unsalted butter

1 cup buttermilk

1 teaspoon kosher salt

Freshly ground white pepper to taste

Place the potatoes in a medium saucepan and cover with cold water. Lightly salt the water and bring to a boil over medium-high heat, then reduce the heat and simmer until tender (about 12 to 15 minutes).

In a medium saucepan over low heat, melt the butter and warm the buttermilk.

Drain the potatoes and put them through a food mill, adding to the pan with the buttermilk. Whisk until fluffy and smooth, then season with the salt and pepper. Transfer to a large bowl and serve immediately.

The Final Touch: Garnish with fresh herbs.

SMASHED POTATOES WITH RAMPS
WITH CRÈME FRAÎCHE

Serves 4 to 6

CHEF'S NOTE: When choosing potatoes for mashed potatoes, use high-starch varieties such as russet or Yukon gold. Since the potatoes in this dish aren't peeled, it's important to buy organic. Ramps, which are members of the leek family with a bit stronger flavor than leeks or scallions, are abundant in the Northeast and are one of the first signs of spring. They can be foraged (they love moist areas) or purchased at farmers' markets.

2 pounds russet or Yukon gold potatoes, cut into 2" pieces

2 tablespoons unsalted butter

4 ounces ramps, cleaned and cut into 1"-long pieces

¾ cup Vermont Butter and Cheese crème fraîche

Kosher salt and freshly ground white pepper to taste

Place the potatoes in a large saucepan and cover with cold water. Lightly salt the water and bring to a boil over medium-high heat. Reduce the heat, partially cover, and simmer until fork tender, about 20 minutes.

Meanwhile, melt the butter in a sauté pan over medium heat. Add the white portions of the ramps and cook for 1 minute, then add the green portions and cook until tender, 3 to 5 minutes total.

Drain the potatoes and put them through a food mill or ricer into a large stainless steel bowl. Fold in the crème fraîche and ramps until well incorporated. Season with salt and pepper, transfer to a large bowl, and serve immediately.

❧ *The Final Touch:* Garnish with chive blossoms.

ROASTED PEARS AND POTATOES
WITH AUTUMN SPICE RUB

Serves 4

CHEF'S NOTE: This is an interesting side dish with pork or chicken.

---

2 pounds small Maine white potatoes, quartered lengthwise (4–6 pieces per potato)

8 pears, Anjou or Bosc, peeled, cored, and quartered lengthwise

2 tablespoons Autumn Spice Rub (recipe on page 182)

2 tablespoons canola oil

Salt and freshly ground black pepper to taste

Preheat a convection oven to 400°F. Lightly oil 2 baking sheets.

Place the potatoes and pears in separate large bowls. Add 1 tablespoon oil and 1 tablespoon spice rub to each bowl and toss to coat. Season with salt and pepper. Transfer to the baking sheets and roast until tender and beginning to caramelize (the potatoes will take somewhat longer [15 to 20 minutes] than the pears [8 to 12 minutes] to reach this point). Transfer to a rack and let cool slightly. Combine in a serving bowl and serve warm.

SPRING PARSNIP AND POTATO PURÉE

Serves 4 to 6

CHEF'S NOTE: If parsnips have been mulched well and endured the frosts of winter, the tubers will be sweeter in spring than in fall. Be sure to get the first harvest because they become woody and stringy if allowed to age in the ground.

1½ pounds parsnips

2 large Maine potatoes

¼ cup (½ stick) butter

½ cup heavy cream

Salt and freshly ground black
  pepper to taste

Peel the parsnips and potatoes, cut the potatoes in half lengthwise, and then cut both into 1- to 2-inch long pieces and place in a large saucepan. Add enough water to cover, salt lightly, and bring to a boil over medium-high heat. Reduce the heat, partially cover, and simmer until fork tender, about 20 minutes.

In a small saucepan, combine the butter and cream and heat gently until the butter has melted and the mixture approaches a simmer. Put the potatoes and parsnips through a food mill or ricer into a medium stainless steel bowl. Fold in the butter mixture until light and fluffy, then season with salt and pepper.

❧ *The Final Touch:* A perfect complement might be steamed fresh spring sweet peas or a hearty braise or stew.

SPICED MAPLE SWEET POTATO SPEARS

Serves 4 to 6

CHEF'S NOTE: There are many varieties of North American sweet potatoes, ranging in color from dark orange to white, any of which work well for this recipe. The freshest sweet potatoes are available from August through October; look for firm, unblemished, heavy tubers.

---

1 teaspoon dark chili powder

1 teaspoon maple sugar

1 teaspoon ground cumin

1 teaspoon granulated garlic

2 large sweet potatoes (10–12 ounces each)

2 teaspoons olive oil

Salt and freshly ground black pepper to taste

1 teaspoon fresh-picked thyme leaves or blossoms

Preheat the oven to 425°F. Line a large baking sheet with parchment paper or foil and oil lightly.

In a small bowl, combine the chili powder, sugar, cumin, and garlic.

Scrub the potatoes well and dry with paper towels, then halve lengthwise and cut each half into 4 spears. Place in a large stainless steel bowl and toss with the oil, then sprinkle with the spice mixture and toss well. Transfer to the baking sheet and roast, turning once, until tender and lightly browned, about 25 minutes.

❧ *The Final Touch:* Season with salt and pepper and garnish with some fresh thyme leaves and/or blossoms. Cilantro and lime also go very well with these sweet potatoes.

LENTIL AND BROWN RICE CASSEROLE

Serves 4

CHEF'S NOTE: Since legumes are harvested from the soil, they often contain small stones and twigs. Be sure to rinse them well in cold water and pick out any debris that floats to the surface. For a vegetarian option, use vegetable broth instead of chicken broth and omit the cheese.

---

2 tablespoons olive oil

1 medium onion, finely chopped

2 cloves garlic, finely chopped

1½ cups diced heirloom tomatoes

1 small bay leaf

¼ teaspoon chopped fresh-picked thyme leaves

½ cup red wine

1½ cups chicken broth

½ cup brown lentils, rinsed

1 cup brown rice

Salt and freshly ground black pepper to taste

Preheat the oven to 350°F.

In a small skillet over medium heat, melt the butter or add the oil, then cook the onion until translucent, about 2 minutes, then add the garlic and cook for 2 minutes. Add the tomatoes, bay leaf, and thyme and cook until fragrant, 2 to 3 minutes. Add the wine and broth.

Place the rice, lentils, and tomato mixture in a baking dish, stir, and cover with a tight-fitting lid. Bake until the rice and lentils are tender and the liquid is absorbed, 40 to 45 minutes. Discard the bay leaf, fluff with a fork, and season with salt and pepper.

❧ *The Final Touch:* Top with ½ cup grated Gruyère cheese and return to the oven until the cheese melts.

LE SOMMELIER: The simple but elegant flavors in this dish are nicely served by an equally simple but elegant beer. Long Trail Brewery's classic Long Trail Ale is a great match, with its creamy texture and roasted malt characteristics. This is one of the original Vermont microbrews and is widely available across New England.

BRAISED LENTILS WITH VERMONT SMOKE AND CURE BACON

Serves 4 to 6

CHEF'S NOTE: French lentils, often called *lentils du puy* (for Le Puy-en-Velay in the Auvergne region of France, where the lentils originally grew in the volcanic soil), are small and dark green.

---

1 cup diced Vermont Smoke and Cure bacon

1 medium carrot, peeled and cut into small dice

1 stalk celery, peeled and cut into small dice

1 medium onion, peeled and cut into small dice

2 cloves garlic, minced

2 cups French lentils, picked over

4½ cups chicken broth or stock

1 bay leaf

1 teaspoon fresh-picked thyme leaves

Salt and freshly ground black pepper to taste

Preheat the oven to 325°F.

In a Dutch oven over low heat, cook the bacon until the fat is rendered, about 10 minutes. Add the carrot, celery, and onion and cook for 5 minutes, then add the garlic and cook for an additional 2 minutes. Add the lentils, broth, bay leaf, and thyme, then cover and bake until the liquid is absorbed and the lentils are tender, 45 minutes. Discard the bay leaf, season with salt and pepper, and serve immediately.

MAPLE BAKED BEANS

Serves 4 to 6

CHEF'S NOTE: Every good New England cook has a good maple baked bean recipe; this is ours. The secret is the Vermont Smoke and Cure bacon—and using Grade B maple syrup.

---

1 pound navy beans

8 ounces Vermont Smoke and Cure smoked bacon, cut into medium dice

1 cup minced Spanish onion

3 cloves garlic, minced

2 cups diced heirloom tomatoes

½ cup ketchup

3 tablespoons dry mustard

⅓ cup Grade B maple syrup

1 tablespoon molasses

1 bay leaf

3 tablespoons apple cider vinegar

Salt and freshly ground black pepper to taste

In a large bowl, combine the beans and enough water to cover by 6 inches and refrigerate overnight. The next day, sort through the beans and remove any that have not swollen or are damaged.

Preheat the oven to 300°F.

In a Dutch oven or ovenproof baking dish over low heat, cook the bacon until the fat is rendered and the bacon is slightly crisp and golden brown, about 10 to 12 minutes. Add the onion and garlic and cook until fragrant and lightly browned. Add the tomatoes, ketchup, mustard, syrup, molasses, bay leaf, vinegar, salt, and pepper and bring to a simmer. Cover and bake for 5 hours, stirring every hour or so. If the mixture becomes thick and pasty-looking while cooking, add water ½ cup at a time until the desired consistency is reached. Uncover, stir, and bake for 1 hour. Serve hot or continue to stir occasionally while cooling (to 70 degrees within 2 hours), then refrigerate.

NEW ENGLAND CHANTERELLE RISOTTO

Serves 4 to 6

CHEF'S NOTE: Because Arborio rice has an enormous capacity to soak up liquid, it's perfect for risotto. Chanterelles are abundant on the slopes of the Northeast, especially around stands of mixed hemlock and birch trees. They are a beautiful, rich egg-yolk color when fresh.

1½ quarts vegetable broth or stock

2 tablespoons canola oil

2 shallots, finely minced

2 cups Arborio rice

1 cup dry white wine

8 ounces chanterelles, wiped clean and trimmed but not washed

2 tablespoons butter

2 tablespoons grated Pecorino Romano cheese

Salt and freshly ground black pepper to taste

Bring the broth to a simmer in a medium saucepan over medium heat. Reduce the heat to low and cover the pan.

Heat the oil in a large, heavy saucepan over medium heat. Add the shallots and cook until translucent, about 5 minutes. Add the rice and stir to coat with oil. Add the wine and cook until almost completely absorbed, about 10 to 12 minutes. Fold in the chanterelles and add 2 cups broth. Increase the heat to medium-high, bring to a simmer, and stir until the liquid is absorbed. Continue adding broth 1 cup at a time, simmering until the liquid is absorbed after each addition and stirring often until the rice is just tender, about 20 minutes. Stir in the butter and cheese and season with salt and pepper. Spoon the risotto into a bowl and serve immediately.

LE SOMMELIER: The slight earthiness of the chanterelles in this dish calls for an earthy wine. Sharpe Hill Vineyards in Connecticut produces a great red wine called Red Seraph, a blend of Merlot and St. Croix grapes that would be a fine accompaniment to the wonderful flavors in this dish.

BUTTERNUT SQUASH AND PANCETTA RISOTTO WITH THISTLE HILL FARM TARENTAISE

Serves 4 to 6

CHEF'S NOTE: Thistle Hill Farm Tarentaise is an aged, raw-milk, farmstead organic cheese that's handmade by John and Janine Putnam on their family farm in North Pomfret, Vermont, from the certified organic milk of their grass-fed Jersey cows.

---

6 cups chicken broth or stock

2 tablespoons canola oil

3 ounces pancetta, cut into small dice

2 cups large-dice peeled butternut squash

½ cup finely chopped onion

1 cup dry white wine

2 cups Arborio rice

2 tablespoons butter

2 tablespoons grated Thistle Hill Farm Tarentaise cheese

2 tablespoons fresh thyme leaves

2 tablespoons chopped flat-leaf parsley

Salt and freshly ground black pepper

Bring the broth to a simmer in a medium saucepan over medium heat. Reduce the heat to low and cover the pan.

Heat the oil in a large heavy saucepan over medium heat. Add the pancetta and cook until heated through, about 5 minutes. Add the squash and onion and stir to coat with oil, then add the rice and stir to coat. Add the wine and then increase the heat to medium high, bring to a simmer, and stir until the liquid is absorbed. Start adding the broth 1 cup at a time, simmering until the liquid is absorbed after each addition and stirring often until the rice is just tender, about 20 minutes. Add the butter, cheese, thyme, and parsley and season to taste with salt and pepper. Spoon the risotto into a bowl and serve immediately.

🍀 *The Final Touch:* Top with grated Tarentaise.

WILD RICE, CRANBERRY, AND PECAN PILAF

Serves 4 to 6

CHEF'S NOTE: Wild rice is not actually a rice grain but the seed of a semi-aquatic grass. After harvesting, it's fermented for several weeks in large vats and dried. It is graded by the length of the grain; any type will work well for this recipe.

---

1 cup coarsely chopped pecan halves

¼ cup canola oil

1 large onion, cut into small dice

2 cloves finely minced garlic

2½ cups wild rice, rinsed well and drained

4½ cups chicken broth or stock

½ cup dried cranberries

Salt and freshly ground black pepper to taste

¾ teaspoon chopped fresh thyme leaves

Preheat the oven to 350°F. Place the pecans on a baking sheet and toast until fragrant, about 5 to 7 minutes. Heat the oil in a medium saucepan over medium heat. Add the onion and cook for 3 to 5 minutes, until translucent, then add the garlic and cook for 3 minutes. Add the rice and stir to coat with oil, then add the broth and cranberries. When the rice is simmering, partially cover, reduce the heat to low, and cook until tender, for at least 45 minutes (longer for softer rice). If it begins to stick, add more broth ¼ cup at a time. Depending on the desired firmness of the rice, there may still be liquid remaining, which can be drained once the rice is cooked. Season with salt and pepper and add the thyme. Fluff lightly with a fork and serve immediately.

AUTUMN WILD RICE SALAD WITH CURRANT AND CRANBERRY

Serves 4

CHEF'S NOTE: Wild rice can take longer to cook than white rice, so plan accordingly. This recipe can easily be adjusted to use any fruits or nuts you have on hand.

Dressing

¼ cup rice wine vinegar

1 tablespoon fresh lemon juice

Salt and pepper to taste

2 tablespoons honey

½ cup olive oil

¼ cup dried cranberries

Salad

2 cups wild rice

1 teaspoon chopped fresh sage or
  ½ teaspoon dried sage

Salt and freshly ground black
  pepper to taste

¼ cup dried currants

¼ cup chopped dried apricots

½ small red onion, diced

¼ cup chopped dates

¼ cup slivered almonds or pecans

To make the dressing: In a large bowl, combine the vinegar, lemon juice, salt, pepper, and honey. Slowly whisk in the oil. Add the cranberries and season with salt and pepper.

To make the salad: In a large saucepan, cook the rice like pasta in a large amount of salted water until tender, probably about 45 minutes for firmer rice. Drain and transfer to a large bowl, then let cool. Add the sage to the rice and season with salt and pepper

In a small bowl, soak the currants and apricots in water for 5 to 7 minutes, then drain well. Add the currants, apricots, red onion, and dates and toss with the dressing. Garnish with the almonds.

SUMMER WHEAT BERRY SALAD WITH FRESH FENNEL, SUGAR SNAP PEAS, AND MINT

Serves 4 to 6

CHEF'S NOTE: Wheat berries are whole wheat grains—actually unprocessed wheat seeds, also known as kernels. They contain the whole grain, endosperm, bran, and germ.

---

2 cups wheat berries

2 quarts water

6 tablespoons extra-virgin olive oil

1 teaspoon grated lemon zest

2½ tablespoons fresh lemon juice

1 clove garlic, minced

⅛ teaspoon roasted fennel seeds

¼ teaspoon sea salt

¼ teaspoon freshly ground black pepper

1 fennel bulb, cut into large dice

4 cups cooked wheat berries

2 cups sugar snap peas, trimmed by pinching to remove both ends of the pea, then halved widthwise

2 tablespoons minced Italian parsley

2 tablespoons minced fresh mint

Rinse the wheat berries, then cook in the water until tender, about 1 hour. In a medium stainless steel bowl, combine the lemon zest and juice, salt and pepper, garlic, and fennel seeds, then whisk in the oil. Add the diced fennel, wheat berries, peas, parsley, and mint, and toss well. Adjust the seasoning with additional salt and pepper if needed.

❧ *The Final Touch:* Crumbled goat cheese or feta could be added to make this an entrée salad.

SWEET CORN PANCAKES

Makes approximately 2 dozen 3-inch pancakes

CHEF'S NOTE: Corn cakes may seem simple and somewhat bland if you have never eaten them made with corn fresh from the field. In Vermont, we like to wander down to the garden, grab a few ears, bring them back to the kitchen, and get to work. That's when this recipe becomes a celebration of country life.

---

3 ears fresh corn

¼ cup minced onion

1½ tablespoons unsalted butter

¼ cup small-dice cored and seeded red bell pepper

2 free-range eggs

½ cup milk

⅓ cup yellow cornmeal

¾ cup all-purpose flour

½ teaspoon kosher salt

¼ teaspoon ground white pepper

1 tablespoon chopped fresh chives

Remove the kernels from the corn (you should have about 1½ cups) and place in a medium bowl. Scrape the cobs to remove the sweet milk and add the milk to the bowl. Add the onion and stir until well combined. Transfer to a food processor with a medium blade and pulse 2 or 3 times to form a coarse purée.

Melt the butter in a small sauté pan over medium-high heat. Add the bell pepper and cook for 2 minutes.

In a large stainless steel bowl, combine the eggs and milk. Add the cornmeal, flour, salt, and pepper and stir until smooth. Add the corn mixture, bell pepper, and chives.

Heat a medium nonstick skillet over medium heat and spray lightly with canola oil or cooking spray. Add the batter to the pan 2 tablespoons at a time to make batches of 3 pancakes at a time in a 12-inch skillet. Cook until small bubbles form, about 2 minutes, then flip and cook for an additional 1½ minutes. Transfer to a warm plate and keep in a low (225°F) oven until all the pancakes are cooked.

🍀 *The Final Touch:* To serve as appetizers or hors d'oeuvres, make the pancakes a little smaller and add a dollop of Vermont Butter and Cheese crème fraîche and a slice of smoked salmon. Garnish with small-dice red onions and capers, fresh lemon, and dill.

BAKED POLENTA

Serves 4 to 6

CHEF'S NOTE: The French of the Northern Alps cook their polenta like a rice pilaf. This recipe may be adapted by substituting an equal amount of unsaturated fat such as olive oil for the butter. You may also use any type of broth you choose.

4½ cups chicken broth

¼ cup unsalted butter

1 medium yellow onion, peeled and cut into small dice

1½ cups coarse cornmeal

Salt and freshly ground black pepper to taste

Preheat the oven to 300°F. Bring the broth to a boil in a large saucepan.

Melt 2 tablespoons butter in a 2-quart cast-iron Dutch oven over medium heat. Add the onion and cook until translucent, about 3 to 5 minutes. Add the cornmeal and toss with the onion. Add the broth, season with salt and pepper, and stir. Cover, transfer to the oven, and cook until the broth is absorbed, 30 to 40 minutes. Transfer to a serving bowl, add the remaining 2 tablespoons butter, and fluff with a fork. Serve immediately.

WINTER

A THIN WINTER SUN dips low behind the trees, the surrounding hills merge into the night's darkness, and an icy crust begins to form on the thick blanket of snow that reaches far across the Canadian border and into the northern wilderness.

The silence is total. No one can hear the faint, slow breathing of a mother bear and her yearling hibernating under an outcropping of rocks a few hundred yards up-slope, or the sigh of a fox snuggled into her den at the foot of an 11,000-year-old boulder not far away. There is not even the whisper of icy crystals over newfallen snow, or the sudden crack of frozen wood in a nearby forest.

But down in the valley, a light appears in a distant farmhouse. A thin column of smoke begins to rise into the star-scattered sky, a door opens, and two thickly furred farm dogs launch themselves joyfully off the porch and into the snow. They break trail from farm-house to barn, pausing only to take care of evening business and sniff at the fresh tracks of a snowshoe hare. Then they circle the barn and head out across the meadow where, two days ago, a fierce wind out of the Canadian wilderness had cleared the pond and meadow of all but a foot of packed snow — perfect for cross-country skiing.

Winter in Vermont is a time of cold and darkness. Temperatures drop to −20°F at night and the sky lightens for less than 8 hours a day.

Those of us who live here, particularly in the mountains near the New England Culinary Institute, make sure we have four-wheel drive and wide snow-grabbing tires when we set out — with emergency flares, flashlights, an artic sleeping bag, snow shovel, snowshoes, snowboots, skis, and maybe a 50-pound bag of kitty litter in the back. It tends to give our vehicles a cluttered look, but there isn't one Vermonter who hasn't used every item at least once or lent it to a stranded neighbor — and not one who hasn't stopped beside an inviting break in the trees to take off on snowshoes or skis to see what lies beyond.

The fact is that we understand the cold, the darkness, and our own human need for warmth, light, and connection.

Our winters are celebrated with bonfires at the winter solstice, candles on Christmas night, torchlit runs down ski slopes on New Year's Eve, and neighborhood gatherings around the woodstove all winter long.

They're also celebrated with food. Church suppers, neighborhood potlucks, firehouse breakfasts, community dinners, and gatherings of friends and multigenerational families at local pubs and restaurants characterize our communities. Rich, hearty chowders, seductively sweet lobster soufflés, gut-warming vegetable stews, farmhouse-roasted free-range chicken, soft cheeses from neighboring cows and goats, fresh fish from under the ice, and maple syrup drawn from our trees give us sustenance.

Our food connects us — to the snow-covered place in which we live, and to one another.

8

THE DESSERT CART

To retreat from the nippy cold of a Vermont winter morning into the warmth of La Brioche, the New England Culinary Institute's pastry shop and café in downtown Montpelier, is to stroll into heaven. The students have been baking bread since 4 a.m., and the smell of brioche, croissants, muffins, scones, bear claws, cinnamon rolls, coffee cakes, and the like reaches out to every person who opens the door.

A peek into the kitchen reveals a small group of white-coated and toqued students who are just finishing up the morning baking. The amazing Chef Adrian is still talking passionately to a small knot of students — explaining, gesturing, sketching shapes in the air with his hands, bending over a cake, and igniting a fire in every student's soul to create the perfect pastry.

The recipes on the following pages will encourage you to explore your own creativity. Use only the freshest dairy products, and freshly ground flours in small batches from local millers. Both can frequently be found at farmers' markets throughout the country. As for chocolate, we ask that you query your sources before you buy, and make sure that the cocoa in it is from sustainable sources and harvested by people who are paid a livable wage. The sad truth is that most chocolate is not. By paying attention to these issues, however, you can turn that around.

VERMONT APPLE PIE

CHEF'S NOTE: Vermonters love their apples, and in the fall we make more than our fair share of apple pies. You can make your own pie shell using our Multipurpose Pie Dough or (if you really have to) buy a readymade one. For a real Vermont experience, try replacing some or all of the brown sugar with maple sugar or maple syrup. You can play with the apples, too, by replacing some or all of the Granny Smiths with another type. Using half McIntoshes will give your pie a saucier consistency, while Honey Crisps will yield a very distinct sweet taste and honey aroma.

8 Granny Smith apples, peeled and sliced

1 cup brown sugar

¼ teaspoon ground nutmeg

¼ teaspoon ground cinnamon

¼ cup cornstarch

2 tablespoons bourbon

Juice of 1 lemon

¼ cup (½ stick) butter

1 baked pie shell (see Multipurpose Pie Dough recipe on page 257)

In a large bowl, toss the apples with the brown sugar, nutmeg, cinnamon, and cornstarch. Add the bourbon, lemon juice, and butter, then transfer to a medium saucepan over low heat. Cook, stirring constantly, just until boiling, then spoon into the pie shell. Let stand to cool and set the filling.

❧ *The Final Touch:* Ben and Jerry's Homemade Vanilla, what else?

SUMMER BLUEBERRY PIE

2 cups blueberries, washed and stems removed

1 cup sugar

½ cup cornstarch

Pinch of salt

Juice of 1 lemon

1 baked pie shell (see Multi-purpose Pie Dough recipe on page 257)

In a large bowl, combine the blueberries, sugar, cornstarch, salt, lemon juice, and ¾ cup water. Transfer to a medium saucepan and cook, stirring, just until boiling. Spoon into the pie shell and chill before serving.

FALL PUMPKIN PIE

CHEF'S NOTE: This dessert represents everything about fall in New England. Usually, fresh ingredients are key to the flavor of a dish, but here we suggest using canned pumpkin. While you can make your own filling by roasting and puréeing fresh pumpkin, it often doesn't have the flavor of canned purée. The pumpkin used for canning is picked at the peak of its flavor and processed quickly, so little of the flavor is lost.

---

2 cups pumpkin purée	3 free-range eggs
1 cup sugar	½ cup milk
Pinch of salt	1 cup heavy cream
1 teaspoon ground cinnamon	½ teaspoon vanilla extract
½ teaspoon ground ginger	1 baked pie shell (see Multi-purpose Pie Dough recipe on page 257)
½ teaspoon ground nutmeg	

Preheat the oven to 350°F.

In a large bowl, combine the pumpkin, sugar, salt, cinnamon, ginger, and nutmeg and whisk until smooth. Whisk in the eggs 1 at a time, then slowly whisk in the milk, cream, and vanilla. Continue whisking for 5 minutes. Pour into the pie shell and bake until the filling jiggles only slightly when the pie is tapped, about 40 minutes. Let stand until cool.

The Final Touch: Can you resist making little cutouts of maple leaves from some of the dough and scattering them over the surface before you bake the pie?

GREEN MOUNTAIN CAPPUCCINO MOUSSE

Makes one 9" pie or eight 4-ounce ramekins

CHEF'S NOTE: This lovely chocolate dessert is creamy but light. If time is short, you can use a store-bought graham cracker pie shell.

Pie Shell

2 cups graham cracker crumbs

2 tablespoons (¼ stick) unsalted butter, melted

Filling

1½ cups heavy cream

¾ teaspoon powdered gelatin

3 tablespoons brewed Green Mountain espresso coffee

5 free-range egg yolks

2 tablespoons + 2 teaspoons honey

2 tablespoons coffee-flavored liqueur

6 ounces semi-sweet chocolate, melted

To make the pie shell: In a 2-quart bowl, combine the graham cracker crumbs and butter and mix with a fork until evenly moistened. Press into the bottom and sides of a 9-inch pie plate and refrigerate for 2 hours.

To make the filling: In a medium bowl, whip the cream until soft peaks form. Place the gelatin in a small microwavable bowl and pour in the coffee. Let stand until thickened, about 5 minutes.

In a 3-quart bowl, whip the egg yolks until ribbons form, about 4 minutes. In a microwavable cup, microwave the honey just until boiling, then carefully pour into the egg yolks, whipping until cool. Microwave the gelatin to dissolve, being careful not to boil. Using a rubber spatula, add to the egg yolk mixture, then stir in the liqueur and chocolate. Add ½ of the whipped cream and carefully fold in with the spatula, then fold in the rest. Quickly pour into a 9-inch pie plate or eight 4-ounce ramekins, then refrigerate for 1 hour before serving.

❧ *The Final Touch:* Serve with crème fraîche or fresh local blueberries.

SUMMER LEMON-STRAWBERRY TART

Makes one 9" tart

CHEF'S NOTE: This is a tangy and refreshing summertime dessert that's best when made with fresh local strawberries. Pouring the lemon curd into the pie shell while it's still hot gives a more professional finish to the tart.

¾ cup fresh lemon juice

½ cup (1 stick) unsalted butter

3 free-range eggs

3 free-range egg yolks

½ cup + 1 tablespoon sugar

1 baked sugar dough tart shell (see Sugar Dough recipe on page 256)

1 pint fresh strawberries

Confectioners' sugar

In a 2-quart saucepan over medium-high heat, bring the lemon juice and butter to a boil. In a 2-quart bowl, whisk together the eggs, egg yolks, and sugar. Carefully stir in the lemon juice mixture and pour back into the saucepan. Reduce the heat to medium and cook, stirring constantly, until thick enough to coat the back of a spoon, being careful not to boil. Pour through a fine mesh sieve into the tart shell. Refrigerate until cool, about 2 hours, then decorate the top with whole or sliced strawberries. To serve, slice and dust heavily with sifted confectioners' sugar.

FRESH FRUIT FLAN

Makes one 9" tart

CHEF'S NOTE: This tart is bursting with local seasonal fruit. Brushing the tart shell with warmed apricot jam keeps it from becoming soggy. If you make the tart more than a few hours before serving, you can brush it with more jam to prevent the fruit from oxidizing.

¼ cup apricot jam

1 baked sugar dough tart shell (see Sugar Dough recipe on page 256)

1 recipe cold Diplomat Mousse (recipe on page 240)

Soft, fresh seasonal fruits of your choice, such as sliced strawberries, raspberries, or blueberries

In a microwavable cup or small bowl, microwave the jam until warm, then brush onto the inside of the tart shell, reserving any remaining jam. Place on a flat serving plate and spread the mousse into the shell, making the center of the tart slightly deeper than the edges. Decorate with the fruit, starting from the outside edge and working toward the center of the tart. Warm the reserved jam and lightly brush on the fruit to give the tart a glossy shine and a professional appearance. Refrigerate for 3 hours before serving.

DIPLOMAT MOUSSE

Makes 2¼ cups

¼ cup orange juice

¾ teaspoon powdered gelatin

1 cup Pastry Cream (recipe on page 260)

1 cup heavy cream

Pour the orange juice into a small microwavable bowl, sprinkle with the gelatin, and let stand for 10 minutes. Place the pastry cream in a 2-quart bowl and whisk until a smooth custard forms. Microwave the gelatin mixture on high until the gelatin melts, 20 seconds. Pour into the pastry cream and stir to incorporate.

In a medium bowl, whip the cream until soft peaks form; then, using a rubber spatula, fold into the pastry cream. Refrigerate for 10 minutes before using.

CARAMEL-APPLE TARTE TATIN

Serves 4

CHEF'S NOTE: This is a longtime favorite in the restaurants of the New England Culinary Institute. To successfully flip the tarte tatin onto a round serving platter, place the platter upside down and centered on top of the hot pan. Wearing oven mitts, hold the pan and platter firmly between your hands and flip so the pan is on top of the platter (be careful of any hot juices that may run out). Slowly lift the pan. If the apples stick to the pan, use a rubber spatula to remove them and replace on the tarte tatin.

Sauce

1 cup sugar

¼ cup (½ stick) cold butter

2 tablespoons heavy cream

Tart

6 tablespoons (¾ stick) butter, melted

1 cup sugar

4 Golden Delicious apples, peeled, seeded, and quartered

1 sheet puff pastry dough, cut into an 8 circle

Vanilla ice cream

Preheat the oven to 350°F.

To make the sauce: In a small saucepan over medium-high heat, combine the sugar and 1 tablespoon water. Without stirring, heat until the sugar boils and is a light golden brown. Remove from the heat and stir in the butter and cream (be careful; the sugar may splatter). Pour into an 8-inch cake pan.

To make the tart: In a medium bowl, combine the butter, sugar, and apples, then spoon into the pan over the caramel. Place the pastry dough on top of the apples and prick with a fork. Bake until the apples are tender, 25 minutes. Carefully remove the pastry and set aside. Place the pan over medium heat and simmer until the juices are completely evaporated, watching carefully to prevent scorching.

Replace the pastry and flip the tart onto a large round platter (see Chef's Note). Slice and serve warm with a scoop of vanilla ice cream and a squiggle of caramel sauce.

TIRAMISU

Makes one 8" cake

CHEF'S NOTE: This is a New England version of the creamy Italian dessert whose name is derived from the coffee it contains (*tiramisu* means "pick-me-up").

---

1 recipe Ladyfingers (recipe on page 258)

¾ cup strong-brewed coffee

1¾ cups mascarpone cheese

½ cup sweet Marsala wine or sherry

3 free-range eggs, separated

5 tablespoons sugar

1 ounce semi-sweet chocolate, grated

Line the sides of an 8-inch soufflé dish with 1 strip of ladyfingers, making sure not to leave a gap at the end. Break the other strip into separate fingers and arrange in 1 layer to cover the bottom of the dish. Brush with ½ of the coffee.

In a 2-quart bowl, soften the cheese with a spoon. Add the wine and stir to incorporate. In a medium bowl, combine the egg yolks with ½ of the sugar and beat with a hand-held mixer until light and foamy, about 3 minutes. Wash and dry the mixer blades; then, in another medium bowl, combine the egg whites and the remaining sugar and beat until soft peaks form.

Add the egg yolks to the cheese mixture and stir gently, then fold in the whites with a rubber spatula. Pour ½ of the filling into the soufflé dish. Cover with more ladyfingers and brush with the remaining coffee. Pour in the remaining filling and spread evenly, then sprinkle with the chocolate and refrigerate for 2 hours. Dust the dessert plates with sifted cocoa powder and top with a slice of cold tiramisu.

❧ *The Final Touch:* The flavor of tiramisu is enhanced when accompanied by Sambuca, a licorice-flavored liqueur.

Autumn Wild Rice Salad with Currant and Cranberry

Autumn Spice Rub

Vermont Maple Crème Brûlée

Caramel-Apple Tarte Tatin

Flourless Chocolate Cake

Cheddar Bread Pudding with Apple Butter and Dark Beer Caramel Sauce

Chocolate Bombe Cakes

Gratinée of Berries with Citrus Sabayon

PUMPKIN CHEESECAKE

Makes one 8" cheesecake

CHEF'S NOTE: This cheesecake is best baked in a water bath to keep cracks from forming on the surface as it cools. You can change the spices to suit your taste, using those similar to your favorite pumpkin pie recipe.

Crust

1¼ cups graham cracker crumbs

2 tablespoons (¼ stick) unsalted butter

Cheesecake

¾ cup pumpkin purée

½ teaspoon ground cinnamon

¼ teaspoon ground nutmeg

¼ teaspoon ground cloves

¼ teaspoon ground allspice

2½ packages (8 ounces each) cream cheese, softened

¾ cup sugar

2 tablespoons all-purpose flour

3 free-range eggs

1 free-range egg yolk

2 teaspoons vanilla extract

To make the crust: Preheat the oven to 350°F. Grease the bottom and sides of an 8-inch round cake pan and line the bottom with a disk of parchment paper, making sure the disk is flat and doesn't curve up the sides of the pan.

Place the graham cracker crumbs in a 2-quart bowl. Melt the butter in a small saucepan over low heat. Pour over the crumbs and stir with a fork, evenly coating all the crumbs. Sprinkle into the bottom of the cake pan and press into a thin, even layer, then wipe any excess crumbs from the sides. Bake for 10 minutes. Let stand to cool completely.

To make the cheesecake: In a small bowl, combine the pumpkin, cinnamon, nutmeg, cloves, and allspice.

In the bowl of an electric mixer with a paddle attachment, cream together the cream cheese and sugar. Add the flour, mix to incorporate, and scrape down the sides of the bowl with a rubber spatula. Slowly mix in the eggs, egg yolk, and vanilla, scraping the bowl between additions. Mix in the pumpkin.

Pour the batter into the cake pan. Place a 12 x 16–inch baking pan in the oven and pour in 6 cups water. (If using a springform pan, wrap the bottom with foil to keep water from leaking into the crust.) Place the cake pan in the water bath and bake until the cake wobbles when shaken gently, 50 to 60 minutes. Cool on a rack for 2 hours, then wrap in plastic wrap and refrigerate overnight. (To remove the cheesecake from a regular pan, warm the base of the pan over low heat for a few seconds. Place a flat plate on top of the pan and flip it so the cheesecake falls onto the plate. Remove the parchment and repeat with another plate to turn the cheesecake right side up.)

❧ *The Final Touch:* Serve with cinnamon whipped cream. (In a cold medium bowl, beat 2 cups heavy cream with an electric mixer until it begins to thicken. Add 4 teaspoons confectioners' sugar and 1 teaspoon ground cinnamon and continue to beat until thick.) Top the cheesecake with the whipped cream or place a dollop on each plate.

MARBLED CHEESECAKE

Makes one 8" cheesecake

CHEF'S NOTE: This recipe is based on the classic New York cheesecake. For variety, you can add flavorings such as orange zest and orange juice, coffee extract, or cinnamon.

Crust
1¼ cups graham cracker crumbs
2 tablespoons (¼ stick) unsalted butter

Cheesecake
2½ packages (8 ounces each) cream cheese, softened

¾ cup sugar
2 tablespoons all-purpose flour
3 free-range eggs
1 free-range egg yolk
2 teaspoons vanilla extract
¼ cup heavy cream
3 ounces semi-sweet chocolate, melted

To make the crust: Preheat the oven to 350°F. Grease the bottom and sides of an 8-inch round cake pan and line the bottom with a disk of parchment paper, making sure the disk is flat and doesn't curve up the sides of the pan.

Place the graham cracker crumbs in a 2-quart bowl. Melt the butter in a small saucepan over low heat. Pour over the crumbs and stir with a fork, evenly coating all the crumbs. Sprinkle into the bottom of the cake pan and press into a thin, even layer, then wipe any excess crumbs from the sides. Bake for 10 minutes. Let stand to cool completely.

To make the cheesecake: In the bowl of an electric mixer with a paddle attachment, cream together the cream cheese and sugar. Add the flour, mix to incorporate, and scrape down the sides of the bowl with a rubber spatula. Slowly mix in the eggs, egg yolk, and vanilla, scraping the bowl between additions. Add the cream and mix on slow speed until combined.

Place the chocolate in a medium bowl, add 2 cups batter, and stir until combined. Pour ½ of the plain batter into the pan, covering the crust. Spoon on the chocolate batter, leaving gaps, then repeat with the remaining plain batter. With the tip of a knife, swirl the batters together to form a marbled pattern, being careful not to cut through the crust.

Pour the batter into the cake pan. Place a 12 x 16–inch baking pan in the oven and pour in 6 cups water. (If using a springform pan, wrap the bottom with foil to keep water from leaking into the crust.) Place the cake pan in the water bath and bake until the cake wobbles when shaken gently, 50 to 60 minutes. Cool on a rack for 2 hours, then wrap in plastic wrap and refrigerate overnight. (To remove the cheesecake from a regular pan, warm the base of the pan over low heat for a few seconds. Place a flat plate on top of the pan and flip it so the cheesecake falls onto the plate. Remove the parchment and repeat with another plate to turn the cheesecake right side up.)

✤ *The Final Touch:* Serve with whipped cream and fresh fruit.

GRATINÉE OF BERRIES WITH CITRUS SABAYON

Serves 4

CHEF'S NOTE: This dessert is a true celebration of summer.

---

1 cup blackberries

2 cups strawberries, washed and stems removed, halved

Sabayon

4 free-range egg yolks

½ cup sugar

Grated zest of 1 lemon

Grated zest of 1 orange

2 tablespoons Grand Marnier

2 tablespoons sweet white wine

1 cup cold heavy cream

Coulis

1 cup raspberries

1 tablespoon sugar

In the center of a chilled wide, shallow bowl or 4 individual bowls, arrange the blackberries and strawberries in a circle, then refrigerate.

To make the sabayon: In a medium stainless steel bowl, lightly beat the egg yolks, sugar, lemon zest, orange zest, Grand Marnier, and wine. Bring a saucepan of water to a boil and place the bowl over the pan. Beat the mixture until fluffy but still firm, then remove from the heat.

In a chilled medium bowl, beat the cream until it forms stiff peaks. Fold into the egg yolk mixture, then spoon over the berries.

To make the coulis: In a blender, process the raspberries and sugar until smooth. Pour through a mesh sieve into a bowl.

Using a blowtorch, caramelize the top part of the sabayon, heating until a clear brown syrup forms. (Alternatively, place under the broiler, watching carefully until caramelized.) Spoon the coulis around the berries and serve immediately.

FLOURLESS CHOCOLATE CAKE

Makes one 8" cake

CHEF'S NOTE: This soft flourless cake with a hint of coffee is best at room temperature. Serve in very thin slices, as it's quite rich.

½ cup (1 stick) unsalted butter

4 ounces semi-sweet chocolate, chopped

3 tablespoons strong-brewed coffee

½ cup cocoa powder, sifted

3 free-range eggs, at room temperature

¾ cup sugar

Preheat the oven to 350°F. Grease an 8-inch round cake pan and line the bottom with a disk of parchment paper.

Heat a saucepan of water, but don't boil. Place the butter and chocolate in a 3-quart heatproof bowl, place over the pan on low heat, and stir until melted. Add the coffee and stir until blended. Remove from the heat, stir in the cocoa, and mix until smooth.

In a 2-quart bowl, combine the eggs and sugar. Using a handheld mixer on high speed, beat until a thick foam forms, about 3 minutes. Using a rubber spatula, fold into the chocolate mixture. Pour into the pan and smooth with the back of a spoon.

Place a 12 x 16–inch baking ban in the oven and pour in 6 cups water. Place the cake pan in the water bath and bake until the cake jiggles when shaken gently and the center is firm, about 30 minutes. Cool in the pan for at least 4 hours. To remove from the pan, invert on a rack and remove the pan and parchment. Place a flat serving plate on the bottom of the cake and invert. To serve, dust dessert plates with small amounts of cocoa and confectioners' sugar and top with thin slices of cake.

CHOCOLATE BOMBE CAKES

Makes eight 4-ounce ramekins

CHEF'S NOTE: These brownie-like cakes are delicious served alone or with vanilla ice cream and chocolate sauce. One caveat: Be vigilant when baking them because they're easily overbaked. They're best when served in the ramekins at room temperature.

---

8 ounces semi-sweet chocolate

1 cup (2 sticks) unsalted butter

1 cup packed light brown sugar

4 tablespoons all-purpose flour

Pinch of salt

3 free-range eggs

2 teaspoons vanilla extract

Preheat the oven to 350°F.

Heat a saucepan of water, but don't boil. Place the chocolate and butter in a medium bowl, place over the pan on low heat, and stir until melted.

In a 2-quart bowl, combine the brown sugar, flour, and salt. Slowly add the eggs and whisk to incorporate. Add the vanilla and stir until smooth.

Place eight 4-ounce ramekins in a baking dish and carefully fill with batter, leaving ¼ inch at the top. Bake until puffed and just beginning to crack, 20 to 25 minutes. The cakes will fall when removed from the oven, and the center will be soft.

❧ *The Final Touch:* Glaze the tops of the cakes with Chocolate Ganache (page 259) and drizzle some passionfruit and raspberry sauce on the plates.

SUMMER GARDEN CAKE

CHEF'S NOTE: This sunflower cake was created for a summer party, but by changing the colors, you can make it a daisy, dahlia, or chrysanthemum. You can find fondant at cake shops and some supermarkets.

1 cake (9" x 13") of your choice
Fruit jam of your choice
1 recipe Vermont Buttercream Icing (recipe on page 250)

1 pound 10 ounces rolled colored fondant
2 ounces rolled brown fondant

Slice the cake horizontally into 2 layers. Spread the bottom layer with jam and icing and replace the top layer, pressing gently to even the surface. Refrigerate for 10 minutes.

On a piece of thin cardboard, draw an oval petal shape about 4 inches wide and 5½ inches long. Place the template on the cake and cut out 6 petals. Using a 2½-inch round cutter, cut the center of the flower from the remaining cake. Place the center piece on a 16-inch round base (a cake circle or platter) and arrange the petals around it so they are spaced evenly and touching at the bases. Smoothly spread the top and sides of the cake with icing, then refrigerate for about 10 minutes.

Roll out the fondant about ⅛ inch thick and carefully cover the cake, smoothing the top surface with your flattened hand and gently pushing the fondant to the sides of the flower. When the cake is covered, remove excess fondant with a small paring knife.

Roll the remaining fondant about ⅛ inch thick and use the template to cut out 6 petals, then place on a piece of Styrofoam or soft foam. Using the back of a knife, score lines in the petals to simulate veining. Using a paring knife, cut a line about 1 inch inside the edges of each petal, following the shape of the petal and extending to just above the base, being careful not to cut the foam. Carefully remove from the foam and place on the cake petals. Gently lift the tip of each inside petal so it curves upward and support it with a crumpled paper towel. Keep the towel in place for 24 hours; the petal will attach to the cake surface.

Roll out the brown fondant ⅛ inch thick and cut a disk the same size as the cake center, then add texture with the tip of a pastry brush handle or thermometer so it resembles a flower center. You can add a border by cutting tiny squares and placing them around the center, pinching to a point toward the edge. Brush the cake center with a little water and attach the flower center.

❧ *The Final Touch:* Enhance the edges of the petals by piping with chocolate or dusting with edible colored powder.

VERMONT BUTTERCREAM ICING
Makes 5 cups

CHEF'S NOTE: This is a classic icing used by pastry chefs. It's smooth, creamy, and versatile, and it flavors and colors well. It also freezes very well; remove from the freezer 24 hours ahead and keep at room temperature until ready to use.

1¼ cups + 2 tablespoons sugar
¾ cup free-range egg whites

4 cups (8 sticks) unsalted butter, softened, chopped

In a 2-quart saucepan, combine 1¼ cups sugar and enough water to form a mixture with the consistency of wet sand. Bring to a boil over medium heat until it reaches 240°F.

In the bowl of an electric mixer, combine the egg whites and 2 tablespoons sugar. When the boiling sugar reaches 238°F, start to beat the egg white mixture into soft peaks at high speed. Turn the mixer to slow speed and slowly add the sugar. Continue to beat on medium speed until cool, adding the butter a few pieces at a time, then increase the speed and beat for about 10 minutes. Use immediately or refrigerate for later use (it will keep for 1 week).

NEW ENGLAND CRUNCH COOKIES

Makes 36 cookies

CHEF'S NOTE: These cookies are quite popular because they don't contain flour. You can be as creative as you like with the add-ins. Any combination of the following is great: sunflower seeds, pumpkin seeds, dried cranberries, dried blueberries, chopped dried apricots, golden raisins, chocolate chips, or chopped walnuts or pecans.

3½ cups rolled oats

1 teaspoon baking soda

2 cups add-ins of choice

3 free-range eggs

¾ teaspoon vanilla extract

¾ cup sugar

1 cup brown sugar

½ cup (1 stick) unsalted butter, softened

1⅓ cups crunchy peanut butter

Preheat the oven to 350°F. Line 2 baking sheets with parchment paper.

In a large bowl, stir together the oats, baking soda, and add-ins. Place the eggs in a small bowl and stir in the vanilla.

In the bowl of an electric mixer with a paddle attachment, cream together the sugar, brown sugar, and butter on slow speed just until combined, being careful not to overmix. Add the peanut butter and mix thoroughly.

With the mixer at medium speed, gradually add the egg mixture. Remove the bowl from the mixer and scrape the sides with a rubber spatula, then return the bowl to the mixer and mix for a few seconds until smooth.

Add the dry ingredients and pulse a couple of times, then mix on slow speed until thoroughly combined. Remove the bowl and scrape the sides. Return the bowl to the mixer and mix for a few seconds.

Using a 2-ounce scoop (a small ice cream scoop with a squeezable handle) or forming balls about 2 inches in diameter, place portions of dough on the baking sheets. Bake until light brown and firm on the edges, about 16 minutes, rotating the baking sheets after 8 minutes (underbaked cookies will be gooey and may not hold together when cooled). Let cool slightly on the baking sheets, then transfer to a rack to cool completely.

REVERSE CHOCOLATE CHIP COOKIES

Makes 24 cookies

CHEF'S NOTE: Natural cocoa is different from the more common Dutch process cocoa and is available in many supermarkets. If the label says only "cocoa," it's probably Dutch process and will not work in this recipe. Natural cocoa is slightly acidic and creates a leavening effect when combined with the baking soda in the recipe. Serve only to true chocolate lovers; these cookies are intensely flavorful.

---

2 cups all-purpose flour

1 cup natural cocoa powder

¾ teaspoon baking soda

½ teaspoon salt

3 free-range eggs

1 teaspoon vanilla extract

1 cup sugar

1 cup brown sugar

1 cup (2 sticks) unsalted butter, softened

12 ounces white chocolate chips or chunks (or a combination of white and semi-sweet chocolate chips or chunks)

Preheat the oven to 350°F. Line 2 baking sheets with parchment paper.

In a medium bowl, whisk together the flour, cocoa, baking soda, and salt, breaking up any lumps. Place the eggs in a small bowl and stir in the vanilla.

In the bowl of an electric mixer with a paddle attachment, cream together the sugar, brown sugar, and butter on slow speed just until combined, being careful not to overmix.

With the mixer on medium speed, gradually add the egg mixture. Remove the bowl and scrape the sides with a rubber spatula, then return the bowl to the mixer and mix for a few seconds until smooth.

Add the dry ingredients and chocolate to the bowl and pulse a couple of times, then mix on slow speed until thoroughly combined. Remove the bowl and scrape the sides. Return the bowl to the mixer and mix for a few seconds.

Using a 2-ounce scoop (a small ice cream scoop with a squeezable handle) or forming balls about 2 inches in diameter, place portions of dough on the baking sheets. Bake until the tops look dry and begin to crack and the edges are firm, about 14 minutes total, rotating the baking sheets after 7 minutes (underbaked cookies will be fudgier inside). Let cool slightly on the baking sheets, then transfer to a rack to cool completely.

WINTER MAPLE-WALNUT COOKIES
Makes 24 cookies

CHEF'S NOTE: These are crisp, shortbread-style cookies, sophisticated and not too sweet.

Use high-quality maple extract from a specialty food store or online spice vendor or omit it, but don't use the kind from the supermarket spice aisle. Use lower-grade maple syrup, which is best for cooking and has the most concentrated flavor.

---

1 free-range egg yolk
½ teaspoon vanilla extract
½ teaspoon maple extract
⅛ cup maple syrup

½ cup sugar
1 cup (2 sticks) unsalted butter, softened
2½ cups all-purpose flour
1 cup walnuts, chopped

Preheat the oven to 350°F. Line 2 baking sheets with parchment paper.

In a small bowl, combine the egg yolk, vanilla and maple extracts, and syrup.

In the bowl of an electric mixer with a paddle attachment, cream together the sugar and butter on slow speed just until combined, being careful not to overmix. With the mixer on medium speed, gradually add the egg mixture. Remove the bowl and scrape the sides with a rubber spatula, then return the bowl to the mixer and mix for a few seconds until smooth.

Add the flour and walnuts and pulse a couple of times, then mix on slow speed until thoroughly combined. Remove the bowl and scrape down the sides. Return the bowl to the mixer and mix for a few seconds.

Place a 12 x 16–inch piece of parchment paper on a work surface. Transfer the dough to the parchment and fold the parchment over the dough. Using your hands, push the dough into the fold of the parchment, forming a log about 12 inches long. Roll the log in the parchment over the counter to even it out (if you like, you can flatten the sides to form a "square" log). Refrigerate for a minimum of 30 minutes or freeze for up to 1 month. When the dough has hardened, cut into ⅜-inch-thick slices and place on the baking sheets. Bake until the edges are golden brown and firm, about 12 minutes, rotating the baking sheets after 6 minutes. Let cool slightly on the baking sheets, then transfer to a rack to cool completely.

VERMONT MAPLE CRÈME BRÛLÉE

Makes five 4-ounce ramekins

CHEF'S NOTE: Crème brûlée is a classic dessert. This recipe is a New England favorite, using Vermont maple syrup in place of most of the sugar and vanilla.

---

1 tablespoon sugar

2 cups heavy cream

½ cup pure maple syrup

7 free-range egg yolks

5 teaspoons sugar

Preheat the oven to 350°F.

In a 2-quart saucepan over medium heat, heat the cream and sugar just until simmering. In a 2-quart bowl, whisk together the syrup and egg yolks, then gradually add the hot cream, whisking constantly. Strain through a fine mesh sieve into a bowl, then divide among five 4-ounce ramekins.

Place a 12 x 16–inch baking pan in the oven and pour in 6 cups water. Place the ramekins in the water bath, cover with foil, and bake until set like Jell-O, 25 minutes. Watch carefully while baking, as they can overbake quickly; do not let them boil.

Carefully remove the ramekins from the water bath, transfer to a wire rack, and let cool to room temperature. Refrigerate for 2 hours. To "brûlée," sprinkle 1 teaspoon sugar on each and place under the broiler until melted and golden brown, watching carefully so they don't burn.

❧ *The Final Touch:* Serve with fresh local blueberries.

CHEDDAR BREAD PUDDING WITH APPLE BUTTER AND DARK BEER CARAMEL SAUCE

Serves 6

CHEF'S NOTE: This incredibly rich caramel-drizzled pudding is the crowning touch to a cold winter's night feast. And it's so simple to make you won't believe it.

Apple Butter
6 Granny Smith apples
1 tablespoon unsalted butter
1½ teaspoons cinnamon
½ teaspoon nutmeg
2 teaspoons granulated sugar

Caramel Sauce
1 quart dark beer, any style
2 cups granulated sugar

Bread Pudding
1 loaf brioche or challah bread
  (or other rich soft bread)
6 eggs
1 pint heavy cream
1 pint whole milk
½ cup sugar
1 teaspoon vanilla extract
2 cups sharp cheddar cheese

To make the apple butter: Preheat the oven to 325°F. Peel, seed, and core the apples. Cut them into quarters. Combine apples, butter, cinnamon, nutmeg, and sugar in a 2-inch-deep 9 x 9–inch pan. Cover with aluminum foil and bake for 50 minutes or until tender. Purée the apple mixture in the food processor until smooth.

To make the caramel sauce: Reduce the beer in a saucepot until 2 cups remain. In a sauté pan, heat the sugar over medium heat until it is a dark honey color, then remove from heat. Add in the reduced beer, and stir to combine the two. Pour into a metal pan and cool.

To make the bread pudding: Slice the bread into ½-inch-thick slices. Set aside to dry out for 2 hours.

Preheat the oven to 300°F.

In a large bowl, whisk together the eggs, heavy cream, milk, sugar, and vanilla. In a buttered 9 x 9–inch pan, place a layer of bread, cutting to fit as need be. Evenly cover the bread with the cheese, then place another layer of bread over the cheese. Pour the custard mixture over the bread, allowing it to sink in evenly. Bake in the oven for 30 minutes or until the custard is set and the top is golden brown.

Serve the bread pudding warm with the apple butter and caramel sauce.

SUGAR DOUGH

Makes three 9" tart shells

CHEF'S NOTE: Sugar dough is very versatile and can be used for piecrusts as well as tart shells. It's important to keep the mixture cold while rolling, to keep the dough from getting sticky as well as to prevent shrinkage during baking.

1¼ cups (2½ sticks) unsalted butter, softened

2 cups + 4 tablespoons confectioners' sugar, sifted

3 free-range eggs

1 teaspoon vanilla extract

3½ cups all-purpose flour

In a large bowl, cream together the butter and confectioners' sugar. Add the eggs and vanilla and mix until smooth. Scrape the sides and bottom of the bowl with a rubber spatula. Add the flour and mix just until the dough comes together. Place in a plastic bag and refrigerate for at least 2 hours.

Grease a 9-inch fluted tart pan with a removable bottom. Divide the dough into thirds and place 1 portion on a lightly floured work surface (refrigerate the remaining portions in the plastic bag until needed; it will keep for about 10 days). Roll out to about 12 inches in diameter, then carefully fold the dough in half, then into quarters. Place in the pan and gently unfold to cover the entire pan. Press your fingers around the fluted edge of the pan to remove excess dough. Refrigerate or freeze for 10 minutes.

Preheat the oven to 350°F. Line the shell with foil, being careful to keep the edges tight by pinching the foil to the sides of the pan. Bake for 30 minutes, carefully remove the foil, and bake until light golden brown, 10 minutes. Cool on a wire rack, then remove from the pan. Hold the pan by the bottom in one hand and carefully press down on the sides with the other. The pan's outer ring will slide down your arm. Switch the tart to the other hand, set the ring aside, and place the tart on a plate.

To make sugar cookies, roll out the dough and cut into the desired shapes with cookie cutters. Bake on parchment-lined baking sheets at 350°F for 10 to 12 minutes.

MULTIPURPOSE PIE DOUGH

Makes one 9" pie shell

CHEF'S NOTE: There are a lot of specialized doughs that can be used for piecrusts, and they're nice when you have time to make them. Sometimes, though, you need dough right away. This is definitely that dough. Best of all, you can use it for a blueberry pie in the summer, a pumpkin pie for Thanksgiving, and a quiche when the chickens start laying beautiful eggs in the spring.

1½ cups pastry flour
1 tablespoon sugar
1¼ teaspoons salt

⅓ cup butter, cubed
½ teaspoon vinegar

In a large bowl, sift together the flour, sugar, and salt. Add the butter and cut into the flour by rubbing the mixture between your hands until it resembles coarse crumbs.

Form a well in the center and add the vinegar and 2 tablespoons cold water, then knead to form a dough. Refrigerate for at least 1 hour.

Place the dough on a well-floured work surface and roll it into a circle about ¼ inch thick. (If the dough sticks, roll it between 2 pieces of waxed paper instead of using flour.) Carefully lay the dough in a pie pan, making sure no air is trapped underneath, then use your fingers to crimp the dough around the top edge. Freeze for 15 minutes.

Preheat the oven to 350°F. Line the shell with foil and bake until light golden brown, about 15 minutes for a metal pie pan and 40 minutes for a glass one. Let cool completely before filling.

LADYFINGERS

Makes two 16" strips (enough to make one 8" charlotte)

CHEF'S NOTE: This is a classic recipe in which sponge cake batter is piped into "fingers" that are used to create desserts with moist fillings. They're generally used on the outside or as a layer within the dessert, such as in tiramisu. When whipping egg whites, be sure that the bowl and beaters are absolutely clean and free of grease; otherwise, the whites won't increase in volume.

½ cup free-range egg yolks
¼ cup sugar
½ cup free-range egg whites

¾ cup all-purpose flour, sifted
Confectioners' sugar

Preheat the oven to 350°F. Line a 16 x 12–inch baking sheet with parchment paper.

In a 3-quart bowl, combine the egg yolks and 2 tablespoons sugar. Using a hand-held mixer, beat on high speed until thick, creamy, and pale yellow, about 3 minutes. In a 2-quart bowl, combine the egg whites and the remaining 2 tablespoons sugar and beat to form soft peaks. Using a rubber spatula, alternately fold the whites and flour into the yolks, being careful not to deflate the batter.

Carefully spoon the batter into a 16-inch pastry bag fitted with a ½-inch plain round tip (or cut ½ inch from the corner of a gallon-size resealable plastic bag). Pipe 3½-inch lines of batter down the length of the baking sheet so they are touching each other; there should be enough batter for 2 strips. Dust with powdered sugar and bake until lightly browned, about 20 minutes. Cool on a wire rack and carefully remove the parchment before using. The ladyfingers can be frozen for up to 1 month.

CHOCOLATE GANACHE

Makes 3½ cups

CHEF'S NOTE: Ganache is one of the basics in the pastry kitchen and is used as a garnish, a flavoring, and even a dessert, as truffles. If you want a different flavor, you can try flavored liquors or even fruit purées. You can use freshly made ganache to glaze a cake or let it set, then cover and refrigerate for later use (it will keep for 10 days). When it's set, use a very small ice cream scoop or a melon baller to scoop small portions, then chill and hand roll them in cocoa powder, ground nuts, or anything else you like, to make truffles.

12 ounces semi-sweet chocolate, chopped

2 cups heavy cream

Place the chocolate in a medium bowl. In a large saucepan, bring the cream to a simmer, then pour over the chocolate and stir gently to combine.

PASTRY CREAM

Makes 2½ cups

CHEF'S NOTE: Pastry cream is a staple custard used by pastry chefs. It's extremely versatile and can be used as filling for éclairs, Napoleons, cakes, and tarts or as a rich vanilla pudding.

1½ cups milk

1½ teaspoons vanilla extract

¾ tablespoon unsalted butter

½ cup sugar

1 free-range egg

1 free-range egg yolk

2½ tablespoons cornstarch

In a heavy-bottomed 2-quart saucepan, bring the milk, vanilla, butter, and ¼ cup sugar to a boil. In a 2-quart bowl, whisk together the egg, egg yolk, cornstarch, and the remaining ¼ cup sugar. Add the milk mixture to the egg mixture 1 ladle at a time, whisking constantly, then pour into the saucepan. Place over medium heat and whisk constantly as it comes to a boil. Cook for 3 minutes, whisking constantly. Pour into a heatproof bowl and place a piece of plastic wrap directly on the surface of the cream. Let cool to room temperature, then refrigerate (use within 6 days).

To serve as a pudding, pour into dessert bowls while still warm. Top with fresh fruit and whipped cream.

ACKNOWLEDGMENTS

One of the joys of turning a simple idea into a book like *A Master Class* is the collaborative nature of the work.

From the moment the idea was first suggested, the New England Culinary Institute's founder and CEO Fran Voigt and his senior vice president for education Dick Flies were enthusiastic supporters — figuring out how to shift resources and get the book done even as their chefs were running six restaurants on two campuses, working with 500 students, preparing for culinary competitions, and feeding thousands of people every day.

Master Chef Michel LeBorgne, M.C.F., vice president for culinary affairs, inspired the entire project from beginning to end. His extraordinary passion for food, combined with his insight into how it should be approached, prepared, and presented, lends a note of grace to every page in this book.

Chef David Miles, the New England Culinary Institute's director of operations, Chef Lyndon Virkler, dean of culinary affairs, and Chef Jason Gingold, dean of academic affairs, all extraordinary chefs, made room in their complex schedules to review every single one of the recipes in this book and made sure that they reflected the Institute's demanding standards. In particular, Chef David was always available to advise, explain, and suggest solutions to every challenge that arose.

Most of the recipes in this book have been drawn from the New England Culinary Institute's recipe database, which has been developed by hundreds of chefs, past and present. The chefs who tested, tinkered with, and in some cases totally recreated recipes for *A Master Class* included chefs Dina Altieri, Sarah Langan, Emma Cutler, Dan Tabor, Louise Duhamel, Bob Long, John Barton, Adrian Westrope, John Belding, Tom Bivins, John Dowman, Bryan Severns, Diana Faryniarz, Chuck Hoffert, Jennifer Toce, Jill Lanpher, John Brown, Joshua Gibbs, and John McBride.

Chef Joe Buley, an instructor in the meat fabrication program and a farmer passionately committed to sustainable agriculture, advised, prodded, and held our feet to the fire to make sure that we offered our readers the best possible information on sustainably sourced ingredients, while chef Claire Menck checked the foods we suggested to make sure that we had met those goals.

Wine and spirits faculty David Garaventa and Dellie Rex made wine and beer recommendations throughout the book.

Patti Cook, Ed.D., dean of faculty development, selected the chefs who would test the recipes and facilitated their initial involvement.

Andrea Ziga coordinated the movement of recipes among chefs, author, and recipe copyeditor, and marketing coordinator Donna Hepinstall undertook the gargantuan task of finding and sorting the wonderful photographs of food and people that illustrate this book.

Jane Sherman took the chefs' recipes and copyedited them into perfection.

And, finally, Lisa Ekus and Jane Fala, our intrepid agents, supported us throughout the entire project and guided us to our publishing home.

I am delighted that I had the opportunity to work with such an amazing, talented, and passionate group of people.

Ellen Michaud

INDEX